Species of Mind

Species of Mind
The Philosophy and Biology of Cognitive Ethology

Colin Allen
Marc Bekoff

A Bradford Book
The MIT Press
Cambridge, Massachusetts
London, England

First MIT Press paperback edition, 1999

© 1997 Massachusetts Institute of Technology

Set in Sabon by The MIT Press.
Printed and bound in the United States of America.

Library of Congress Cataloging-in-Publication Data

Allen, Colin.
    Species of mind : the philosophy and biology of cognitive ethology / Colin Allen,
    Marc Bekoff.
        p.   cm.
    "A Bradford book."
    Includes bibliographical references (p.   ) and index.
    ISBN 0-262-01163-8 (hc : alk. paper), 0-262-51108-8 (pb)
    1. Cognition in animals.   2. Consciousness in animals.   3. Animal behavior.
I. Bekoff, Marc.   II. Title.
QL785.A585   1997
591.5'13—dc21   97-3263
                                                                        CIP

Contents

for our parents

Preface

There is a lot of interest in studying the minds of nonhuman animals and in the need for interdisciplinary connections between empirical and theoretical approaches. The importance of interdisciplinary discussion means that philosophers who would like their theorizing to appeal and be relevant to scientific colleagues must spend an increasing amount of time keeping up with the empirical literature, perhaps even going out to gain firsthand experience of the ordeals of fieldwork. And scientists who have not read technically difficult philosophical papers and books must do so if they are to stay abreast of developments. We hope that this book contributes to the understanding of what can be achieved by direct collaboration between philosophers and scientists.

Our book has the title it does not only because we want to stress the interdisciplinary nature of the field called cognitive ethology but also because we want to emphasize how essential are comparative inquiries into animals' minds. Defined briefly, cognitive ethology refers to the comparative, evolutionary, and ecological study of animal thought processes, beliefs, rationality, information processing, and consciousness. Cognitive ethology can trace its beginnings to the writings of Charles Darwin, an anecdotal cognitivist, and some of his contemporaries and disciples. Their approach incorporated appeals to evolutionary theory, interests in mental continuity, concerns with individual and intraspecific variation, interests in the mental worlds of the animals, close associations with natural history, and attempts to learn more about the behavior of animals in conditions that are as close as possible to the environments in which natural selection has occurred or is occurring. When needed, research on captive animals also can inform the comparative study of animal cognition. But cognitive ethologists are resistant to suggestions that field studies of animal cognition are impossible (they are difficult, yes, but certainly not impossible), that they should give up their attempts to study animal minds under natural conditions, and that studies of learning and memory alone are sufficient for a complete understanding of animal cognition. In addition to being concerned with the diverse solutions that living organisms have found to common problems, they emphasize broad taxonomic comparisons and do not focus on a few select representatives of a limited number of taxa.

Typically, philosophers of mind have developed their theories anthropocentrically and have applied those theories only secondarily to questions about animal mentality. We believe a more thoroughly naturalistic approach that begins with a consideration of the evolution and biological continuity of human and nonhuman mentality has the potential to produce a more nearly complete understanding of the nature and the evolution of mind. A basic assumption of our approach is that some organisms—humans, at least—are accurately described as having mental states. In making this assumption we are setting aside the worries of "eliminativists" who argue that all talk of minds is hopelessly confused and should be eliminated from the behavioral sciences. Perhaps the eliminativists are right. But, while we are ready to concede that there is confusion about concepts such as belief and consciousness, we do not yet think that the situation is hopeless. It is our view that the best way to understand mental-state attributions across species boundaries is within the comparative, evolutionary, and interdisciplinary framework provided by cognitive ethology. One goal of this book is to make that framework as explicit as possible. Where there are shortcomings in our account, we hope to convince our readers that the difficulties are tractable within the interdisciplinary approach. Ultimately, cognitive ethology will be viable only if a mentalistic approach to the study of animal behavior is capable of sustaining a viable, empirical research program. A major goal that we have in writing this book is to indicate how such a research program might be sustained.

Although there is a great deal of activity by empirical researchers in the comparative study of animal minds, many research programs are narrowly primatocentric, giving only passing attention to animals other than nonhuman primates. We are not the first to urge a broader taxonomic approach to the study of animal minds. It has, for example, been suggested that, in order to learn more about human social behavior and cognition, it is worthwhile to study social carnivores. These animals may provide excellent models for the evolution of cognitive capacities. Many social carnivores are subject to changing environmental conditions, social and nonsocial, that require individuals to show flexible behavior depending on the social composition of their group and the nature of their food supply (Schaller and Lowther 1969; Tinbergen 1972). These carnivores' groups are also characterized by complex networks of social relationships and divisions of labor that may change unpredictably. Complex social and environmental conditions also appear to have been operating in the evolution of cognition in birds. Our attempt to broaden cognitive ethology is only a beginning, and some might even find our concentration on birds and mammals to be narrower than they like. For example, a good deal of interesting work is already being done on cephalopods (Mather 1995), and a mature cognitive ethology will have to consider the full range of vertebrates and invertebrates. Thus, we hope to correct the primatocentric trend by encouraging our readers to consider the behavior of many of the other animals with whom we share this planet. A "speciesist" cognitivism will impede progress in this exciting and challenging area of inquiry, and it will preclude the amassing of a database that would allow sufficiently motivated claims about mental continuity and animal minds.

We stress the importance of conducting empirical, evolutionary, comparative, and ecological studies of animal minds. (See also Yoerg 1991; Yoerg and Kamil 1991; Shettleworth 1993.) We believe that arguments about evolutionary continuity are as applicable to the study of animal minds and brains as they are to comparative studies of kidneys, stomachs, and hearts. We also stress how important it is for those interested in the study of animal minds to make their ideas tractable to empirical research. Cognitive ethology can raise new questions that may be approached from various levels of analysis. For example, detailed descriptive information about subtle behavior patterns and neuroethological data may inform further studies in animal cognition, and may be useful for explaining data that are already available. Such analyses will not make cognitive ethology superfluous, because behavioral evidence is necessary for the interpretation of anatomical or physiological data in assessments of cognitive abilities.

We also hope to show that debates about animal minds and cognition really do not come down to a confrontation between "us" (people who argue that many animals have rich cognitive lives) and "them" (methodological or radical behaviorists who view animals as mere stimulus-response machines). We favor pluralism in all areas. Our view is underscored by the assertion that some animals sometimes need to deal with changing social and nonsocial environments, and the best way for them to do this is to store information when it is available so as to be able to extrapolate from it later (Toates 1995). In other situations, it might be better to respond more mechanically, using time-tested responses that have worked in the past.

We come to the study of animal minds with the perspective that many animals have minds and rich cognitive lives. Some researchers who come from the behaviorist side of the fence, including Toates, also remain open to the idea that single-minded appeals to a particular explanatory framework are unpromising. Maintaining that one type of explanation is always better than the other is stifling and, we believe, incorrect. If nothing else, ideological and narrow appeals lead us to devalue animals (and this has serious moral implications—see Rachels 1990 and Bekoff 1994a); much more important, this type of closed-minding thinking can impede the work that is sorely needed if we are to improve our understanding of the behavioral capacities of individuals of many species.

Cognitive ethologists and comparative or cognitive psychologists can learn important lessons from one another. On the one hand, cognitive psychologists who specialize in highly controlled experimental procedures can teach something about the importance of experimental design and control to those cognitive ethologists who do not perform such research. On the other hand, those who study humans and other animals under highly controlled and often contrived and impoverished laboratory conditions can broaden their horizons and learn more about the importance of more naturalistic methods: they can be challenged to develop procedures that take into account possible interactions among stimuli within and between modalities in more natural settings.

We have chosen the topics that we consider in detail not only to emphasize the need to go beyond primates but also because we want to discuss some behavior patterns that do not typically receive detailed discussion in the comparative literature. In a much longer book we could also have considered bee communication; studies of language in primates, cetaceans, and psittacines; tool use; food caching and recovery; teaching; imitation; and self-recognition. (For ample reviews of these topics see Byrne and Whiten 1988; Cheney and Seyfarth 1990, 1992; Allen and Hauser 1991; Ristau 1991; Griffin 1992; Bekoff and Jamieson 1990a,b, 1996a; Dawkins 1993; Kamil 1987; Byrne 1995; Roitblat and Meyer 1995; Bekoff and Allen 1996; Bekoff 1996; Galef 1996b; Nicol 1996; Vauclair 1996; Cummins and Allen 1997.) Griffin, with his broad-based approach to animal cognition and consciousness, considered numerous topics, some of which do not appear to fall squarely within what we view to be the primary domain of cognitive ethology: the study of behavior patterns in natural (or close-to-natural) settings from an evolutionary and ecological perspective. (Of course, this view does not discount entirely the importance to cognitive ethology of research on captive animals.) With respect to ape language, for example, only future research will tell if the behavior of the few captive individuals who have been intensively studied is related to the behavior of wild members of the same species (see e.g. Savage-Rumbaugh et al. 1996), or if the data demonstrating behavioral plasticity and behavioral potential in captive animals are more significant. For similar reasons we have had little to say about the studies in which mirrors have been used to study self-recognition.

We have chosen to focus on social play and on antipredatory (vigilance) behavior for a number of reasons. First, it seems to us that these are important areas because there are many points of contact with philosophical discussions of intentionality and representation. Second, we want to discuss areas in which there is a good database but one that needs to be filled out by additional comparative field studies. A return to basics is needed, for many studies have been conducted using simplistic and misleading presuppositions. So, for example, in our discussions of social play and antipredator behavior, we want to learn in detail about what the animals are doing and also to compare different sorts of explanations (e.g., those that appeal to intentionality and representation versus those that appeal to stimulus-response contingencies). In regard to both social play and vigilance, we will argue that noncognitive rule-of-thumb explanations (e.g., "Play this way if this happens or if this happened" and "Play that way if that happens or if that happened," or "Scan this way if there are this number of birds in this geometric array" and "Scan that way if there are that number of birds in that geometric array") are cumbersome and do not seem to account for the data and the flexibility in animals' behavior as well or as simply as explanations that appeal to cognitive capacities of the animals under study. Of course, more research is needed in these and other areas.

Methodology must also be given serious attention, for it is highly unlikely that the same methods can be used to study cognition and theories of mind in fishes, birds, carnivores, and nonhuman primates. There is a need to develop and implement species-fair tests that tap the sensory and motor worlds of organisms belonging to different taxa. Furthermore, individual differences must be taken seriously. Sweeping generalizations at the species level of explanation can be misleading, and they are often based on studies of a very few individuals or on small data sets. It is important to know as much as possible about the sensory world of the animals whose behavior one is studying. Experimenters should not ask animals to do things that they are unable to do because they are insensitive to the experimental stimuli or unmotivated by them. The relationships between normal ecological conditions and differences between the capabilities of animals to acquire, process, and respond to information are in the domain of a growing field called "sensory ecology." Many good ethologists begin by attempting to develop an awareness of the senses that the animals use singly or in combination with one another. It is highly unlikely that individuals of any other species sense the world in the same way we do, and it is unlikely that even members of the same species sense the world identically all the time. It is important to remain alert to the possibility of individual variation.

We begin chapter 1 with a difficult question: How widely are mental phenomena distributed in nature? We also stress the importance of a seriously motivated interdisciplinary approach to this question, and as part of our attempt to argue convincingly for this view we discuss intentionality and consciousness and how interdisciplinary and naturalistic approaches to these topics will help us to make progress. Different ideas about philosophical naturalism and about how to naturalize cognitive ethology are presented. The project of studying animal minds should be broadly naturalistic, although there are various formulations of naturalism that might prove satisfactory and deserve independent investigation. We see Darwinian continuity as one plausible route to a naturalistic theory of mental phenomena and ethology, and cognitive ethology as essential to the pursuit of this route. (We recognize our debts to Darwin and Griffin here and elsewhere.) Our project, then, is to explore how evolutionary accounts of mental phenomena can inform and be informed by philosophical accounts. The current philosophical literature on mental phenomena is dominated by discussions of two major aspects of mentality: intentionality (in Franz Brentano's sense) and consciousness (in who knows what sense!). The common strategy of treating these phenomena as independent is not unanimously applauded. Throughout this book, we shall be concerned with the benefits and risks of a divide-and-conquer strategy. We shall come out on the side of careful division.

It is important to know about some of the historical underpinnings of cognitive ethology. In chapter 2 we briefly consider the historical roots of classical and cognitive ethology and how these two fields may be related. We discuss Darwin's anecdotal cognitivism and the importance of his ideas about mental continuity between humans and other animals. We then discuss various forms of behaviorism, the rise of classical ethology, and Griffin's emphasis on consciousness and the versatility of behavior. We conclude that cognitive ethology does not represent a major departure from the practices of classical ethologists such as Konrad Lorenz and Niko Tinbergen, but that the explanatory constructs provided by the application of cognitive science to ethology are conceptually richer than Lorenzian constructs such as "action-specific energy" and "drive." Careful observation, description, interpretation, experimentation, and explanation form the raw material for just about all analyses of behavior, regardless of one's position on matters of mind, and advances in the philosophical analysis of cognitive concepts provide good prospects for empirical investigation of the applicability of these concepts to animal behavior.

In chapter 3 we ask "What is behavior?" We discuss some general but very important methodological topics, including the difference between actions and other movements (that is, between what an animal does and what happens to it) and how behavior patterns are categorized. We also consider the natures of various types and levels of description (for example, acontextual description with reference to muscular contractions and description with reference to function or consequence), and we come down on the side of pluralism. Descriptions can come in many different flavors—none is always correct and none is always incorrect. Rather, the questions being asked (and perhaps the animals being studied) drive the selection of the type of description (and other methods) that should be used.

A balanced view of cognitive ethology requires consideration of critics' points of view. We attempt to give serious attention to various critics' challenges in chapter 4, and also in other chapters as the need arises. Criticisms of cognitive ethology come in many forms but usually center on the notion that nonhuman animals do not have minds; on the idea that (many, most, all) animals are not conscious, or that so little of their behavior is conscious (no matter how broadly defined) that it is a waste of time to study animal consciousness; on the inaccessibility to rigorous study of animal mental states (they are private) and whatever (if anything) might be contained in them; on the assumption that nonhuman animals do not have any beliefs because human language is incapable of expressing anything other than the contents of human beliefs; on the belief that there is too much human subjectivity about animal subjectivity; on the rigor with which data are collected; on the lack of large databases (anecdotes are far too prevalent); on the nature of explanations that rely too heavily on theoretical constructs (e.g., minds and mental states) that are regarded as anthropomorphic, folk-psychological, and merely instrumentalistic; and on the reliance on behavior to the exclusion of neurological or physiological explanations of behavior.

Much of the criticism of cognitive ethology comes from those who ignore its successes, those who dismiss it in principle because of strong and radical behavioristic leanings, or those who do not always appreciate some of the basic philosophical principles that inform it. The more mechanistic approaches to the study of animal cognition are not without their own faults. Kamil (1987), a comparative psychologist himself, faults many of his colleagues for disregarding external validity (i.e., how relevant a study is to the natural existence of the animals under study) and for paying too much attention to internal validity (i.e., the logical structure of the experiments being performed).

In our response to critics, we introduce the notions of *stimulus-bound behaviors* (i.e., behavior patterns that occur almost invariably in response to some stimulus, with external stimuli predominating over internal factors) and *stimulus-free behaviors* (where internal factors predominate over external stimuli). There are different ways of conceiving these internal factors, ranging from interoceptive phenomena to representational accounts of mental states. Here interdisciplinary input is necessary, and Jerry Fodor shakes hands with Niko Tinbergen. For much of the twentieth century, psychology, especially comparative psychology, was on a behavioristic track that explicitly denied the possibility of a science of animal mind. We argue that this halving of psychology depends on unsound arguments about the privacy of mental phenomena and on unsound views about the relationship between observation and theory. The appearance of the adequacy of behavioristic explanations to account for any observed behavior may be an artifact of the way in which comparative psychologists identify behaviors to be explained. When the full complexity of the behaviors is considered, behavioristic explanations can seem rather less straightforward than cognitive or mentalistic ones.

Other challenges to cognitive ethology center on the use of folk-psychological explanations—appeals to animals' desires and beliefs. In chapter 5 we consider what folk psychology is, consciousness and content, the semantic properties of mental states, and evolutionary explanations of content. We discuss the possibility of traveling smoothly from folk psychology to science and transforming folk psychology into something respectable. We also consider serious criticisms of the notion of belief, concluding that they do not threaten the enterprise of cognitive ethology—that intentional explanations are alive and well and can be used to explain behavior. We argue that a notion of content is essential to the explanatory project of cognitive ethology in that it provides a level of abstraction that is important for comparative accounts of behavior. A common objection to the use of mentalistic terms to explain animal behavior involves both a mistaken understanding of what such terms are best at explaining and an overoptimistic assessment of the scope of nonmentalistic explanations of behavior. We also argue that there are fewer grounds for pessimism about the precise specification of the content of animal beliefs than critics have supposed. The fact that the conceptual schemes of nonhuman animals do not exactly correspond to classifications that are of anthropocentric interest does not mean that more precise specification of content is impossible for the cognitive states of animals.

Our first case study, presented in chapter 6, concerns social play behavior, especially in canids (members of the dog family). Darwin thought that playful behavior indicated pleasure, and many observers would agree that animals play because it is fun for them to do so. It also is fun to watch animals at play! This aside, there is much of directly cognitive interest in the study of play, including the requirement to communicate intentions about play and the possibilities that the study of play may afford for the development of understanding the context in which various actions may occur in order to distinguish playful actions from their nonplayful counterparts.

In addition to the fact that social play exemplifies many of the theoretical issues faced by cognitive ethologists and philosophers, empirical research on social play has benefited and will benefit further from a cognitive approach, because social play involves communication, intention, role playing, turn taking, and cooperation. Furthermore, social play occurs in a wide range of species and thus affords a good opportunity for a comparative investigation of cognitive abilities. Finally, our choice of social play is in keeping with our major goal of discussing behavior patterns—tractable, evolved behavioral phenotypes—that lend themselves to detailed empirical study. Because the social play of canids and other animals involves the use of behavior patterns from other contexts, such as predation, aggression, and reproduction, it is important that when the same patterns are used in play they are not misinterpreted. Thus, in this chapter we concentrate on how individuals communicate that they want to play with others, rather than to eat, fight, or mate with them.

Our second case, study presented in chapter 7, centers on antipredatory behavior, mainly in birds—how individuals scan their social and nonsocial surroundings looking for predators or looking at who is nearby and what they are doing. Many of our observations about social play as a cognitive domain also apply to the study of vigilance. However, perhaps even better than play, the vigilance behavior of animals lends itself to broad taxonomic comparisons and is amenable to neurobiological studies and to studies of perceptual abilities. Many vertebrates and invertebrates show minute-by-minute, daily, and seasonal changes in their vigilance behavior. In many cases, the causes of these changes, which are not amenable to simple, single-factor explanations, seem amenable to cognitive analysis. Studying vigilance could allow cognitive ethologists to break away from the tendency to focus on a few select representatives of a few taxa. In short, vigilance studies might allow cognitive ethologists to escape the primato-centrism that plagues much of comparative psychology, and also might make possible real comparative studies of a variety of taxonomic groups. In chapter 7 we use a study of western evening grosbeaks to illustrate the application of cognitive approaches to vigilance behavior. This study con-cerned the sorts of information accessible to these birds as they feed in small to medium-size groups and scan for potential predators and the expectations they might have about the behavior of other flock members.

In chapter 8 we turn to the topic of consciousness. Although some of the classical ethologists (especially Tinbergen) were skeptical or hostile toward the idea that animals' subjective experiences could be investigated rigor-ously (Burkhardt 1997; van den Bos 1997), Griffin placed the topic at the top of his agenda for cognitive ethology. We wait so long to get to this important but highly controversial and muddled area because we wish to illustrate that there is much of interest in cognitive ethology that can be pursued even in the absence of a completely satisfying account of con-sciousness. We try in chapter 8 to reorient the debate about animal con-sciousness away from Thomas Nagel's famous question "What is it like to be a bat?" and back toward the question of which creatures possess con-sciousness. We discuss the lack of a need to provide a stipulative definition of consciousness; we consider qualia, sensations, and information; and we stress the importance of learning about how animals detect misinforma-tion. We hope to convince our readers that some questions about animal consciousness may be empirically tractable, even if others seem at present intractable.

Without a doubt, the difficulty of understanding consciousness is the single biggest bludgeon used to bash cognitive ethology. We think that to focus on this difficulty is to be very unfair to cognitive ethologists, for many interesting questions about the evolution of mentality can be pur-sued in the absence of solutions to all the problems of consciousness. Many philosophers have focused on how one can know what it is like for anoth-er organism to be in a particular conscious state. We argue that the more fundamental epistemological question concerns which organisms *have* conscious states, not what it is like to be those organisms. For many philosophers, however, the epistemological problems of consciousness pale in comparison to the ontological problem of saying just what conscious-ness is. We do not think that the project now facing cognitive ethologists and comparative psychologists requires us to say anything explicit about the ontological problem of consciousness. For present purposes it is enough to point to cognitive and behavioral capacities that exhibit some of the characteristics associated with consciousness and to target those for further empirical investigation and philosophical analysis. Only this kind of interdisciplinary research will tell whether those capacities are the ones to which we should be pointing.

In chapter 9 we attempt to provide a synthesis of philosophical, psy-chological, and ethological approaches to the study of animal minds. We directly head off the attempt by Cecilia Heyes and Anthony Dickinson (1990, 1995)—severe but cogent critics of cognitive ethology—to argue that only in the laboratory is it possible to rigorously test hypotheses about the intentionality of animal behavior. Heyes and Dickinson's arguments are flawed, we believe, by an excessively narrow dedication to Daniel Dennett's (1983, 1987) conception of intentionality and by a lack of atten-tion to the natural history of their laboratory subjects.

In summary, we argue that the following should figure prominently in cognitive ethological studies:

remaining open to the possibility of surprising findings about animals' cog-nitive abilities

concentrating on comparative, evolutionary, and ecological questions

sampling many different species, including domesticated animals—going beyond primates, and avoiding talk of "lower" and "higher" animals (or at least laying out explicit criteria for using these slippery and value-laden terms)

naturalizing the methods of study by taking the animals' points of view (communicating with them on their terms) and studying them in condi-tions that are close to the conditions in which they typically live

trying to understand how cognitive skills used by captive animals may function in more natural settings

studying individual differences

using all sorts of data, ranging from anecdotes to large data sets

appealing to a variety of types of explanation in the search for the best explanations of the data under scrutiny.

Cognitive ethology need not model itself on other fields of science, such as physics or neurobiology, in order to gain credibility. Envy of the "hard" sciences is what led to the neglect of animal and human minds in the early part of the twentieth century.

All in all, we hope that our readers will come away from this book recognizing that the comparative and evolutionary study of animal minds is a most exciting and challenging interdisciplinary field of inquiry that is worthy of respect from those who think it a soft science: it is not. Interdisciplinary research is difficult, and it becomes even more so when impassable boundaries are established between academic disciplines (Bekoff 1994b; van Valen 1996). Our hope is that traditional academic territories will be abandoned in areas where friendly overlap is essential to the advancement of knowledge; cognitive ethology is such an area. We recognize that not everyone will be satisfied. Some may wish to see more experimentation and less theorizing. We agree that more experimentation is desirable, but a solid theoretical approach is equally important. Most of all, we hope that our critics will come forth and mount serious challenges to what we have written, for in this way we can continue to develop and to refine ideas that will make the worlds of other animals more understandable to us.

We would like to thank Joe Allen, Peter Bednekoff, Andy Brown, Diana Bushong, Simon Dembitzer (who also prepared the index), Ted Friend, Jim Grau, Chuck Hamilton, Robin Joynes, Tamara King, Chris Menzel, Eric Saidel, Sue Townsend, Adrian Treves, Gary Varner, and Mary Wicksten for providing us with comments on the manuscript. Donald Griffin, Herb Roitblat, Kim Sterelny, and an anonymous reviewer commented extensively on the penultimate draft. We also benefited from discussions with David Hatfield, Dale Jamieson, Steve Lima, Carron Meaney, Paul Moriarty, Carolyn Ristau, and members of the TAMU Animal Behavior Discussion Group. The National Science Foundation (NSF SBR-9320214), Texas A&M University, and the University of Colorado at Boulder provided partial financial support. We thank E. J. Brill, Blackwell Wissenschafts-Verlag GmbH, and Blackwell Publishers Ltd. for permission to use material from previously published essays. Portions of Allen and Bekoff 1994 are reprinted with kind permission of Kluwer Academic Publishers. Marc Bekoff thanks Carron Meaney, Marjorie Bekoff, and Bruce Gottlieb for their support during the preparation of this book. Colin Allen thanks Lynn for her love, patience, and understanding.

1

Cognitive Ethology and Philosophy of Mind: An Interdisciplinary Approach

If no organic being excepting man had possessed any mental power, or if his powers had been of a wholly different nature from those of the lower animals, then we should never have been able to convince ourselves that our high faculties had been gradually developed. But it can be shewn that there is no fundamental difference of this kind. We must also admit that there is a much wider interval in mental power between one of the lowest fishes, as a lamprey or lancelet, and one of the higher apes, than between an ape and a man; yet this interval is filled up by numberless gradations.

—Charles Darwin (1871, p. 445)

Only the most benighted of evolutionary gradualists could be sanguine that the apparently radical intellectual discontinuity between us and other creatures will prove to be merely quantitative.

—Jerry Fodor (1994 p. 91)

How widely are mental phenomena distributed in nature? Are the capacities for thought and feeling unique traits of humans, or are these and other mental states also found in nonhuman animals? If they are found in nonhuman animals, how similar are the mental states of those animals to the mental states of humans? Are human mental states different in kind, or are there "numberless gradations" filling the interval between humans and lampreys (as Darwin hypothesized)? Answers to questions such as these about continuity between the minds of humans and those of other animals are central for understanding both the evolution and the nature of mental capacities. But many scientists have been reluctant, for various reasons, to take seriously the attribution of mental states to nonhuman animals.

Unless this reluctance can be overcome, it will not be possible to assess Darwin's gradualist hypothesis scientifically.

Many nonscientists find the reluctance of scientists to admit the existence of nonhuman mentality to be contrary to common sense. Common sense does not always, however, provide clear intuitions about the mentality of nonhuman animals. On the one hand, it is normal to talk about companion animals and other familiar animals in mentalistic terms: it is not uncommon to hear of cats who are angry when their owners return after a weekend away, or of dogs who think they are going for a walk. Starting as young children, humans attribute mental characteristics to a variety of objects, both animate and inanimate. But these common-sense, "folk-psychological" judgments are typically taken more seriously when applied to animals, and as such they seem to support the view that mental states are not uniquely human traits. On the other hand, it is also commonly recognized that there are large gaps between the mental abilities of humans and those of other animals; for example, many people talk to their pets but do not expect them to understand much of what is said. The existence of these gaps raises questions about the extent to which other animals really are like us. And it is common sense to many people that the psychological dissimilarities of other animals from humans are sufficient to permit farming, hunting, various types of research, and other practices that would be considered unacceptable if applied to humans. Furthermore, unmitigated appeals to common sense are unlikely to be effective in changing the attitudes of scientists toward animal mentality. Science has a history of overturning the opinions of common sense.

From a psychological or an epistemological point of view, differences between humans and other animals make it difficult for us to imagine or know what the subjective experiences of other organisms might be like. From an evolutionary point of view, there are difficult questions about how such gaps could have arisen by natural selection. The task of bridging these gaps and understanding the bases for mental-state attributions is at the same time a philosophical project and a scientific project. It is a philosophical project because it requires philosophical investigation of mentalistic concepts and of the aims and methods of cognitive ethology; it is a scientific project because impoverished knowledge of animal behavior results in impoverished arguments and faulty conclusions.

Cognitive ethology provides a tractable approach to obtaining such knowledge.

Our approach is to assume that at least some organisms (minimally, humans) do have mental lives and that the best way to understand mental-state attributions across species boundaries is within the comparative, evolutionary, and interdisciplinary framework provided by cognitive ethology. A goal of this book is to make that framework as explicit as possible. Where there are shortcomings in our account, we hope to convince our readers that the difficulties are tractable within the interdisciplinary approach. By assuming a realist attitude toward mental states, we choose to set aside the worries of "eliminativists," who believe that talk of minds is hopelessly confused and will be dispensed with in the future. Although ordinary mentalistic talk may be confused, we will work with the assumption that it is not *hopelessly* confused. Of course, much ordinary mentalistic language is bound up in cultural practices, such as determining innocence, guilt, or responsibility for various actions. For this reason, we also accept that it may be necessary to reconceptualize much of folk psychology if we are ever to have a clear view of the cognitive similarities among different species.

In the course of the book we shall address a variety of arguments that have been put forward to establish the hopelessness, misguidedness, or sheer impossibility of studying the minds of animals. All these arguments—even those given by scientists—have something of a philosophical character, but they differ with respect to the degree of attention they pay to empirical research on animal behavior. Not so long ago, undergraduate philosophy majors were taught that if a question had an empirical component it was not a philosophical question. Many science undergraduates were also taught that if a question could not be directly answered empirically then it was of no concern to scientists. Although these attitudes persist in some quarters, there is now much greater understanding of relationships between theory and evidence, especially the fact that theories are always underdetermined by evidence because there are many theories that are compatible with the same set of evidence (Quine 1953). There is consequently more respect for interdisciplinary efforts such as the one undertaken here. However, there is still much to be learned about the relationships between theory-motivated philosophical arguments and empirical work. In this book, we hope to contribute by example to the understanding of what can be achieved by direct collaboration between scientists and philosophers.

Although Darwin proposed his ideas about mental continuity more than 120 years ago, the dominant present-day view among animal-behavior researchers is that such issues are beyond the pale of respectable scientific research. Related developments in both philosophy and psychology have much to do with this prevailing attitude. In philosophy, empiricism is the a class of views that maintain that all human knowledge must ultimately be derived from sensory experience. In the early twentieth century empiricism reached its zenith in the movement known as logical empiricism (or logical positivism) which emphasized that the meaningfulness of any concept depended on its reducibility to logical constructions from observable, verifiable experiences. In psychology, the behaviorists implemented the positivist program with a strict operationalism that allowed the use of mentalistic terminology only insofar as individual terms could be "defined" strictly using observable relationships between stimuli and responses. These "definitions" were not intended to capture the ordinary meanings of terms, but to replace the ordinary terms with a "more scientific" vocabulary.

Donald Griffin, in a series of books and articles dating back to 1976, has urged that the comparative, evolutionary study of animal behavior cannot be completed if issues of animal mind are ignored, and has urged the development of the field for which he invented the label "cognitive ethology." Griffin's writings have been attacked as anecdotal and anthropomorphic, as bad science, and as just plain muddled thinking. Some of the critics of his work in particular and of cognitive ethology more generally bring behavioristic presuppositions to their arguments; thus, it is our view that, in defending cognitive ethology, it is not feasible to ignore the behavioristic challenge.

Cognitive ethology, however, requires more than a convincing response to the behaviorists. Behaviorism is no longer the force that it once was, even within comparative psychology. But even those who are sympathetic to cognitive ethology worry that, hard as it is to make progress on difficult issues of mind when the subjects are human, it is many times harder when one is working with nonhuman animals, with whom linguistic communication is either impossible or highly limited. Although human cognitive psychology relies very little on verbal introspective reports by research subjects, the ability of subjects to respond to complex verbal instructions is nonetheless essential to the design of many experiments. Cognitive ethology will be shown viable only if it can be shown that a mentalistic approach to the study of animal behavior is capable of sustaining an empirical research program despite the challenges presented. A major goal of this book is to indicate how such a research program might be sustained.

Naturalism about the Mind

In contributing to the development of cognitive ethology, we believe ourselves to be contributing to the philosophical project of naturalizing the mind. Naturalism is a broad philosophical stance that denies either the existence of supernatural or nonphysical entities or their relevance for understanding any given phenomenon. Another major strand in philosophical naturalism (see Quine 1953) is that the methods of science and philosophy are intertwined. When naturalism is concerned with what kinds of entities exist, it is part of the philosophical subdiscipline of ontology— the theory of existence. ("Ontology" should not be confused with "ontogeny," the development of individual organisms.) When naturalism is concerned with how a phenomenon can be understood, then it is part of the philosophical subdiscipline of epistemology—the theory of knowledge.

The phrase "naturalizing the mind" has a variety of meanings to different authors. We take the central idea behind naturalism about the mind to be an ontological view to the effect that mental phenomena are in some sense a part of the physical world. Naturalism in this sense is opposed to the Cartesian view that mind is substantially distinct from the rest of nature, and it is generally opposed to theories of mind that link mental properties with notions such as the possession of an immaterial soul or spirit. (See Shapiro 1997 and the discussion below for a disagreement with this characterization of naturalism.)

Of what consequence is this issue about naturalism for cognitive scientists in general, and cognitive ethologists specifically? One can do good work on memory or planning without worrying about the philosophical underpinnings of these concepts, just as one may do excellent experimental work in particle physics that is not affected by one's opinion about the relative merits of the "Copenhagen" and "many-worlds" interpretations of quantum mechanics. But whether or not a particular scientist is personally attracted to such issues, the discipline as a whole is affected by them. Theories are accepted both for their ability to account for observations and for their coherence with the rest of science. In this vein, the notion of a mental representation is puzzling because mental representations have features that are hard to account for in ordinary causal terms. Consider planning, which requires the ability to represent future events that have not yet occurred and may never occur. Clearly such events cannot be causes of their representations. So how is it possible to understand representation of future goals from within a causal perspective? This is one aspect of the problem of naturalizing representation, which if not resolved leaves cognitive scientists with an unpaid debt no matter how empirically successful their theories are (von Eckardt 1993, especially p. 197).

In order to assess the prospects for naturalism about the mind, it is necessary to get clear about what would satisfy the desire for a naturalistic theory.

Three Forms of Reductionism

Opinions vary on what must be done to establish naturalism with respect to mental phenomena. We ultimately reject the suggestion that it means showing how mentalistic terms or predicates (the language of mentalistic psychology) can be *reduced* to nonmental predicates. According to the strongest versions of reductionism, the successful reduction of a mentalistic term, M, requires a definitional *analysis* of M in nonmentalistic terms. This would be achieved if one could complete the schema "x has mental property M if and only if x is F" in such a way that F provides a definition of M. Under a very strong conception of definition, the defined term (the *definiendum*) and the defining phrase (the *definiens*) must be completely synonymous. But this very strong requirement is extremely unlikely to be met by any suggested definition. For example, it is extremely unlikely that one could find a statement about neural states with exactly the same meaning as a statement about mental states that it is intended to analyze. For this reason, most naturalists do not believe that it is necessary to provide this kind of analysis to support naturalism.

A weaker version of reductionism requires the nondefinitional analysis of mentalistic terms or predicates. That is, one must specify necessary and sufficient conditions for the application of a mentalistic term *M* in non-mentalistic, naturalistic terms, but the *analysandum* (the expression being analyzed) need not be equivalent to the *analysans* (the expression providing the analysis). Thus, it is still required that the schema "*x* has mental property *M* if and only if *x* is *F*" be completed, but the stronger requirement of synonymy between *M* and *F* is dropped. For example, it has often been suggested that possession of a particular brain or neural state is both necessary and sufficient for possession of a particular mental state. The standard philosophical example, almost certainly wrong, is that *x* is in pain if and only if *x*'s C fibers are firing. If successful, this analysis would provide identity conditions for pain—the mental state of being in pain would be identified with (or reduced to) the neural state of C fibers' firing—even though, for linguistic and historical reasons, no one would suppose that "John is in pain" and "John's C fibers are firing" had the same meanings. Unfortunately for those who favor this version of reductionism, it has been remarkably difficult to provide successful analyses (Stich 1992; Tye 1992). Consequently, many naturalists have favored weakening the requirements for naturalism still further.

One obvious move is to drop the joint requirement for necessary and sufficient conditions in favor of an approach that allows naturalists to get by with specifying, in naturalistically acceptable terms, merely sufficient or merely necessary conditions for the application of mentalistic terms. If successful in doing this, a naturalist would have managed to establish connections that, although weaker than equivalence or identity, would still support the naturalistic claim that mental phenomena are not inherently supernatural. For example, if C-fiber stimulation turned out to be sufficient (in the context of a functioning nervous system) although not necessary for pain, then it would be known that at least some cases of pain do not depend on anything supernatural. In such a case, the notion of pain would not have been completely reduced (other cases of pain might occur without C fibers' firing), but the partial reduction would nonetheless provide some support to naturalism about pain.

Emergent Properties and Reductionism

So much for the cold touch of technical philosophy. Much of the broader scientific debate about the status of mental properties is conducted in terms of the notion of an emergent property. One is told that consciousness and other mental properties "emerge" in an unpredictable way from the actions of neurons. Such claims are sometimes taken to have antireductionistic consequences. But is emergence an antireductionistic notion? With respect to ontology, we believe that the correct answer to this question is negative. An emergent property is, very roughly, a property that belongs to an aggregate of entities but is not a linear sum of the properties of the parts. This means that the mass of a large object would *not* count as an emergent property of the object, as the total mass is simply the sum of the masses of all its parts.

Uncontroversial examples of emergent properties are harder to find. The solvent property of water is one candidate, for neither hydrogen atoms nor oxygen atoms in isolation possess this property and neither do they possess scaled-down versions of the property. Solvent action seems to emerge from a nonlinear combination of the properties of hydrogen and oxygen. One can, of course, produce a solvent using nothing more than hydrogen atoms and oxygen atoms in the ratio 2:1, so from an ontological standpoint nothing more is required. In this sense, chemical combination of these atoms is sufficient for producing a solvent. Thus, a naturalistic stance toward the solvent property of water is justified.

The nonlinear relationship between the properties of hydrogen and oxygen and the properties of water (if typical for emergent properties) might be taken to entail that the doctrine of emergent properties supports an epistemological version of antireductionism. If one could not infer the properties of the brain from the properties of its neurons and glial cells, then, it would seem that one could not fully understand a reductionistic explanation of the brain's properties in terms of the properties of its cellular parts. Connections between reduction and understanding often lead philosophers of science to characterize reductionism as having an epistemological component, because epistemology is concerned with questions of knowledge and understanding. We prefer to avoid this characterization of reductionism, however, for it depends on rather vague claims about what one could or could not understand on the basis of given information. Who is the "one" whose understanding is at issue here? Trying to take a God's-eye view is fruitless. From the point of view of a mere mortal, what one may or may not understand can change. Though it was puzzling in the past, scientists now have a pretty good understanding of how the polarity of a water molecule accounts for water's ability to act as a solvent, and of how that polarity is due to the electron structure of a water molecule's component atoms. Thus, what seems irreducible today may not seem irreducible tomorrow, and it would be shaky to pin one's views about the understandability of mental properties on the limitations of current theories.

The common thread in all the varieties of ontological reductionism is the idea that it should be possible to show how mental phenomena arise from or are constituted by suitable arrangements of the basic materials that make up the rest of the natural world. Because science purports to tell us about the natural world, naturalistically inclined philosophers commonly turn to science as the source for necessary or sufficient conditions relevant to mental phenomena; computer science, cognitive psychology, the neurosciences, evolutionary biology, and quantum mechanics have all been enlisted for support. Stich (1992) and Tye (1992) both suggest that such appeals to science have been unsuccessful in supporting reductionism as a viable approach to naturalism about mental phenomena. We do not wish to go into the details of their arguments, but their general point is easy to state: Despite a long history of attempts to provide reductionistic accounts of mental phenomena, there is not even one case of a widely accepted partial reduction—for example, of a neurally specific sufficient condition for a specific mental property. Although we think ontological reduction is a worthy goal, in view of this miserable history it seems that naturalists would be well advised to consider alternative approaches.

Alternative Approaches to Naturalism

Tye (1992, p. 436) states his own version of naturalism as follows: "Mental states participate in causal interactions which fall under scientific laws, and are either ultimately constituted or ultimately realized by microphysical phenomena." This view has two components. The second part—

concern for the ontological issue of what mental states are "constituted" or "realized" by—is a feature (shared by most reductionistic approaches) that, in accordance with Shapiro (1997), we will label *ontological naturalism*. Shapiro also labels such views, somewhat disparagingly, as "Lego naturalism," because of their concern with the nonmentalistic building blocks of mental phenomena. Tye's version of ontological naturalism differs from others by being less optimistic about the likelihood of providing analyses of mental terms in terms of either necessary or sufficient conditions. The first part of Tye's view—insistence on the place of mental states in law-governed causal interactions—has much in common with Shapiro's (1997) *methodological naturalism,* according to which naturalism about mental states requires only that there be a productive, systematic, empirically tractable theory that includes mental-state predicates within its theoretical vocabulary.

Shapiro's view lacks the ontological component of Tye's. For Shapiro, it doesn't matter what mental states are made of so long as they can be studied by methods that are acceptable to scientists. Indeed, whereas Tye's view combines ontological and methodological components, Shapiro explicitly rejects an ontological component to his naturalism; he thinks that the ontological approach is unable to make the distinction that, on his view, really matters to naturalism. Shapiro believes that naturalists are not really concerned with whether mental phenomena are natural or supernatural. Rather, he writes (1997, p. 11), "we should expect of a naturalistic thesis that it allows us to distinguish scientific kinds and properties from nonscientific kinds and properties."

We agree with Shapiro that methodological unity between the study of mental phenomena and other natural sciences would provide support for naturalism. We disagree, however, with Shapiro's rejection of ontological concerns. On our view, both the ontological and the methodological strand of naturalism provide useful characterizations of criteria that might be satisfied by a naturalistic theory of mind. In our view it is premature to decide now what is likely to be the best approach to naturalizing the mind. Neither ontological nor methodological approaches to naturalism require reductionism (although they are compatible with it), and the fact that there are alternative approaches to naturalizing the mind is valuable. There are various ways in which mental phenomena might be assimilated to other natural phenomena, and naturalism gains support whether that assimilation is reductionistic, ontological, or methodological, or if it takes some other form that we have yet failed to consider.

For scientists, most philosophical attempts to characterize naturalism do not provide adequate advice on how to achieve the goal of a naturalistic theory of mind (other than "Keep doing whatever you are doing"). In general, knowing what would count as satisfying some goal is not the same thing as knowing how to achieve it—one might well know that one would be rich if one had a million dollars yet have no clue how to make that much money. Likewise, many philosophical views about naturalism purport to specify what scientists are or should be aiming at but do not give much help with the practicalities of taking aim. It is fair to respond that most philosophical discussions do not aim to provide practical suggestions for scientific research. But the naturalist's cause could be advanced if such suggestions were forthcoming. It is not entirely surprising that suggestions are infrequent. Philosophers often do not know enough about the relevant sciences to be able to make practical suggestions and the task is difficult even for those who are relatively knowledgeable. For example, after visiting the Kenyan research site of Dorothy Cheney and Robert Seyfarth (Cheney and Seyfarth 1990), Daniel Dennett (1987) admitted that his earlier methodological suggestions for cognitive ethology (1983) did not take account of the complexities and difficulties presented by ethological fieldwork. Similarly when one of us (C.A.) was given the opportunity to conduct field studies of bird behavior (described in chapter 7) with the other (M.B.), the sheer practical difficulties of implementing certain research ideas meant that many ideas were shelved. Conversely, scientists often do not know enough about the intricacies of philosophical theories of mind to be able to identify the ways in which their work is relevant to those theories. In view of the difficulties for any individual of becoming completely conversant in two fields, a collaborative, interdisciplinary approach seems necessary.

By pushing cognitive ethology as an approach to naturalizing the mind, we do not suggest that it is the only possible approach, or even that it is the only approach that is likely to succeed (and perhaps we should not suggest that it is likely to succeed at all). Rather, we intend this book as an extended investigation of the prospects for understanding naturalism about mind within an ethological framework. In particular, we shall attempt to show that achieving a thorough understanding of the evolution and the phylogenetic distribution of mental phenomena might facilitate the assimilation of mental phenomena to other natural phenomena. Although we shall often be somewhat critical of those who insist that only in the laboratory can one conduct properly controlled experiments, this is not to say that we reject the relevance of laboratory investigations of animal behavior; it is only to say that they alone cannot provide a complete picture of the comparative and evolutionary aspects of animal cognition.

Cognitive Ethology and Naturalism

The idea that mental phenomena are found in nonhuman organisms is not essential to a naturalist position with regard to mind; one might, for example, identify mental properties with a level of computational complexity not found in nonhumans. Nevertheless, skepticism about animal minds is one of a number of pieces of the Cartesian legacy whose defeat would go some way toward vindicating naturalism. In this context, the Darwinian idea of mental continuity between the species provides a framework for constructing a naturalistic view of mind.

Using Darwin as his guide, Griffin has argued persistently for the claim that ethological observations of animals support attributions to them of thought, consciousness, and other mental states. Griffin does not, however, provide a clear account of the grounds for attributing mental states on the basis of behavioral observations other than in his metaphor that communication provides a window on animal minds. For this he has been criticized both by those who are sympathetic toward cognitive ethology (including Allen and Hauser (1993), Jamieson and Bekoff (1993), and Bekoff and Allen (1997)) and by those who are not sympathetic (e.g., Heyes (1987a,b)). A number of unsympathetic critics, including Premack (1988) and Heyes and Dickinson (1990), have suggested that ethology, which relies heavily on observing animals in their natural habitats, simply cannot support the kinds of mental-state attributions that interest cognitive ethologists, and that progress on issues of comparative cognition can be made only under laboratory conditions. We favor the more pluralistic view that both laboratory work and fieldwork are important to the study

of comparative cognition, but fieldwork is essential to the proper interpretation of the results of laboratory experimentation. In chapter 9 we will
illustrate this point with respect to the argument of Heyes and Dickinson.
Here we will provide a more general argument for the centrality of ethology in studies of comparative cognition.

Natural selection generally acts on the functional properties (in the
sense of Cummins 1975) of organismic traits; the material properties of
an organism or its traits are important only insofar as they affect the
functional capacities of those traits. Nervous systems of animals are no
exceptions—the functions for which they are selected include the control
of behavior. Nervous systems are also, at least in humans, the organ of the
mind. Thus, in trying to understand the evolution of mentality it is reasonable to consider the evolution of nervous systems. The branch of ethology specifically concerned with relationships between behavior and
neurobiology is known as neuroethology. If selection acts on traits in virtue
of their functional characteristics, then it acts on nervous systems in virtue
of the behavioral functions they support. Thus, in order to understand
nervous-system function from an evolutionary perspective, it is essential to
understand the functional aspects of behavior. This is one of the tasks clas-
sically taken to define ethology; therefore, ethology is a cornerstone of any
attempt to understand the evolution of mentality. Ethologists study animal behavior from a variety of perspectives, including the examination of
relationships between behavioral phenotypes and selective pressures. Thus,
ethologists favor observations and experiments on animals under conditions that are as close as possible to the environments in which selection
occurs—that is, they favor fieldwork.

Theories of Mind: A Pluralistic Approach

No one knows whether mentalistic terms provide the right vocabulary
for cognitive ethology, or whether evolutionary accounts of behavior
provide the key to a naturalistic account of mentality. Potentially,
philosophers have as much to learn from ethologists as vice versa.
Philosophical theories of mind, insofar as they are empirically tractable,
can provide suggestions for empirical investigation. In return, ethological research into cognition provides data points for the refinement of

philosophical theories—for example, with respect to the importance or unimportance of language for mentality. Much of the rest of this book will explore specific examples of this two-way interaction.

Our approach is pluralistic. Owing to the complexities involved, the more points of departure available the greater will be the chances of success. Thus, we are less concerned with producing a complete theory of mind than with showing how different theories of mind have different consequences for making the scientific study of animal mind empirically tractable.

Two aspects of mentality have been the major targets of contemporary philosophical theorizing. Both are important to cognitive ethologists. One is consciousness, particularly in the sense that some mental states *feel* like something to their possessors. A puzzle that worries many philosophers is how the machinations of neurons could add up to such feelings. Some philosophers, including Nagel (1974), put this in terms of wonder at *how* it could be that events in the cortex could give rise to the subjective quality of experience. Others, such as Jackson (1986), put the point in terms of the existence of knowledge that is not available from a purely physical (or neurological) description. Clearly, anyone who wonders about the experiences of nonhuman animals must hope to find some philosophical clarity on the notion of consciousness.

The other major target of contemporary philosophers of mind is the *intentionality* of mental states. Owing to the nineteenth-century psychologist Franz Brentano (1874), the use of the term "intentional" and its cognates by philosophers has a special sense that differs from the ordinary sense of the term. In ordinary language the term "intentional" can be used as a synonym for "purposeful," but in the philosophy of mind it has come to have a broader but more technical meaning. Although there is disagreement about exactly how the term should be defined, the general idea it is intended to capture is that mental states have semantic or representational content, sometimes described by saying that they represent (or are "directed toward," or "about") other states of affairs.

Intentional notions, in this sense, appear in several topics that are of concern to cognitive ethologists. For instance, an ethologist who considers the possibility of planning in nonhuman animals is wondering about an intentional notion, for a plan involves the representation of future actions.

Many of the terms that appear in folk psychology are also intentional in Brentano's sense. For example, beliefs and desires are intentional, for to have a belief one must have a belief *about* something and to have a desire one must have a desire *for* something. Intentionality, in Brentano's sense, is not limited to the so-called propositional attitudes, such as belief and desire, found within folk psychology. Mental representation, information, and other notions widely used by cognitive scientists are also intentional in the sense that one cannot have information without its being information about something and one cannot have a representation without its being a representation of something.

Why is intentionality puzzling? One reason is that it appears to fall outside the usual causal order of the world. Consider an organism that is capable of formulating a plan. The plan represents future actions, yet these are actions that have not yet occurred and can therefore not be causes of that plan or of its content. Thus, although it might be tempting to think that a belief is about a leopard because it was caused by a leopard, this cannot be a completely general account of intentionality.

Within recent philosophy of mind it has been common to follow a divide-and-conquer strategy of treating consciousness and intentionality independently. Not all philosophers who agree that it is appropriate to consider intentionality independent of consciousness. Searle (1992) is among those who disagree, on the grounds that genuine intentionality requires the subject's awareness of the contents of his or her own mental states. We shall address this concern in chapter 8.

During the last quarter of the twentieth century, philosophers have generally moved away from attempts to provide language-based criteria for understanding mental phenomena and toward approaches that are more grounded in scientific practice. A number of these approaches will be covered in later chapters. For the moment, we wish to illustrate some consequences of this trend by briefly introducing the work of Ruth Millikan (1984), which is of special interest to ethologists because it attempts to provide an evolutionary analysis of intentionality that is divorced from the notion of consciousness. According to Millikan, intentionality is a property derived from the biological or "proper" functions of those things that possess it. Millikan uses bee dances as examples of what she calls "intentional icons." According to her account, bee dances are about the location of nectar because (presumably) the ancestors of current bees were able to pass on the behavioral trait of dancing to current bees as a consequence of the selective advantage afforded to those who exploited correlations between features of dances and the locations of nectar.

Millikan's account is historical in the sense that a thing's intentionality depends not on its present characteristics but on its being the product of a selective process that allows us to say what the thing is for. For example, her theory leads her to say (1984, p. 93) that an exact duplicate of a human being produced by a random process (e.g., an extremely unlikely quantum accident), although it might be conscious or have other mental states, would not have any intentional states (beliefs, desires, etc.), since (initially at least) the creature's brain states would lack the right selectional history to explain their existence. It is also a consequence of Millikan's theory that certain features of the behavior of plants exhibit intentionality. These consequences of her theory might at first seem to make it of questionable relevance to an investigation of the nature of minds. We shall return to this issue; here we only want to point out the extent to which the notion of intentionality has been divorced from the notion of consciousness. This is not to the liking of some philosophers of mind—especially John Searle (1992)—who believe that the separation of issues of consciousness from issues of intentionality is symptomatic of what is wrong with current philosophy of mind.

Empirical Approaches to Intentionality

Different notions of intentionality have the potential to cause confusion about the role of intentional terms in the description and explanation of animal behavior. But rather than see disagreement about the correct account of intentionality as a problem for cognitive science, we see it as an opportunity for developing an empirical account of intentionality. This attitude may seem to present a problem. We are a long way from being able to give an uncontroversial definition of intentionality, but many behavioral scientists believe it is not possible to study a phenomenon without a rigorous (preferably operational) definition of that phenomenon. That this idea is false should be obvious from the early investigations of the chemical natures of gold, carbon, and other elements. Before gold's atomic structure was understood, overt properties such as density, hardness, color, and reactivity were used to determine whether a given specimen was indeed gold. It would have been premature to define gold in terms of those properties, since, like carbon, gold could have turned out to occur in more than one form. A precise definition of "gold" formulated before comparative work had been done on numerous putative examples of gold would have begged certain questions about the nature of gold, since by definition things that shared the overt properties would have been gold and things that lacked the properties would not have been gold. Rough characterizations in terms of overt properties provide an initial classificatory scheme which is then revised by careful comparative work (such as the work that led to revisions in the concept of gold to include ideas about atomic structure within an empirically productive theoretical framework). (See Kripke 1972 for a general account of scientific terms on which these considerations are based; see Crick 1994 for an application to the notion of consciousness.)

The motivation for a comparative approach to the study of intentionality should now be clear. The empirical utility of a notion of intentionality will depend on whether it can be fit into an appropriate theoretical framework. This cannot be decided *a priori* by philosophers any more than philosophers could have decided whether gold, carbon, etc. was a better classification scheme than earth, air, fire, water. Cognitive scientists would be ill-advised to look to philosophers for a crisp and empirically rigorous definition of intentionality (even if some philosophers promise to provide it). Philosophical conceptions of intentionality distinguish a certain class of phenomena from others. Given a particular classification scheme based on a particular philosophical conception, further investigation may show whether there is a scientifically useful theoretical basis for including all the phenomena initially characterized in this way. Phenomena initially included may come to be dropped from the categorization scheme, and some phenomena initially omitted may be usefully included. Or the phenomena picked out by the philosophical categories may turn out to be so heterogeneous that no useful theory can be built around them. From this perspective, the variety of philosophical views about intentionality is a good thing insofar as they suggest different bases for comparative studies.

The question whether to treat intentionality as a property of minds, as a property of sentences, as an aspect of biological function, or in some other way takes on a different significance from this perspective. Brentano, Millikan, and other authors of theories of intentionality provide criteria for distinguishing some phenomena (intentional ones) from others (non-intentional ones). Some of these criteria are more easily applied than others. The resulting categorization schemes may not agree in all cases, but they may provide equally useful starting points for more detailed comparisons of the phenomena. The results of comparative work may lead to refinements in the notion of intentionality, or to its abandonment, but this cannot be predicted reliably when the empirical work has not been done. The main point here, though, is that choosing to start from a particular categorization scheme does not commit one to accepting that it is the correct scheme. Indeed, investigation of conflicting categorization schemes might even hasten convergence on a more useful scheme.

Ethology, Intentionality, and Consciousness

Griffin has placed the issue of animal consciousness firmly in the center of cognitive ethology. Somewhat ironically, those philosophers who have turned their attention to cognitive ethology have had rather little to say about consciousness, and rather more to say about intentionality in Brentano's sense and about the associated phenomena of representation and meaning. Because "intentionality" in this sense is a technical term within philosophy, it has received comparatively little attention from ethologists, although there are notable exceptions, including Cheney and Seyfarth (1990) and Beer (1991) (also see Bekoff and Allen 1992). It is also the case that although not explicitly discussed in these terms, much of the current research on deception and self-recognition is about intentionality (see Byrne 1995).

We believe that to elucidate the relationship between consciousness and intentionality is the most difficult task facing all existing attempts to naturalize the mind. It is a task that we do not expect to accomplish fully within these pages. However, we will try to indicate how a comparative, ethological approach may have something to contribute to the project.

Many recent philosophical discussions of consciousness have stressed the heterogeneity of the notion. For some, including Wilkes (1984, 1995), this has called into question its scientific utility; for others, including Dennett (1991), Flanagan (1992), and Nelkin (1993), it suggests that empirical progress may be possible if one is careful to treat different aspects of consciousness independently. Most recent discussions of intentionality specifically dissociate it from consciousness, as we have already indicated with respect to Millikan's account.

According to Searle (1980, p. 454), intentionality requires "some awareness of the causal relation between the symbol and the referent." This appeal to awareness requires further elucidation. Searle's claim that this awareness probably arises from the biochemical properties of nervous systems does not help to elucidate the idea. He draws an analogy to the biochemistry of digestion, but because digestion is identified as the mechanical and chemical breakdown of ingested substances it is clear why biochemistry is important to digestion. It is less clear why it should be important to consciousness, which is not identified in chemical terms. We shall argue (in chapter 8) that a comparative approach with cognitive ethology as a major component has the potential to demystify the notion of awareness to which Searle appeals. We believe that progress is possible by paying attention to the cognitive ability to detect perceptual errors.

Concluding Remarks

Our aim in this book is to promote an interdisciplinary approach to theories of mind. The perspective should be broadly naturalistic, although there are various senses of naturalism that might prove satisfactory and deserve independent investigation. We see Darwinian continuity as one plausible route to a naturalistic theory of mental phenomena and ethology, and cognitive ethology as essential to the pursuit of this route. Our project, then, is to explore how evolutionary accounts of mental phenomena can inform and be informed by philosophical accounts. Wherever possible, we will concentrate on available data or suggest studies that will promote understanding of animal minds.

2

A Brief Historical Account of Classical Ethology and Cognitive Ethology

Every realm of nature is marvellous . . . so we should venture on the study of every kind of animal without distaste; for each and all will reveal to us something natural and something beautiful. If any person thinks the examination of the rest of the animal kingdom an unworthy task, he must hold in like disesteem the study of man.

—Aristotle (*Parts of Animals* 645 a 17-27, quoted on p. 44 of Robinson 1989)

Concepts such as "play" and "learning" have not yet been purged completely from their subjectivist, anthropomorphic undertones. Both terms have not yet been satisfactorily defined objectively, and this might well prove impossible . . .

—Niko Tinbergen (1963, p. 13.)

We are not like other animals; our minds set us off from them.

—Daniel Dennett (1995, p. 371)

In this chapter we consider some major strands in the history of approaches to the study of animal behavior and cognition. These range from the "anecdotal cognitivism" of the late nineteenth century to present-day cognitive ethology via behaviorism and classical ethology. Our aim is to provide a historical context for understanding the origins of certain views about the attribution of mental states to animals and the continuing controversy surrounding those views. The incipience of different points of view can be attributed to attempts to repair apparent deficiencies in earlier views. The return to a form of anecdotal cognitivism that came with the publication of Donald Griffin's book *The Question of Animal Awareness: Evolutionary Continuity of Mental Experience* (1976) seemed to many to be a return to past ills. Nonetheless, Griffin's work too can be seen as a necessary antidote to overly narrow views about the nature of scientific theorizing about animal minds.

We have not aimed to provide a comprehensive historical review (for that, we recommend Burghardt 1973, Burghardt 1985, Thorpe 1979, Burkhardt 1981, Burkhardt 1983, Boakes 1984, Richards 1987, Dewsbury 1989, and Lorenz 1996). Rather, our brief historical analysis serves to underline our point that cognitive ethology is truly an interdisciplinary enterprise with a broad agenda that is very much grounded in classical biological thought.

Darwin, Continuity, and Anecdotal Cognitivism

A number of people contributed to the foundations of animal-behavior studies, but it seems to be little disputed that Charles Darwin's ideas were the most important contributions of the third quarter of the nineteenth century (Burkhardt 1983; Boakes 1984; Krushinsky 1990). Indeed, Donald (1991, p. 25) claims that "modern theories of our mental origins should really be dated from the publication of Charles Darwin's landmark book *The Descent of Man.*"

Darwin, as we saw in chapter 1, stressed mental continuity between humans and other animals. There are two aspects of Darwin's ideas about mental continuity that deserve separate discussion. The first is a commitment to mental continuity over evolutionary history. This has its basis in a theoretical commitment to the idea of modification by descent and selection of physical and behavioral phenotypes. The second is Darwin's commitment to mental continuity among extant organisms, which is based on attributing mental states by the method of observing animals.

Darwin's general ideas about continuity among the species were not always well received by his contemporaries. His claims about mental continuity were especially controversial because they were taken to undermine the idea that humans are uniquely rational beings and therefore to undermine the moral separation between humans and animals (Rachels 1990). Even today, some champions of Darwinian thinking emphasize the division between humans and other animals. For example, Dennett (1995, p. 371) writes of "a huge difference between our minds and the minds of other species, a gulf wide enough even to make a moral difference."

Against the background of Darwin's theory, the default assumption for any heritable characteristic of any organism is that it developed by a process of gradual change from the characteristics of ancestral organisms. If one imagines a design space of possible organismic phenotypes (Dennett 1995), then this assumption amounts to the view that life has evolved by walking its way through that space, rather than by jumping. This distinction between walking and jumping is somewhat fuzzy, for even walkers do not touch every part of the ground they traverse. Nonetheless, the guiding idea behind the default assumption is that large jumps in design space are very unlikely and demand special explanation. A kangaroo's producing an offspring that sprouted wings and took to the air would have radical implications for the Darwinian view of evolution by gradual modification, for most of our understanding of the fossil record is based on the extreme improbability if not the downright impossibility of such an occurrence. For any flying organism, we expect there to have been a series of intermediate forms with limbs that were less adapted for flying and perhaps more suited to gliding.

Thus, for any trait T that is supposed to be an ancestral form of another sufficiently different trait T', the Darwinian idea of continuity presumes that there are viable intermediate forms between T and T'. It is possible, of course, that no extant organisms display those intermediate forms, for the possessors of those traits may have all died a long time ago. But if it is to be maintained that T' evolved from T, the possibility of those intermediate forms must be recognized. Whether one thinks that the sequence from T to T' was gradual or that it was punctuated by short periods of rapid change followed by long periods of relative stability doesn't matter. As long as one believes that *naturam non facit saltum* (nature does not make jumps), one accepts a version of Darwin's continuity hypothesis.

But there is another sense of continuity that is sometimes associated with the theory of evolution, and it too is suggested by Darwin's writings. This is the idea that all extant organisms, taken together, constitute a continuous lineage (from lamprey to ape to human, as Darwin suggests in the passage we quoted as an epigraph to chapter 1). It is reminiscent of the ancient idea of a *scala naturae,* according to which all species may be arranged from higher to lower. But there is no justification for such a view. Although it is true that between any two extant species there must be at least one continuous sequence of relatively small modifications (through a common ancestor), it is not necessary that any such path pass through other extant species.

Nonetheless, Darwin did write as if there is continuity among extant organisms of nonmental and mental characteristics. He argued for mental continuity of extant organisms in a fashion that is appropriately labeled "anecdotal cognitivism" (Jamieson and Bekoff 1993). He thought that scientists often underestimated the mental abilities of nonhuman animals, and he freely used anecdotes to make his case. Darwin attributed cognitive states to many animals on the basis of observations of particular cases rather than controlled experiments. In addition to making a strong case for mental continuity (along with Herbert Spencer) between humans and nonhumans ("There is no fundamental difference between man and the higher animals in their mental faculties"—Darwin 1871, p. 448), in Darwin's writings we also see the clear attribution of feelings and emotions to nonhumans. (For a discussion of how Darwin's anthropomorphism informed his ideas about continuity, see Crist 1996.) For example, Darwin (1871, p. 448) claimed that "the lower animals, like man, manifestly feel pleasure and pain, happiness, and misery." He also observed that monkeys are capable of elaborate deceit, and he even studied problem solving in insects (1896). Furthermore, Darwin used behavioral evidence, such as pausing before solving problems, to support his contention that even animals without language are able to reason (Donald 1991; see also Krushinsky 1990).

Anecdotal cognitivism also found a home in the work of Darwin's disciple George Romanes (1883). For both Darwin and Romanes, Boakes (1984, p. 51) writes, "the potential science of animal behavior was a form of natural history, with methods and theories not very different from those of mid-century anatomy or geology." Although Romanes collected and classified anecdotes concerning cognitive abilities and the nature of animal minds, he was more critical than many of his contemporaries, including Darwin (Boakes 1984). Romanes also believed that the ability to reason was important in helping animals adapt to novel situations, especially during first encounters with novel environments (Krushinsky 1990). Griffin (1984, 1992; see also Dawkins 1993) also believes that adaptive versatility in behavior is a strong indicator of animal thinking.

Darwin did not rely solely on anecdotal evidence, and in several ways his methodological suggestions presaged the field of comparative ethology. He appears to have been the first person to apply the comparative phylogenetic method to the study of behavior, having done so in his attempt to answer questions concerning the origin of emotional expression (Darwin 1872). Darwin used six methods to study emotional expression, some of which did not work well and others of which seem naive nowadays (Burghardt 1973, p. 326): observations of infants, observations of the insane (who were less able than normal adults to hide their emotions), judgments of facial expressions created by electrical stimulation of facial muscles, analyses of paintings and sculptures, cross-cultural comparisons of expressions and gestures (especially of non-Europeans), and observations of animal expressions (especially those of domestic dogs, *Canis familiaris*). According to Thorpe (1979, p. ix), by using the comparative method Darwin "showed the way forward"; however, his ideas were slow to catch on, possibly because his other contributions overshadowed his efforts in the comparative study of behavior.

Conway Lloyd Morgan, a contemporary of Romanes who also was very interested in animal minds, is well known for his canon: "In no case may we interpret an action as the outcome of the exercise of a higher psychical faculty, if it can be interpreted as the outcome of the exercise of one which stands lower in the psychological scale" (Lloyd Morgan 1894, p. 53). Although Lloyd Morgan did not give much credence to anecdote, it is important to note that he largely accepted Darwin's and Romanes's views of the continuity of mental phenomena. Indeed, Lloyd Morgan's canon presupposes animal mentation: "lower" psychological states are, after all, psychological states (for discussion see Rollin 1989 and Rollin 1990). (On what Lloyd Morgan meant by "lower" and "higher" psychological faculties, see Sober 1997.)

Psychological Behaviorism: The Common Sense of Science and the Shrinking of the Mind

Behaviorism in psychology arose as an attempt to bring rigor to the study of animal behavior. The much-discussed case of Clever Hans, a horse who was reputed to be able to solve arithmetic problems (Boakes 1984; Fernald

1984; Smith 1986; Wilder 1996), provides a prime example of what was perceived to be wrong with anecdotal cognitivism. Many Germans suspected fraud, but in September 1904 a commission of thirteen men, including the prominent scientists Oskar Heinroth (Konrad Lorenz's mentor) and Wilhelm Stumpf, put their names to a report that failed to find any evidence that Clever Hans was being cued by his trainer. Later that year, however, Stumpf and Oskar Pfungst issued a report showing, by the use of proper experimental controls, that Hans was in fact responding to unintentional cues from the people around him. For many psychologists, the initially mistaken conclusions about Clever Hans were taken as indicative of the nature of behavioral studies as "soft science" and led to attempts to bring psychology more in line with "hard sciences" such as physics and chemistry (Boakes 1984; Smith 1986).

By insisting on replicable, controlled experimentation that manipulated only measurable stimuli and recorded only observable behavior, behaviorists such as J. B. Watson (1930) and B. F. Skinner (1974) sought to apply the methods of the hard sciences to psychology. Many behaviorists went further and adopted the logical positivists' insistence on operationalizing all theoretical terms by reducing them to observable or measurable phenomena. The hope was that by these methods it would be possible to control behavior and to provide explanations that covered the behavior patterns that animals (including humans) display under a wide variety of conditions.

Philosophical Behaviorism: The Interpretation of Mind Talk

Psychological behaviorism should be carefully distinguished from philosophical behaviorism, which is most associated with Gilbert Ryle (1949). Although these two movements arose contemporaneously, their objectives and their philosophical outlooks were rather different. Philosophical behaviorism was first and foremost a doctrine about the meaning of ordinary mentalistic language, not about scientific method. Whereas the psychological behaviorists were heavily influenced by logical empiricist (or positivist) views of science, the philosophical behaviorists were often more influenced by Ludwig Wittgenstein's (1953) rejection of positivism. Proponents of philosophical behaviorism often regarded the attempt to bring science to bear on philosophical issues about the mind as a form of scientism—exaggerated trust in the power of science to answer questions in any domain of enquiry. Philosophical behaviorism is no longer a popular view among philosophers, although many regard the work of Dennett (1969, 1987, 1991; see also Dahlbom 1993) as a continuation of some major aspects of its tradition, albeit within the framework of cognitive science. Psychological behaviorism has proved more durable, partly because its methods and goals have remained more flexible (it is thus much harder to pin down exactly what behaviorism amounts to besides skepticism about the appropriateness and utility of mentalistic notions for the purposes of science) and partly because it is often promoted as a theory about the boundaries of science (thus it contains an internal critique of alternative attempts to theorize about animal behavior). The roots of these attitudes lie in positivism.

During the years just after the First World War, a group of scientists and philosophers (including Ernst Mach and Rudolf Carnap) met regularly in Vienna and became known as the Vienna Circle. This group wedded newly developed techniques of formal logic to philosophical empiricism (the view that all human knowledge is derived from experience). This logical empiricism later was called logical positivism, and its practitioners positivists. The positivists looked to science, particularly to physics and chemistry, for their ideal model of human enquiry. Using verifiability by empirical means as their test of meaningfulness for any statement, they sought to draw a hard distinction between the meaningful statements of empirical science and the unverifiable and therefore nonsensical statements of pseudo-science, metaphysical philosophy, religion, and ethics. Philosophy owes much to positivism insofar as it encouraged rigorous standards of argumentation and clarity of expression in philosophical discussions. But perhaps positivism did too much to encourage scientists to ignore of a variety of important issues, including ethical concerns (Rollin 1989).

Another effect of positivism was that questions about consciousness and other aspects of mind came to be regarded as unscientific. The Darwin-Romanes approach to mental continuity virtually vanished from the scientific mainstream, because the new breed of psychologists regarded Darwinian hypotheses about animal mentality as completely untestable by empirical means. Rollin (ibid., p. 51) points out a curious aspect of this state of affairs when he asks: "Why, by 1930, had the Darwin-Romanes approach to mind virtually vanished from mainstream scientific activity, whereas Darwinian biology has flourished?" Many of those who are critical of mentalistic explanations on the ground that they appear to be merely "just-so" stories nonetheless readily accept evolutionary explanations that, in many cases, are also just-so stories based on confidence in our ability to reconstruct the past. Some may think "so much the worse for evolutionary explanations," but we think that this would represent an excessively narrow view of science. Rollin (p. 106) puts it this way: "Behaviorism was both a cause and effect of . . . the common sense of science. It is an outcome of the fact that the common sense of science ignores moral and value questions, that it stresses observables as the only material of science, that it is ahistorical and has a simplistic positivistic bias, that it values science that leads to control, and exalts nineteenth-century physics and chemistry as the model to which all science should aspire, and emphasizes laboratory experiments." The important point here is that the development of a fully evolutionary cognitive ethology may be hampered by comparisons to physics that do not respect fundamental differences in the complexity of the phenomena studied.

Behaviorism in its strictest stimulus-response incarnation has few adherents today, but many present-day psychologists urge a behavioristic theoretical outlook and behavioristic methods, and even adopt the label "behaviorist." These neobehaviorists are willing to theorize about unobserved processes internal to an organism ("intervening variables" in behavioristic jargon) in order to explain the organism's behavior. Different approaches to these ideas can be traced back to Clark Hull (1943) and Edward Tolman (1951), two early proponents of the utility of intervening variables for psychological explanations who differed on the types and the theoretical status of these variables. Hull, a strict mechanist, recognized only a very small set of intervening variables, such as thirst and habit (about eight in all, according to Bower and Hilgard 1981). Hull also sometimes wrote as though the intervening variables were merely convenient fictions, not to be accorded any real status in the psychology of the organism. Tolman recognized a much richer set of internal processes, and he is now sometimes credited with being the first of the modern cognitivists.

One effect of behaviorism in the study of animal behavior was that, as Rollin (1990) colorfully puts it, animals lost their minds. Another significant effect was that psychology became debiologized. Neither of these effects is fully mitigated by neobehaviorist acceptance of the importance of internal processes for explaining behaviorists. Organisms treated as black boxes were the domain of the behavioristic psychologists, whose task it became to find general learning rules or other rules relating environment to behavior that could be generalized across species. (In practice, however, the application of behavioristic experimental techniques has not gone much beyond the study of laboratory-reared rats and pigeons, which are typically many generations removed from the wild.) The biology of an organism, including its evolutionary history, was important to psychologists only insofar as it was necessary to keep animals healthy and motivated for the duration of the experiment.

The Rise of Classical Ethology

The growth of classical ethology signified a return to some of the ideas of Darwin and the early anecdotal cognitivists, especially with respect to appeals to evolutionary theory, close associations with natural history, and the use of anecdote and anthropomorphism to inform and motivate more rigorous study. Eibl-Eibesfeldt (1975, p. 8) defines ethology as "a natural science, a branch of biology, from which it took the comparative method for the study of behavioral morphology and the analytic method for the causal analysis of behavioral physiology." "Its philosophical stance," Eibl-Eibesfeldt continues, "is critical realism. Its orientation is neo-Darwinistic. . . ." Thorpe (1979, p. 3) also notes that one may think of ethology as one of two main aspects of natural history (the other being ecology). According to Burghardt (1973), ethologists try to separate description and interpretation, each of which is a part of observation. However, description and interpretation cannot readily be separated—it is difficult, if not impossible to describe without engaging in some interpretation, because observation depends on theory (Popper 1959; see also Enç 1995).

According to Eibl-Eibesfeldt (1975), classical ethology emerged primarily in Europe, from zoology, mainly through the work of Konrad Lorenz and Niko Tinbergen, and it is based on the notion of phylogenetic adaptations in behavior. The direct forerunners of ethology are Charles Darwin, Charles Otis Whitman, Oskar Heinroth, and Wallace Craig (see also Dewsbury 1989). Lorenz once claimed that ethology could be defined as "the subject that Heinroth invented" (Thorpe 1979, p. 54).

Lorenz, trained as a physician, comparative anatomist, psychologist, and philosopher, was among the first to appreciate fully the importance of behavioral characters for taxonomic endeavors. He stressed that, because animals perceive only parts of their environments (key stimuli), their behavioral responses are due to perceptual filtering (Lorenz 1996). Tinbergen (1963, p. 430) wrote: "The central point in Lorenz's life work thus seems to me his clear recognition that behavior is part and parcel of the adaptive equipment of animals. . . ." Lorenz's contributions are also important for their emphasis on how innate and acquired components of behavior are integrated ("innate-learning intercalation"), perhaps most famously in his studies of imprinting in geese. (Lorenz's conceptualization of the nature-nurture problem was not readily accepted among his colleagues; see, e.g., Lehrman 1953, 1970.)

Lorenz did little fieldwork, but his knowledge of animal behavior was enormous (Dewsbury 1990). Mainly he watched various animals, both domestic and wild, who lived near his homes in Austria and Bavaria. He freely used anecdote and anthropomorphism, stressed that it was important to empathize with nonhumans, and believed that animals had the capacities to love, be jealous, experience envy, and be angry. Lorenz focused mainly on description rather than experimentation. "The emphasis on blind, quantitative experimentation without prior observation is based," he wrote, "on the erroneous assumption that scientists already know the questions to ask about the natural world" (Lorenz 1991, p. 7). Lorenz also believed that human emotion and intuition were important in understanding animals, and that natural science could not be pursued to the exclusion of human emotion "in the belief that it is possible to be objective by ignoring one's feelings" (ibid., p. 259). In his recent biography—which lacks even one table or graph of data—Lorenz (1991, p. xiii) claimed, "without modesty," that "this represents the most complete investigation to date of the ethology of a higher organism and its social system."

Lorenz is not without his critics. Beer (1982, p. 326) claims that in his 1981 book *The Foundations of Ethology* Lorenz "adopts an attitude of isolation so splendid that he assumes himself absolved from having to keep up with his subject or maintain even minimum standards of scholarship in writing about it." But Lorenz's lack of concern for careful experimentation was more than compensated for by his theoretical contributions and by his relationship with the more careful experimentalist Niko Tinbergen, with whom he would share the Nobel Prize for physiology or medicine in 1973. (The prize was also shared with Karl von Frisch, who worked on the dance language of bees.)

Tinbergen, often called "the curious naturalist" (see Tinbergen 1969 and Dewsbury 1990), complemented Lorenz's more naturalistic and anecdotal approaches by doing elegant, simple, and usually relatively noninvasive field experiments. He was adept at "finding simple problems which he could put to his animals in the wild without disturbing them unduly" (Thorpe 1979, p. 75). Whereas Lorenz took a "naked ape" approach to the study of human behavior, Tinbergen believed that the method (but not the results) of animal studies should be applied to the systematic study of humans (Dewsbury 1990)—and indeed he and his wife conducted a classical study of autism in young children (Tinbergen and Tinbergen 1972). Despite their differences, Tinbergen worked with Lorenz on a number of classical problems, including egg rolling in geese. While Tinbergen and Lorenz made substantial contributions to the study of animal behavior, their emphasis on instincts, internal drives, and energy models of motivation (see, e.g., Lorenz 1981)—on behavior's being driven from within until being released, usually but not necessarily by external stimuli (Kennedy 1992, p. 34)—fell out of favor with subsequent generations of ethologists as it became clearer and clearer that explanations of behavior based on forces such as "outward-flowing nervous energy" (Lorenz) or "motivational impulses" (Tinbergen) were too simplistic. Tinbergen also believed that teleological reasoning (explaining causation by appealing to animals' desires to attain future goals) was "seriously hampering the progress of ethology" (1951, p. 4). He thought it idle to speculate on the possibility of subjective experiences because it was impossible to know whether nonhumans had feelings or thoughts of the future.

Lorenz and Tinbergen established ethology as a recognized subdiscipline of biology with its own journal, *Ethology* (originally called *Zeitschrift für Tierpsychologie*), professional meetings, and a body of researchers who considered themselves specialists in ethology.

Donald Griffin's Agenda for Cognitive Ethology: Consciousness and Versatility

Interest in what has come to be called cognitive ethology was rekindled by Donald Griffin's 1976 book *The Question of Animal Awareness: Evolutionary Continuity of Mental Experience* and by the précis (Griffin 1978) and the commentaries that appeared in the journal *Behavioral and Brain Sciences*. The précis and the associated commentaries provide a valuable historical record of Griffin's early efforts in the field of cognitive ethology. By writing in the same stroke about conscious awareness, mentality, and cognition, Griffin sometimes contributed to the failure to distinguish among various ideas associated with these terms. Indeed, he and many of his supporters and critics have often used these terms interchangeably. For a number of reasons, including this one, Griffin's work has not provided a solid theoretical foundation for cognitive ethology. However, Griffin did provide the stimulation that reopened an important field of inquiry.

In his early works Griffin placed the issue of animal consciousness at the forefront of cognitive ethology, and he has continued to do so in his latest book, *Animal Minds* (1992). Although Lorenz and Tinbergen had already appealed on theoretical grounds to internal states that are not directly observable respectable within ethology, it is Griffin's emphasis on consciousness that has generated some of the harshest criticisms of his work.

All Griffin's writings show the influence of Thomas Nagel, whose 1974 paper "What is it like to be a bat?" stimulated Griffin and many others to ask the corresponding question for many other animals. On page 3 of *Animal Minds* Griffin notes that the aim of the book is "to reopen the basic question of what life is like, subjectively, to nonhuman animals," and on page 233 he says "We want to understand what the lives of these other creatures are like, to them." Although we do not think that Nagel's question is the most suitable starting point for investigating animal consciousness, its historical role as a starting point for cognitive ethology cannot be denied.

Griffin has always been a realist concerning animal minds; he believes that animal minds are not merely theoretical constructs that are of instrumental value for informing ethological investigations. He and many others accept that many nonhumans are conscious according to the common usage of the word. For example, animals are conscious in the ordinary sense that they are sometimes awake and they respond and switch attention between various stimuli. Griffin, however, wants to go beyond such minimal attributions of consciousness. Building on Natsoulas's (1978) definitions of consciousness, which allow that there are different kinds and degrees, Griffin (1992, p. 10) maintains that many animals experience *perceptual consciousness* (which "entails memories, anticipations, or thinking about nonexistent objects or events as well as immediate sensory input") and *reflective consciousness* (an "immediate awareness of one's own thoughts as distinguished from the objects or activities about which one is thinking"). Although the states listed under perceptual consciousness may at times be nonconscious, it is not clear how interested Griffin is in investigating nonconscious mental states. Controversy might also be reduced if a clear distinction were drawn between animals' having mental states and animals' being aware of their mental states (Beer 1992, p. 79)— a point with which Griffin agrees. However, even the claim that animals have mental states is contentious to many skeptics. If cognitive ethology is to be advanced, it will be necessary to bring some clarity to the various sorts of cognitive and mental states that are under investigation.

Griffin (1992, pp. 4–5) takes it for granted that "behavior and consciousness in both animals and men result entirely from events that occur in their central nervous systems." He claims to operate on the basis of emergent materialism, from which "it follows that conscious thoughts and subjective feelings are caused by events in the central nervous system" (p. 255). He rejects the epiphenomenalist view that causation flows only in one direction: from the neural to the mental. It is not clear, but his view about the causation of mental phenomena by neural events may preclude the claim that mental states are themselves neural states. When Dennett (1995, p. 370) writes "Of course our minds are our brains, and hence are ultimately just stupendously complex 'machines,'" he is asserting an identity between minds and brains that is popular among philosophers of mind who accept some kind of ontological naturalism. Griffin (1992, p. 259) views consciousness as an emergent property that "confers an enormous advantage by allowing animals to select those actions that are most likely to get them what they want or to ward off what they fear." He stresses the importance of continuity in structure and function of nervous systems across diverse taxa in making such claims. He discusses how brain size may be related to cognitive competence; however, he maintains that size is not the most important criterion for an organism's ability to perform complex cognitive tasks, and he (somewhat curiously) argues that flexible cognition may actually compensate for limited neural machinery. This view is hard to reconcile with the naturalistic view that complex cognition is a function of complex neural machinery. Although Griffin provides relatively undetailed analyses of difficult concepts such as consciousness, intentionality, rationality, and emergent properties, to focus on his shortcomings in this area is to divert attention from his major goal and from the importance of his work.

Griffin's objective is to show, by marshaling evidence from a very wide range of sources, that mental continuity between extant species cannot be dismissed out of hand. Dennett (1995, p. 371) explains his claim about the difference between humans and other animals, quoted above, as follows: "the difference between us and other animals is one of huge degree, not metaphysical kind." Griffin, like Darwin before him, does not accept that there is a "huge degree" of difference between human minds and animal minds. Griffin provides a wide-ranging natural historical account of the behavior of diverse taxa within a broad comparative perspective. He goes to great lengths to find examples of possible cognition and consciousness in a wide range of organisms spanning many taxa. Griffin is not surprised that what are sometimes called "lower" animals can outperform "higher" animals on some tasks that suggest cognition, especially when these performance differences can be related back to the evolution of behavior under different ecological conditions. Along these lines, Whiten and Ham (1992) note that rats and mice seem to outperform monkeys and perhaps chimpanzees on some tests of the ability to imitate. The conclude (p. 270) that "it would seem that a century's assumptions about the supremacy of primate imitation have still to be experimentally confirmed." (See also Beck 1982 and chapter 3 below.)

Griffin's *Animal Minds* is a comprehensive and comparative review of evidence from a variety of sources. Gee-whiz stories, anecdotes, data from careful observations, and experimental findings are all brought to bear on questions of animal consciousness and animal thinking. Griffin discusses how animals find food, how individuals avoid being taken as food, food caching, mate choice, habitat selection, mental maps, language acquisition, artifact construction, deception, and manipulation. By including information from a range of sources, Griffin hopes to continue to develop support for a sophisticated cognitive ethology in which explanations based on appeals to cognition and more reductionistic and behavioristic explanations find a comfortable home. Griffin's openness to the possible utility of both behavioristic and cognitive explanations in the study of animal behavior stands in contrast to the often more single-minded views of his critics. Nonetheless, because his emphasis is on establishing the plausibility of mentalistic explanations, his pluralism is easily ignored or dismissed.

To support his objective of promoting mentalistic explanations of animal behavior, Griffin offers three criteria by which consciousness can be inferred: versatile adaptability to novel challenges, neurophysiological correlates, and the richness of animal communication (1992, p. 27). Griffin claims that many examples of animal communication provide a "window on animal minds." Griffin maintains that animals do not merely utter "groans of pain" that indicate the physiological state of the individual (see also Marler and Evans 1995). Rather, in many cases, animals provide information about their thoughts and feelings. Nonetheless, there is a limit to which analyses of animal communication can provide the kinds of support that Griffin needs to bolster his notion of animal consciousness; communication is not a perfectly transparent window that permits access to other individuals' subjective states. (For an attempt to cash out the metaphor of the window in terms of information communicated, see Allen and Hauser 1993.)

A strong point of Griffin's agenda is that it is clearly interdisciplinary. For example, with respect to the importance of neurobiology in informing and motivating research in animal cognition, Griffin is of the mind that advances in neurobiology and behavior will provide convincing answers to many of the questions that scientists now have about animal consciousness and minds (see also Klemm 1992). Appeals to a future containing a more mature neuroscience can be dangerously vacuous, for the future can always be put off until we like what it brings (Bekoff 1995a). And even when we know a lot more about nervous systems, this knowledge will not necessarily replace appeals to explanations of behavior that use a more psychological vocabulary, perhaps even including folk-psychological terms (Saidel 1992; chapter 4 below). From a comparative perspective too, attempts to infer functional similarity from neurological similarity will always be insecure, because similar structure is no guarantee of similar function (consider bat wings and human hands) and because the mappings between nervous systems in different species will never be exact. (We thank Kim Sterelny for reminding us of these points.)

Because of his critics' strong and in some cases personal attacks on his views, Griffin often comes across as defensive. Defensiveness may have been necessary in his earlier works, but it is not necessary now. We believe that Griffin weakens his case by being so defensive. The plethora of data and the volumes of work that are available now indicate that many scientists are very much interested in animal minds and that they are following Griffin's courageous lead in attempting to study animal cognition more rigorously than has been done in the past.

Another justifiable criticism of Griffin's work is that he does not suggest how we may go about rigorously testing his and others' ideas about animal minds or animal consciousness. Part of Griffin's agenda concerning the question "What is it like to be a ____?" is "to outline how we can begin to answer this challenging question by analyzing the versatility of animal behavior, especially the communicative signals by which animals sometime appear to express their thoughts and feelings" (1992, p. 3). But Griffin often does not tell us *how* to go about empirically testing his and others' ideas. Rather, he primarily tries to convince readers of the possibility of animal cognition by citing numerous examples that indicate consciousness and thinking and by appealing to the notion that cognitive explanations are often more parsimonious than are behavioristic explanations. It is up to others to pick up where Griffin leaves off by using his collection of anecdotes, his discussion of empirical research, and his ideas to motivate new and highly innovative studies, the bases for which might not have been obvious before his work.

There are those who assert that reductionistic approaches in ethology have been more fruitful in furthering our understanding of animal behavior than have other lines of inquiry, especially cognitive investigations. For example, Colgan (1989, p. 67) claims: "There can be no historical doubt that behaviorism has advanced ethology as a science, whereas the methods advocated by cognitivists have yet to prove their worth. Until mental concepts are clarified and their need justified by convincing data, cognitive ethology is no advance over the anecdotalism and anthropomorphism which characterized interest in animal behavior a century ago, and thus should be eschewed." To suggest that cognitive ethologists should hang up their field glasses and have nothing to do with talk about nonhuman intentional behavior (Heyes 1987a) is premature. If we hang up our field glasses, we give up one of the basic pieces of equipment with which we and others inform our knowledge of the behavior of other animals. Reasons for our disagreeing with these pessimistic assessments will be brought forward in the rest of this book.

Concluding Remarks

Despite the great interdisciplinary interest in cognitive ethology, there is no reason why cognitive ethology cannot or should not concern itself with the four areas that Tinbergen (1951, 1963) suggested ethology should be concerned with: evolution, adaptation (function), causation, and development (Jamieson and Bekoff 1993). Thorpe (1979, p. 169) maintains that ethology is an integrative science and is "in many respects essential for the full and satisfactory development of all other disciplines which are concerned with the whole animal." Cognitive ethology is also an important extension of ethology because it explicitly licenses hypotheses about the internal states of animals. In this respect, cognitive ethology does not represent a major departure from the practices of classical ethologists such as Lorenz and Tinbergen. In practice, however, the explanatory constructs provided by the application of cognitive science to ethology are conceptually richer than Lorenzian constructs such as "action-specific energy" and "drive." Careful observation, description, interpretation, experimentation, and explanation form the raw material for just about all types of analyses of behavior, regardless of one's position on matters of mind; there are no substitutes for detailed ethological investigations. Also, advances in the philosophical analysis of cognitive concepts provide better prospects than older analyses for empirical investigation of the applicability of these concepts to animal behavior.

3

What Is Behavior?

One does not become familiar with animals by enclosing them in a cramped laboratory cage and providing them only with opportunity to exhibit quite specific responses to stimuli that are determined by the rationale of an experiment. On the other hand, it is also impossible to become fully familiar with animals, if . . . they are observed exclusively in their natural habitat. . . . Approach the animal as closely as possible without producing a significant disruption of its behavior that cannot be controlled. . . . Observation in the field is equally indispensable as a *control* for results obtained in captivity.

—Konrad Lorenz (1996, p.221)

Of course, it can always be maintained that there *were* publicly observable differences in the dog's behavior from one occasion to the next, if only I had been very careful in conducting my observations. But . . . the number of different individual beliefs attributed to dogs would fill tomes, and it is simply implausible to contend that there is always a nice difference in their behavior from one occasion to the next . . . because, if other dogs are like my dog, the behavioral repertoire of dogs is itself limited; and wagging its tail, barking and jumping back and forth comprise a large part of this repertoire.

—Raymond Frey (1980, p. 115)

The ethologist Adrian Kortlandt once pointed out to Colin Allen how the invention of field glasses had made ethology possible by enabling thousands of budding ethologists to develop their interests at an early age. In these days of big-budget, high-technology science, the idea that field glasses could launch a science seems almost laughable. Yet many of today's ethologists, if they carry more than field glasses and notebooks, still rely largely on relatively low-tech items such as audio recorders and cameras. Because of this low-tech approach, studying animal behavior can appear to be a relatively simple scientific endeavor. How hard could it be just to sit and watch a few animals?

Those who make a living studying animal behavior already know that it is in fact rather difficult. (For general guides see Martin and Bateson 1993 and Lehner 1996; on what it is like to be an ant watcher see Gordon 1992.) Interdisciplinary progress requires a solid appreciation of these difficulties by those who are not trained ethologists. One set of problems are associated with learning to recognize and describe just what it is that animals are doing. We humans little realize how much of our own appreciation for the subtleties of human behavior is rooted in a biological predisposition to notice them. Despite the proclamations of untrained observers, dogs and other animals have rather large behavioral repertoires. Fifty or more different actions might easily be recognized in a single study of canid behavior (Bekoff 1978a). Thus, to turn to the behavior of members of another species and to proclaim (as Frey does in the quotation above) that their behavioral repertoires are limited is to express an uninformed opinion, but one that is not surprising for an untrained observer.

Behavioral studies usually start with the observation and categorization of animals' behavior patterns. The result of this process is the development of an *ethogram* (a behavioral catalog that presents information about an action's morphology and gives the action a name). Descriptions can be based on visual information (what an action looks like), auditory characteristics (sonograms, which are pictures of sounds), or chemical constituents (output of chromatographic analyses of glandular deposits, urine, or feces, for example). Great care must be given to the development an ethogram, for it is an inventory that anyone else should be able to replicate without error. Thus, for example, if one is to call an action a "bow," then others interested in this motor pattern will need to know what it looks like so they will not mistake bowing for another action, such as stretching. Permanent records of observations allow others to check their observations and descriptions against original records. Usually, after a period of training, there is reliable agreement among different observers about the identification of specific behaviors. However, differences in training mean that reliability across different studies can be problematic.

Of course, people differ on how they categorize and distinguish among behavior patterns—for example, when they split one behavior pattern into two and when they lump two behavior patterns into one. The problem of individuation is at the root of the construction of an ethogram for a given species. The number of actions and the breadth of the categories that are identified in a behavioral study depends on the questions at hand, but generally it is better to keep actions separate in the early stages and to lump them together only when the questions of interest have been carefully laid out. Many good ethologists begin with the attempt to develop an awareness of the senses that the animals use (singly or in combination). It is highly unlikely that individuals of any other species sense the world the same way we do. Indeed, it is unlikely that even members of the same species sense the world identically all the time. It is important to remain alert to the possibility of individual variation.

To go beyond the mere observation of behavior requires one to record what has been observed. This in turn requires the selection of a vocabulary. Terminological choices, often made unconsciously at the very beginning of a study, can seriously affect what is subsequently learned. An unfortunate choice of descriptive terms may cause the observer to focus on some aspects while unwittingly excluding other equally important aspects of the many behavior patterns that animals perform under diverse conditions. As the quotation from Frey reveals, an impoverished vocabulary for describing behavior can lead to a failure to appreciate relevant differences.

Behavior vs. Action

Terminological difficulties begin with the very notion of behavior. What is behavior? What should ethologists be looking for if they wish to study it? Most behavior involves observable movements or products of these movements (such as vocalizations, glandular secretions, or excretions). But it would be incorrect to make movement a necessary condition of behavior, for sometimes the *suppression* of movement is a significant feature of an animal's behavioral repertoire (as when an organism freezes upon detecting a predator). Conversely, not all movements are behaviors; some movements may be due to the direct application of external physical force. One would not, for instance, expect an ethological explanation for the motion of an armadillo dragged 50 meters along a highway by a speeding pickup truck. The common-sense distinction implicit in these examples is between something that an animal *does* and something that *happens to* an animal. But, as with many common-sense distinctions, it is hard to make this distinction rigorous.

Philosophers have traditionally discussed a related distinction under the auspices of action theory. Actions are often defined as deliberate (or intended), or as resulting from what Aristotle described as practical reasoning. In a relatively early interdisciplinary attempt to apply philosophical theory to ethology, Purton (1978) argued for the importance of the distinction between actions and other movements. She cited winking at someone as an example of an action, and blinking in response to an air puff as an example of mere movement, and she implicated the same distinction in the difference between raising a limb and a limb's going up. Apparently unmindful of examples of deliberate freezing, Purton erroneously claimed that "logically" an animal cannot perform an action without making some kind of movement. Let us, however, set aside this objection and attend to the issue of whether the distinction between action and mere reflexive movement is significant for ethology, as Purton claimed.

The first thing to note is that the philosophical distinction is not quite the same as the common-sense distinction between what an animal does and what happens to it. Things that merely happen to animals require no input of energy on their part. The kinetic energy of the pickup truck is sufficient to account for the movement of the unfortunate armadillo down the highway, whereas the kinetic energy of the puff of air may be considerably less than is required to move the eyelid down and up. The eyeblink reflex is an "energy-added" system—it depends on energy contributed by the organism beyond the external forces that were immediately applied. In general, an adaptive explanation is required only when energy is added (although perhaps not always when energy is added). Typically, an energy-added system can be given an adaptive explanation when it is possible to say why the cost to organisms of expending this energy is, on average, worth paying. In the case of the eyeblink it may seem obvious that protecting the eyes is a good thing for the organism. In fact, it is not so obvious. Aside from the energy required to contract the muscles involved, the organism suffers a potential cost from being momentarily blind while the eyelid is closed. Providing an explanation of why the organism blinks in some circumstances and not in others lies within the domain of ethology. Thus, the philosophical distinction between action and mere movement does not delimit the proper domain of ethology.

So much for the role of the distinction with respect to classical ethology. What about cognitive ethology? After all, intentionality in the sense of purposiveness is considered to be a defining characteristic of action, and purposeful behavior is also within the domain of cognitive ethology. Certainly the extent to which organisms may deliberate, plan, and act on the basis of those deliberations is one of the interests of cognitive ethologists. But it is by no means the only topic of interest. The broader notion of intentionality that is due to Brentano plays an important explanatory role even in cases where deliberation is not an issue.

The distinction between deliberate behavior or action (on the one hand) and reflexive behavior (on the other) is closely related to the distinction between voluntary and involuntary behavior that is commonly discussed by psychologists. However, the latter distinction is not as clear cut as it may initially appear. With varying degrees of difficulty, humans and perhaps other animals find it possible to learn to control many bodily responses, including bowel movements, eyeblinks, heart rate, and other responses that would typically be considered "hard-wired" or reflexive (or perhaps even "wireless" in the sense that in many species the heart will beat myogenically). There may be differences among species and among individuals in the degree of difficulty involved in bringing different tasks under voluntary control. This blurs the distinction between voluntary and involuntary in a complicated way. Nonetheless, all these responses are energy-adding, so even those toward the reflexive or involuntary end of the scale are going to fall within the domain of ethology. Insofar as cognition affords increasingly sophisticated control of behavioral responses all along the scale from involuntary to voluntary, however, there is going to be no clear point where classical ethology ends and cognitive ethology begins. (There is, of course, a question about whether and when cognitive explanations are most appropriate for various kinds of behavioral systems; we will address this below.)

Purton's distinction between raising an arm and an arm's going up prompts the question of how observed behavior should be described. If all that an observer strictly sees is a limb going up, perhaps the conscientious ethologist should never record that an organism *raised* its limb. A similar controversy arises over so-called functional descriptions of behavior (Hinde 1970)—for example, "threat display" versus "bared teeth" (Millikan 1993; Lehner 1996). Should an ethologist describe a dog as performing a play bow (thereby indicating the function of the bow as a part of a play sequence), or merely as performing a bow? Or should a movement notation that records only relative positions of the dog's anatomical features—e.g, feet on ground, shoulders below hips—be preferred (Golani 1992)?

Function vs. Form

Hinde (1970) notes that in practice there are two broad categories of behavioral description. One involves reference to muscular contractions—patterns of limb or body movements (their strength, degree, and patterning, for example); the other makes reference to the broader context of these contractions—their consequences and their causes. The former scheme involves grouping actions on the basis of similar spatiotemporal patterns of muscular contractions. Phrases such as "head extension," "tail upright," and "bent neck" may be used (see also Golani 1992). The second category involves reference to causes and effects that may lie beyond the organism. Hinde notes that behavior patterns can be classified in terms of consequence, immediate causation, function, or by appeals to history. Classification by consequence allows such phrases as "approaches nest," "picks up nest material," and "rolls eggs." Classification in terms of immediate causation entails grouping activities that share causal factors; for example, all actions that are increased by testosterone can be called "male sexual behavior," and all actions that are influenced by rivals might be called "agonistic behavior." Functional classification involves grouping together behavior patterns that share an adaptive consequence, such as threat, courtship, or hunting. Historical classification can refer to the grouping of patterns that share a common historical origin or to grouping on the basis of a common method of acquisition (e.g., learning or ritualization that has occurred during ontogeny or evolution).

Hinde argues that the second kind of description has the following advantages:

A multitude of variable motor patterns, such as hopping, flying, walking, running, and sidling, can be covered in a brief description when those patterns have common causes or effects.

It allows behavioral units to be described unambiguously in terms of environmental changes. Whether a bird placed grass in her nest, or whether a pigeon pecked at a lever, usually does not lead to disagreements.

Contextualized descriptions are usually more informative than mere physical descriptions. When identical or highly similar actions are used in different contexts (say, hammering with the beak by great tits either to open nuts or to attack rivals), description by consequence calls attention to essential features of the behavior (in this example, the objects to which they are directed).

Hinde stresses that, while descriptions by consequence and other contextualized descriptions are very useful (in general more so than are physical descriptions), there is the danger of overinterpretation. Description and interpretation are intimately linked. When we say that an animal "escaped from a predator" or "avoided the color red by running away," we are not only describing by consequence what happened, but also imputing motivation by suggesting why it happened. The rationales are sometimes regarded as provided by evolution (Dennett 1995) and sometimes thought to be provided by the individual performing the behavior. (Ordinary talk of reasons often mixes adaptive or ultimate reasons with proximate or psychological reasons.) The danger of overinterpretation lies in the fact that seemingly compelling rationales often have no basis in reality. Another reason the classification or grouping together of behavior patterns demands careful scrutiny is that it can lead to spurious claims about common causes or common functions.

Despite Hinde's (1970) arguments, whether there is a proper description of behavior for ethology continues to be controversial. Golani (1992) argues in favor of an acontextual reporting scheme, called Eshkol-Wachmann (EW) notation, that records spatial relations between major anatomical features. Golani claims that EW movement notation is better than ordinary language at revealing commonalities and differences in behaviors. EW descriptions concentrate on the kinematic features of behaviors, and they clearly provide a means for identifying similarities and differences between behaviors with respect to trunk orientation, freedom of movement, and other features that Golani mentions. Golani argues that these features are significant for understanding the neurological organization of behavior. We agree that this is an important goal, but it is not the sole goal of ethological research. Hinde (1970) claims that ethology shares with the rest of biology an interest in questions of "immediate causes" and development. But, following Tinbergen (1951, 1963), he identifies two further questions of special interest to ethologists: What is the function of behavior? How did it evolve? Golani concentrates on neurological mechanisms and ontogeny, and his attention is consequently drawn to the first two questions—questions that Hinde identifies as generic to biology. Although there is some discussion of phylogeny, there is little discussion of function. Golani's use of the EW system plays down the significance of the questions Hinde identifies as characteristically ethological. EW descriptions also seem limited with respect to understanding the evolution and the immediate causes of behavior. The notation does provide one way of assessing similarity across the phylogenetic tree (as Golani illustrates). But, again, complete understanding requires more than EW can provide. Functional demands for a particular behavior can drive the evolution of neurological mechanisms to support that behavior, as well as driving the use of the mechanisms in appropriate circumstances. For example, knowing that play involves maximum freedom of movement does not help us understand why the nervous system provides for such freedom, or why animals play when they do play. A danger of EW notation is that it obscures the function-driven nature of both the evolutionary process and the moment-to-moment expression of behavior.

Coming from a background of philosophical considerations about the nature of psychology, Millikan (1993) argues that ethologists (and psychologists) are interested in explaining behavior only insofar as it is functionally described. A blink involves a motion of the eyelashes toward the toes, but, she claims, it is not the job of ethologists or psychologists to explain why eyelashes move toward the toes. Rather, the eyeblink is of interest to ethology only insofar as it has one or more functions. Millikan (1984, 1993) provides a detailed theory of biological function that explains how a particular behavioral, anatomical, or physiological trait of an organism may possess a function even if it fails to perform that function (Allen and Bekoff 1995a). Whereas Hinde's description by consequence is focused on the actual outcomes of particular behaviors, and his characterization of function refers to "adaptive consequences," Millikan's functional classification scheme depends on facts about evolutionary history.

Although our criticism of Golani's view should make clear that we are sympathetic to Millikan's emphasis on the importance of functional considerations, we think Millikan tends in places to overstate the case against the importance of alternative categorization schemes for ethology. We favor a pluralistic approach according to which it is an empirical question which schemes for categorizing behavior will turn out to be empirically most productive. We doubt that it is possible to predict in advance whether the patterns identified by classifying behavior kinematically will be more helpful for understanding behavior than the patterns identified by classifying behavior functionally. In view of this, the best approach is the pluralistic one of allowing studies to proceed using a variety of classification schemes (Bekoff 1992).

A pluralistic attitude can also be extracted from Purton's (1978) observation that the various frameworks in which behaviors are conceptualized (Purton suggested form, function, causality, and motive or purpose, among which there can be links) lead to the organization of data in different ways. As Hinde (1970, p. 3) noted, behavioral events have to be grouped into classes "by abstracting properties which, to a degree of precision appropriate to the task at hand, recur in more than one event." Some lumping together of distinguishable actions is essential, because each action is probably unique in its exact form. It would simply be cumbersome to deal in any meaningful way with every single action that is performed by any single animal, and composite categories could not be developed for practical purposes. Hinde also suggests that there is no single level of abstraction that provides a single correct method of study for ethologists. *Aristotle*

Concluding Remarks

Cognitive science comprises a number of disciplines, including cognitive psychology, neuropsychology, psycholinguistics, artificial intelligence, and cognitive ethology. What, if anything, do practitioners of these disciplines have in common that makes them all cognitive scientists? An often-suggested answer is that they share a willingness to theorize about the role of internal representations in the production of behavior.

This answer is vague enough to be uncontentious. Trouble arises when one tries to get precise about the notions of representation and behavior that are involved. We shall return to the topic of representation in later chapters. In this chapter we have argued that there is no simple answer to the question "What is behavior?" At one extreme, one might classify behavior in physical terms as changes of position of objects with respect to some frame of reference. At another extreme, one might classify it in the fully intentional terms familiar from philosophical action theory. How one proceeds in this matter is important for psychology, for the two schemes may be completely orthogonal. A certain physical movement of the hand may in one case constitute the action of signing a contract; in entirely different circumstances the very same movement could constitute a breach of contract. Conversely, two entirely different physical movements could both constitute the same action of greeting a friend. The way one chooses to classify these behaviors will affect the way one explains them, for one expects the same explanations for the same behaviors and different explanations for different behaviors.

Because we do not expect there to be a way to decide this choice *a priori*, we favor a pluralistic attitude toward behavioral classification schemes—an attitude that should be sensitive to the questions at hand. An appreciation of methods that are used in the study of animal behavior is necessary. It is important not to be misled by the deceptive simplicity of the question "What is behavior?"

4

But Is It Science?

The awakenings of the 1960s led most psychologists to a search for relevance and to commerce with such concepts as cognition, volition, and consciousness. For many of them, positivism and operationism became dirty words because of the gossip that, back home in philosophy, they were in trouble. This development did psychology great harm.

—Gregory Kimble (1994, p. 257)

There can be no historical doubt that behaviorism has advanced ethology as a science, whereas the methods advocated by cognitivists have yet to prove their worth. Until mental concepts are clarified and their need justified by convincing data, cognitive ethology is no advance over the anecdotalism and anthropomorphism which characterized interest in animal behavior a century ago, and thus should be eschewed.

—Patrick Colgan (1989, p. 67)

Cooperation merely depends upon the behavior of one animal serving as a stimulus that elicits a certain response from the other.

—John Pearce (1987, p. 261)

Must cognitive ethologists rely forever on anecdotal cognitivism and face the ensuing charge of anthropomorphism? Is it possible to investigate mental phenomena in nonhuman animals under natural conditions? Some critics believe that any attempt to investigate the minds of animals must fail to be scientific. Others object specifically to the methods of cognitive ethologists, especially the limitations inherent in fieldwork. Griffin's books have failed to reassure critics that the problems facing cognitive ethology can be solved. Although he provides many examples of behaviors that are suggestive of mental processing, Griffin does not present an adequate theoretical framework for the attribution of mental states.

Here we consider a number of objections to the aims of studying animal cognition and mind that have been raised from within psychology. It is our view that some of these objections are based on differences in vocabulary, but where there are substantive disagreements we hope to make them clear. Later in this chapter we shall outline a framework for the attribution of mental states.

Cognitive Awakenings

Kimble (1994, quoted above) reports as gossip the idea that in the 1960s positivism and operationism were in trouble back home in philosophy. But it was not mere gossip. Quine (1953) had already argued that the logical positivists' theory of meaning relied on principles that were not justifiable from within the positivist framework, and that empirical science and theoretical philosophy are strongly intertwined. Quine revived the following thesis, which he attributed to Pierre Duhem: No scientific hypothesis is ever tested independent of an ensemble of mathematical, logical, theoretical, and empirical beliefs; consequently, the results of any experiment can never be taken as logically refuting any specific hypothesis, only as logically refuting the ensemble as a whole.

These troubles for positivism resulted in a broader conception of the relation between theory and evidence than is allowed by strict operationism. According to strict operationism, any theoretical term must be directly defined in terms of observable phenomena. But if no hypothesis is ever tested in isolation, the failure of an experimental prediction can always be attributed to any of the numerous assumptions that were used to generate the prediction. Any particular theory may be implicated in a large number of predictions, and the rejectability of the theory does not depend on its involvement in the failure of any single prediction. In view of the logical structure of this situation, as elaborated by the Quine-Duhem thesis, there is no objective reason for denying scientific status to theoretical terms that are not directly operationalized.

This view of the relationship between theory and evidence suggests that there are not likely to be any behavioral litmus tests for the attribution of mental states to animals, and that such attributions can be evaluated only in the context of a broad set of observations. Such a view is fully compatible with a thoroughly naturalistic account of mental phenomena that completely rejects dualist ideas about immaterial souls and other supernatural substances. Nonetheless, the idea that there is any room for such notions in science continues to provoke a vigorous negative response from a broad range of psychologists.

It is easy for philosophers of mind to label these responses "behaviorist" and to dismiss them all as results of a conditioned association of mentalistic terms with dualism. Unfortunately, the label "behaviorist" obscures some important distinctions among psychologists. In many cases, however, it does seem that scientists who resist the use of mentalistic terms are reacting against a perceived return to mysterious immaterial causes rather than responding to the careful suggestions that naturalistically inclined philosophers are making. This represents an unfortunate miscommunication about what is really at stake in this dispute.

Such miscommunication is apparent in Howard Rachlin's (1991) discussion of cognitive ethology in his textbook of behavioristic psychology. Rachlin specifically discusses Dennett's (1983) methodological suggestions for cognitive ethologists. Dennett suggests that ethologists frame hypotheses within a hierarchy of intentional attributions. Zero-order explanations of behavior involve only stimulus-response mechanisms. First-order explanations invoke representations of non-intentional facts about the world to explain behavior; for instance, a monkey's ascent into a tree might be explained by the first-order belief that a leopard is present. Second-order explanations involves representations of first-order intentional facts, such as the belief that a leopard wants to eat me. Third-order intentionality involves representation of second-order facts. And so on. Rachlin reports this proposal as a suggestion about levels of consciousness, thus obscuring the distinction between intentionality and consciousness that is so important to much contemporary philosophy of mind (including Dennett's). Rachlin proceeds to reject Dennett's proposal on the ground that the ordinary notion of consciousness is of no scientific value. But Dennett (1991) would agree that the ordinary Cartesian notion of consciousness is of no scientific value, so this critique misses its target by a wide margin.

Cognitive ethologists need not be particularly embarrassed if they are unsure how to pursue questions about animal consciousness. The strategy of condemning cognitive ethology because it has trouble with consciousness is about as creditable as the strategy of so-called creation scientists who seek to undermine astronomy by pointing out that astronomers can't explain what caused the Big Bang. There is much more to astronomy than that, and there is much more to cognitive ethology than questions about animal consciousness.

It is all too easy for participants on both sides of this debate to lapse into name calling, and drawing analogies with religious arguments seems to be a favored strategy. Indeed, the charge of anthropomorphism (Humphrey 1977; Colgan 1989; Kennedy 1992) often leveled against those who would attribute mental states to animals hearkens back to theological disputes about attributing human characteristics to divine beings (Mitchell 1996). Blumberg and Wasserman (1995) also play the religion card against Griffin. They claim that his argument from the complexity of animal behavior for animal mind is analogous to the argument from design for the existence of a creator. But the analogy fails: creators are outside nature (almost by definition), but neither Griffin nor other cognitive ethologists are opposed to naturalistic accounts of mental phenomena. Thus, there is less *prima facie* reason to be suspicious of inferences from apparently intelligent behavior to the intelligence of the actors.

We shall do our best to avoid these religious wars and instead examine the arguments offered by critics of attempts to study animal mind to see whether they really do support the conclusions that are claimed.

Mental Privacy

Many scientists who are sympathetic to the idea that nonhuman animals possess mental states are nonetheless skeptical of cognitive ethology. Underlying this view is the worry that we can never know about the mental states of others. In its most general form, this worry is the same as that traditionally known to philosophers as the problem of other minds. Psychologists concerned with human behavior effectively shelve skepticism about other minds in just the same way that physicists shelve skepticism about the mind-independent existence of physical objects. But many behavioral scientists believe that knowledge of nonhuman minds poses special problems. While they admit that knowledge of other human minds is possible, they regard the mental states of other animals as closed to us forever. To distinguish this from the general problem of other minds, we will refer to this as the *other-species-of-mind problem.*

The other-species-of-mind problem underlies the frequent complaint that attributing mental states to nonhumans is unjustifiable anthropomorphism—defined as an interpretation of what is not human in terms of human characteristics (see Fisher 1996 for a sophisticated analysis of this complaint). The charge of anthropomorphism clearly invokes the other-species-of-mind problem rather than the generic problem of other minds, since attributing mental states to other humans cannot, by definition, be considered anthropomorphic.

A very general argument against scientific knowledge of other minds can be reconstructed as follows (see Williams 1992 and Kimble 1994 for examples that follow this pattern):

Mental phenomena are private phenomena.
Private phenomena cannot be studied scientifically.
Thus, mental phenomena cannot be studied scientifically.

The first thing to note about this argument is that its premises depend on a particular conception of mental phenomena, namely that they are "private," and one might ask what this amounts to. Clearly, none of us is capable of directly seeing, touching, hearing, tasting, or smelling the mental states of others. But neither can any of us directly sense quarks. Thus, if all that "private" means is "not directly sensible," quarks are private phenomena too. Scientific understanding of quarks is based on what philosophers call *inference to the best explanation*: the selection of the most plausible hypothesis among competing alternatives for the explanation of observable phenomena. In the absence of further reasons against taking a similar approach to mental phenomena, the argument from privacy is not convincing. If "private" means "directly sensible only by the individual having the experiences," then inference to the best explanation would still seem to be a viable strategy. Indeed, it would fail to be a viable strategy only if the privacy of a mental state meant that it had no effects whatsoever beyond the individual subject possessing the state. Even if there is no conceptual reason why mental states must have effects (as Strawson (1994) has argued), it does not follow that there are no effects. And if they do have effects, it should be possible to discover the characteristics of mental states by an inference to the best explanation of those effects.

The first premise of the argument is probably untrue if "private" means "having no effects whatsoever," yet the second premise is true only if "private" is given that meaning. Thus, either the first premise is false or the second one is, and either way the argument is unsound. Because this version of the argument says nothing specifically about nonhuman animals, it would also rule out attempts to study human mental states—a view that is strongly at odds with contemporary cognitive science. A more restricted version of the argument must be considered for application to nonhuman subjects, viz.:

Mental phenomena are private phenomena.
Private phenomena cannot be studied scientifically in nonhuman animals.
Thus, mental phenomena cannot be studied scientifically in nonhuman animals.

In this version, the second premise makes special appeal to the fact that our subjects are nonhuman animals. Perhaps, a proponent of it might argue, one can infer the presence of mental states in humans, but one cannot do so for nonhuman animals. A commonly stated basis for this view is that, in the absence of language use by nonhumans, their behavior is not discriminating enough to allow the attribution of mental states. (For examples of this claim see p. 115 of Frey 1980 and p. 40 of Rosenberg 1990.)

We do not intend to get embroiled in the dispute about what constitutes a language and whether nonhuman animals meet the criteria for language possession. In fact we shall have very little to say about attempts to teach artificial languages to nonhuman animals (although in later chapters we shall discuss natural systems of animal communication and the role of human language in specifying mental content). Our aim here is simply to point out that in view of our diagnosis of the state of the discussion, it is up to cognitive ethologists to explain the grounds on which a mentalistic explanation might be considered the best explanation of some aspect of animal behavior. Griffin, relying on little more than the methods of anecdotal cognitivism, has not been entirely successful in doing this (Bekoff and Allen 1996). Progress will be made by identifying various aspects of mentality and showing how each of these aspects might be made amenable to scientific investigation. This, however, is the project of later chapters. Here we shall continue to examine the arguments of critics.

The Behaviorist Challenge

Often philosophers to whom we talk about cognitive ethology are surprised to learn that behaviorism is alive and well in studies of animal behavior. Yet it is. For example, Blumberg and Wasserman (1995, p. 142) chide Allen and Hauser (1991) for having "prematurely announced the demise of behaviorism." McFarland and Bösser (1993, p. 289) write that "the problem for the ethologist is that for every cognitive account of an animal's behavior there is always an equally valid behaviorist account." Coupled with the presumption that considerations of simplicity and parsimony favor behavioristic accounts, prospects for mentalistic explanations can be made to appear quite bleak. There are many of our readers, including philosophers and scientists, who will not have much sympathy with behaviorism. But despite the impression of many that behaviorism collapsed under its own weight, many of its methodological presuppositions continue to exert an influence on the thinking of many scientists about issues of animal mind. We will take some time to clarify these issues.

There is a tendency by philosophers of mind and others outside of psychology to lump all the variants of behaviorism together. Within psychology, however, the differences among followers of Pavlov, Watson, Skinner, Hull, and Tolman are very important. Arguments endorsed by one group would not necessarily be endorsed by the members of another group (Smith 1986; Kamil 1987). We will attempt to tread carefully by discussing the arguments of individual authors on their own merits.

In the passage quoted at the beginning of this chapter, Kimble (1994) self-consciously portrays the second coming of J. B. Watson. We have already mentioned that the demise of positivism in the philosophy of science cannot seriously be dismissed as "gossip." Yet Kimble's main argument for why psychology must be behavioristic (1994, p. 258) is based on just this dismissal:

> If psychology takes the scientific road to truth, it will discover that the only observables available are stimuli and responses. That reality means

that, at bottom, psychology must be behavioristic. After that, it can be as biological, cognitive, or even humanistic as it wants to be. But disciplines that study something else—like brain, mind, or human potential—without connections to stimuli and responses may occasionally be science—even elegant science—but they are not psychology. Psychology is the science of behavior.

The transition from what is observable to what may be theorized is not justified. Although cognitive or biological approaches to mind may employ theoretical notions that are not operationally connected to observable stimuli and responses, this is not the same as saying that they have no connection to observables. To suggest otherwise is to attack a straw man, for few present-day theorists deny that there are connections. At issue is the nature of the connections between theoretical terms and observable phenomena. Positivist theories of the nature of science and meaning were beautiful theories; they were, however, ultimately indefensible (Quine 1953), and no amount of lamenting that fact can change it. Once it is realized that few theoretical notions can be strictly operationalized, the inference from what is observable to what is acceptable as a theoretical posit must be seen in terms more sophisticated than Kimble's. What applies to psychology in this regard applies also to cognitive ethology.

We have already stated our view that mental-state attributions, when justified, are justified by inference to the best explanation. To understand any such inference, it is necessary to understand what is being explained and what the alternative explanations are. In human psychology, it is sometimes possible to take the existence of mentality for granted and to make the mental states themselves targets for explanation (Shapiro 1994). However, ethologists are not in a position to take mental states of animals for granted. Furthermore, because ethology is traditionally the comparative study of behavioral phenotypes, it is not surprising that cognitive ethologists regard behavior as their main target for explanation.

Animals face a variety of environmental conditions that change over a range of time scales. Conceivably it could be advantageous for a given piece of behavior to be "stimulus bound" in the sense that it occurs invariably (or almost invariably) in response to some stimulus. However, in many cases stimulus-bound behavior will not be to an organism's best advantage. For example, it does a sated animal no good to continue to eat when its visual and olfactory systems are being stimulated in a way that normally corresponds to the presence of food. Thus, organisms have internal states that modulate their responses to such stimuli. Indeed, laboratory researchers must often take account of this in the design of their experiments. Many laboratory protocols involve lowering the body weight of animals in order to produce the proper state of "motivation" to work for a food reward.

In admitting the notion of "motivation," one agrees that explanations of behaviors must take into account factors that are internal to the organisms in question. Grounds for disagreement lie in the questions of how complex these internal factors may be and how they are best described. In chapter 2 we touched on the controversy between Hull and Tolman about the status of intervening variables in the explanation of animal behavior. Those who are sympathetic to the Hullian line tend to regard internal factors either as further "internal stimuli" or as simple threshold mechanisms that are relatively isolated from one another. However, in some organisms at least, these internal factors seem to be very complicated indeed. For example, an organism's response to a given stimulus may change as a result of a single experience with an entirely different stimulus at a different time and location. Humans provide clear examples; for instance, a news report about a natural disaster close to home may make an individual more likely to pick up the next telephone he or she encounters. Comparative studies of the extent to which the behavior of nonhuman organisms toward a given stimulus may be affected by stimuli of a rather different type are needed; however, tests of observational learning are of particular interest in this respect, for in such cases an organism may acquire a new behavior on the basis of no direct reward.

The degree of interaction between external and internal factors can be conceptualized as falling along a scale. Toward one end of the scale, external stimuli predominate over internal factors and the behaviors can be considered relatively "stimulus bound"; toward the other end, internal factors predominate over external stimuli and the behaviors may be considered relatively "stimulus free." Behavioristic explanations are to be preferred at or near the end of the scale where external factors predominate over internal factors in the causation of behavioral responses. "Predominate" has two senses here, referring both to the extent to which external stimuli that reliably produce a given response can be identified and to the extent to which explanations of behavior tend to focus on the adequacy of those external factors in accounting for the observed behavior.

Toward the stimulus-free end of the scale, it is necessary to invoke internal factors to account for the observed behaviors. These internal factors may be of varying degrees of structural complexity, understood both in terms of the number of different types of internal events and in terms of the types of possible interactions between tokens of these internal event types. Some relatively stimulus-free behaviors, such as quasi-diurnal cycles, may be explained by relatively simple and relatively isolated internal mechanisms, such as a physiological "clock." Cognitive and mentalistic explanations, by adopting typologies of internal states drawn (respectively) from computational theory and folk psychology, provide models for understanding types of complex interactions between internal states. As the example of an internal clock shows, we do not argue that every stimulus-free behavior should be explained cognitively or mentalistically. Rather, we argue, cognitive or mentalistic explanations may be preferred for stimulus-free behaviors that involve integrating inputs from various contexts over extended time scales.

Fodor (1994, p. 90) uses the term "stimulus free" in a way that is related to our use of it. Fodor is concerned, as we are, with the question which behaviors are best explained by attributing mental representations (with meaningful content) to organisms. According to Fodor, intentional states are causally intermediate between stimuli (p. 89: "the currently impinging environmental forces") and behavior, and can therefore be used to account for behavior that is relatively "autonomous" from environmental conditions. It is important to note here that stimulus conditions and environmental conditions should be strictly distinguished. The presence of a coral snake or a king snake will, under certain conditions, produce the same stimuli in an organism, yet these should be considered different environmental conditions because one snake is deadly and the other is not. This serves to make the point that organisms face the problem of using proximal stimuli to guide their reactions to more distal causes of those stimuli.

Fodor simply asserts that some human and some nonhuman behaviors are stimulus free. However, there is a long tradition in behavioristic circles of denying or downplaying the occurrence of behaviors that are not stimulus bound. Stimulus-bound phenomena prove to be especially suitable for laboratory investigation because of the ease with which the relevant stimulus conditions, and hence the behavioral responses, can be replicated. Indeed, the demands of statistical significance and repeatability tend to favor the study of stimulus-bound behaviors in laboratory settings over the observation of animals in natural habitats. Furthermore, behavioristic learning theory is essentially a theory of how behaviors are bound to stimuli, either by being paired with another stimulus (the unconditioned stimulus) to which the behavior was previously bound, as in classical conditioning, or by subsequent reinforcement of a contingent pairing of stimulus and behavior, as in instrumental or operant conditioning.

Although the terminology of stimulus-bound and stimulus-free behaviors is not found in ethology, the concept of stimulus boundedness is implicit in ethological research. The classical ethological concepts of releasers and sign-stimuli (Tinbergen 1951; Hailman 1967; Hinde 1970; Eibl-Eibesfeldt 1975) were used to explain and describe the tight link between the occurrence of a particular stimulus and the performance of a specific response. Numerous examples of behavior studied by classical ethologists count as relatively stimulus bound. The stereotyped responses of sticklebacks to moving red objects, hatchling gulls to beak models, and ants to objects daubed in oleic acid all provide good examples of relatively stimulus-bound behaviors that have been extensively studied by ethologists. These phenomena are especially suitable for laboratory investigation because of the ease with which the relevant stimulus conditions, and hence the behavioral responses, can be replicated. Classical ethology made the turn toward recognizing internal factors with the Lorenzian notions of "action-specific energy" and "drive," which, like Hullian intervening variables, seem to be modelable as simple accumulator-threshold devices. Although such notions are capable of explaining relatively simple internally motivated behaviors, the interactions they permit are far less complex than those suggested by the application of cognitive or mentalistic notions to the description of the internal states of animals.

For cognitive ethologists, however, behaviors that appear relatively stimulus free are often of great interest. For example, vervet monkeys whose behavior indicates that they have detected a predator do not automatically emit an alarm call. The existence of this "audience effect" has been used to argue in favor of a cognitive "referential" account of vervet communication (Seyfarth et al. 1980; Dennett 1983; Cheney and Seyfarth 1990). Likewise, the fact that rhesus macaques appear to scan for group members before deciding whether to give a food signal shows that they are not bound to call when they detect food (Hauser and Marler 1993a,b) and suggests (but requires further empirical investigation to establish) that these animals are aware of the informational content of their signals (Allen and Hauser 1993). Another example is provided by research showing that bees appear to take stored information about physical features of their environment into account in their responses to the dances of hive members (Gould 1986); this degree of freedom in bees' responses has been cited as evidence for cognitive maps in bees (see Gould and Gould 1994). The interest in behavioral "novelty"—for example, macaques' washing potatoes (Galef 1996a) and vervets' soaking acacia pods in order to extract edible parts (Hauser 1988)—can also be understood as interest in stimulus-free behavior.

Some researchers have tended to downplay the importance of behavior that appears to be stimulus free, often by one of the following strategies:

denying that the behavior in question is really stimulus-free   Heyes, for example, has argued that many behaviors described in the literatures of cognitive ethology and comparative psychology can be explained by the presence of stimuli that were not controlled for in the experiments. In response to a study by Povinelli et al. (1990; see also Povinelli 1994a, 1996) showing that chimpanzees could look at photographs depicting humans trying to solve problems and select items that would enable the problems to be solved, Heyes (1994c; see also Heyes 1994d) suggests that the chimps' performance might be explained by matching to sample. In other words, the photographs contained a sample of the right response, which is the stimulus that elicits the response. Another example of the same strategy applies to the observation that a lone vervet monkey confronted with a predator is much less likely to give an alarm call than one in a group (Cheney and Seyfarth 1990). The common response is to suggest that alarm-call production is actually under the control of a complex stimulus involving the conjunction of predator and conspecifics. We do not deny that in specific cases one may be able to provide a sound empirical case to support the claim that a behavior may be bound to a specific stimulus. However, many critics of cognitive accounts mount their criticism without making the relevant empirical case, relying on the fact that for any behavior it is always possible to imagine some (possibly complex) stimulus to which the behavior is bound that has escaped the notice of the researchers whose cognitive inferences are being questioned. Heyes (1994a) seems committed to the view that there must be such a stimulus even if we do not know what it is. This view can also be found in the writings of several earlier comparative psychologists (see Hearst 1975 for a discussion citing Konorski and Miller 1937a,b and Guthrie 1952). In the absence of the relevant empirical data, this could be viewed as a questionable methodological bias.

attributing the behavior to chance   With respect to the much-discussed case of potato washing in Japanese macaques (Galef 1996a), Heyes (1993) suggests that the alleged discovery that washed potatoes are better to eat may in fact have arisen when a potato was accidentally dropped by an individual who had entered the water for other reasons. Heyes then explains the fact that this individual adopted the practice of washing potatoes in terms of operant conditioning. Furthermore, she argues that it is a plausible explanation for the subsequent spread of the practice to other troop members that each of them went through a similar serendipitous process, perhaps accelerated by the tendency of monkeys to congregate (in this case, in the water). She uses this line of argument to deny the suggestion that observational learning was important in spreading the potato-washing technique. Observational learning presents a puzzle to some learning theories because it involves modification of a subject's behavior by processes that do not involve direct reinforcement of that behavior. The appeal to chance is an attempt to avoid those puzzles. Indeed Heyes (1994b, p. 229) argues that it is possible to subsume various categories of social learning under standard paradigms for asocial learning, and that "perhaps . . . it is time also to reexamine the 'special' status of social learning."

ignoring the variations in behavior as a consequence of statistical averaging   This third way in which stimulus-free behaviors tend to get downplayed is a consequence of the common methodological practice of pooling data, a practice that serves to meet the demand that results be statistically analyzable. Many studies establish a statistically reliable connection between a given stimulus condition and a response, in the sense that (for example) subjects produce the response in 90 percent of stimulus presentations. The 10 percent of cases where the stimulus fails to produce the response tend to be ignored in the analysis. (Labeling observations as "anecdotes" and then dismissing them is also symptomatic of this concern with statistical reliability.) Yet, for really understanding the causal complexity underlying the production of behavior, we argue (chapter 7) that it is a mistake to dismiss these data as noise. Here interest in causal and evolutionary explanations converge. For selection to operate, there must be variance in the expression of a given phenotype. Therefore, it is crucial for ethologists not to dismiss such differences just because they are hard to treat statistically. Even if the number of individuals that make up the "noise" is small, there are ways to handle them rigorously.

Concluding Remarks

Psychology, according to a standard dictionary definition, is the study of mind and behavior. For a major part of the twentieth century, psychology, especially comparative psychology, was on a behavioristic track that explicitly denied the possibility of a science of animal mind. This halving of psychology depended on unsound arguments about the privacy of mental phenomena and on views about the relationship between observation and theory that should be rejected. Although many contemporary studies of animal learning and memory adopt a cognitive approach, the influence of behaviorism is still evident in the writings of a number of behavioral scientists. The appearance of the adequacy of behavioristic explanations to account for any observed behavior (McFarland and Bösser 1993) may be an artifact of the way in which the behaviors to be explained are identified. When the full complexity of the behaviors is considered, behavioristic explanations can seem rather less straightforward than the cognitive or mentalistic alternatives. Byrne (1995, p. 134) makes this point forcefully:

> . . . for the 18 cases [of deception] that seem intentional, any one of them can still be challenged and an explanation devised that is based on a hypothetical series of coincidences in the past that might have given rise to learning by association. However, as the hypothesized coincidences become more and more far-fetched, and the histories of possible events that just might have reinforced these tactics grew longer and longer, we decided at some point it was simpler to accept that some primates can understand intentions.

5

From Folk Psychology to Cognitive Ethology

A plausible and familiar reason for wanting to talk about beliefs would be: because we want to explain and predict human (and animal) behavior. That is as good a reason as any for wanting to talk about beliefs, but it may not be good enough. It may not be good enough because when one talks about beliefs one implicates oneself in a tangle of philosophical problems from which there may be no escape—save giving up talking about beliefs.

—Daniel Dennett (1987, p. 117)

Granting, however, that the theory fails from time to time—and not just when fairies intervene—*I nevertheless want to emphasize (1) how often it goes right, (2) how deep it is, and (3) how much we do depend upon it.* Commonsense belief/desire psychology has recently come under a lot of philosophical pressure, and it's possible to doubt whether it can be saved in face of the sorts of problems that its critics have raised.

—Jerry Fodor (1987, p. 2)

Did President Truman authorize the use of an atomic bomb because he believed it would shorten the war against Japan, or because he wanted to send the Russians a message about the superiority of American military technology (or, perhaps, both)? In attempting to answer this question about Truman's intentions, historians reflexively adopt the framework of psychological explanation (ubiquitous among normal human adults) within which actions are understood as caused by the mental states of actors, and mental states are taken to interact the way they do because of their representational properties. For example, a belief that using the bomb would shorten the war would interact with the desire to shorten the war, because these mental states have overlapping representational content. This common-sense approach to mentalistic explanation is referred to as "folk psychology" by philosophers. (It should not be confused with pop psychology, which is often far removed from common sense.)

Developmental psychologists have only recently begun to identify the structure and acquisition of competence with folk psychology. In normal children, development follows a typical sequence. For instance, very young children will not attribute beliefs to other people that differ in content from their own beliefs. In later development, however, the attribution of divergent beliefs becomes entirely automatic and commonsensical. The abnormal development implicated in autism results in difficulties with social interactions (Baron-Cohen 1995; Byrne 1995).

There are two reasons why cognitive ethologists might be interested in folk psychology. One concerns whether members of other species also attribute mental states to one another. This has been investigated by ethologists and comparative psychologists in terms of whether humans are unique in having a theory of mind or whether the capacity for attributing mental states is found in other species, with nonhuman primates receiving the majority of attention (Premack and Woodruff 1978; Cheney and Seyfarth 1990, 1992; Povinelli 1994b; Byrne 1995; Hauser and Carey 1997). (Morton (1996) asserts that the capacity for mental-state attribution is limited to humans.)

The other reason for interest in folk psychology has to do with a more fundamental issue: whether the framework provided by folk psychology can form the basis for a scientific account of nonhuman animal behavior. Our first step in addressing this is to provide a more detailed account of what folk psychology is.

What Is Folk Psychology?

The attempt to provide careful analyses of folk-psychological notions, such as *belief*, has been a pervasive feature of twentieth-century philosophy. But only more recently have philosophers and psychologists begun to specify with care what they mean by "folk psychology." Among philosophers this care has arisen largely in response to eliminativist arguments that attempt to argue for (or at least make plausible) that our ordinary mentalistic notions refer to fictions that have no place in scientific psychology, just as phlogiston and aether have no place in modern physical science. Among psychologists, this care has arisen as developmental psychologists have taken on the task of describing exactly the competence with mentalistic concepts that is acquired by normal human children.

Developmental psychologists can, up to a point, remain neutral on the question of eliminativism. Whether or not folk psychology can provide a basis for scientific psychology, the fact remains that normal human development involves the acquisition of the competence to attribute beliefs, desires, and other mental states to others. Developmental psychology is, however, relevant to the premise—common to many eliminativist arguments—that a child who gains competence with folk-psychological notions has learned a theory (or perhaps a prototheory) of behavior. This is the so-called "Theory theory" of folk psychology. Its chief rival is the Mental Simulation theory, which claims that acquisition of folk-psychological competence involves the ability to predict the behavior of others by simulating their mental states using one's own mental apparatus. One of the tasks of developmental psychologists is to determine whether the Theory theory or the Mental Simulation theory is, in fact, what children acquire, and whether competence with a theory explains the ability of humans to predict the behavior of others. (For reviews see Gopnik 1993; Smith and Carruthers 1996; Sterelny 1997.)

Once it is granted that folk psychology constitutes a theory, eliminativists typically go on to argue that it is a miserable theory by any scientific standard and hence ought to be abandoned (Churchland 1981; Stich 1983). Specific eliminativist arguments depend on highly specific claims about the nature of folk psychology, so one very general way in which defenders of folk psychology have responded to eliminativists is to show that the conceptions of folk psychology implicit in their arguments are unreasonable conceptions. In the current state of this debate, about all that can be said uncontroversially about folk psychology is that it consists of a rather loose set of generalizations about mind and behavior that are reflected in the things that normal adult humans say about mental states and action. (For surveys of these issues see Bogdan 1991; Greenwood 1991; Christensen and Turner 1993; Stich and Ravenscroft 1994; Lycan 1996.)

Although supporters of folk psychology disagree with its eliminativist detractors, they are united with eliminativists in response to hermeneutic (interpretive) approaches which deny that folk psychology is intended to provide causal explanations at all. According to the hermeneutic approach, folk-psychological explanations are not causal but "interpretive"—aiming to provide a story about behavior that makes it intelligible by giving reasons for behavior rather than causes of it. Philosophers who take such an approach typically believe that all of cognitive science is based on the category error of confusing interpretation with causal explanation. *Interpretationism* is often antinaturalistic (Rosenberg 1988) and is often combined with an antiscience stance. (Dennett may provide an exception as an interpretationalist who is not antiscience.) If interpretationalism is a threat at all, it is a threat to all of cognitive science; it is of no *special* concern to cognitive ethology. Because it is well beyond the scope of this book to defend cognitive science generally, we shall have nothing more to say about interpretationalism.

Our view is that folk psychology does constitute a prototheory of behavior, and we accept the following principles:

The theoretical terms of folk psychology paradigmatically refer to conscious states with semantic content, such as the so-called propositional attitudes (belief, desire, etc.).

The generalizations of folk psychology are intended to provide a causal-explanatory theory of behavior that appears to be highly successful.

The generalizations and theoretical terms of folk psychology may be suitably refined and incorporated into a fully scientific theory of mind and behavior applicable to both humans and nonhumans.

In this chapter we consider the consequences of this conception of folk psychology for the development of cognitive ethology.

Consciousness and Mental Content

When beliefs are attributed to human beings, they are taken to be conscious mental states with semantic content. Consciousness is the most difficult topic facing all approaches to human and animal psychology. Banishing consciousness from science, as some have tried to do, does not make it go away. We have no intention of banishing consciousness from our discussion, but we will postpone discussing it until chapter 8. In this chapter we focus on the semantic properties of mental states.

Beliefs, desires, and a host of other states invoked within folk psychology have semantic content. This means that each instance of a belief or a desire may be associated with an expression representing or describing the content of that state. In the example above, for instance, Truman's desire to scare the Russians is a state whose content may be expressed using the sentence "The Russians become scared." Because the contents of these states may be described in propositional form (as expressed by a declarative sentence), the states of folk psychology are referred to by philosophers as "propositional attitudes."

The idea that mental states have propositional content is a core idea of folk psychology that is shared by all cognitive approaches. To make our discussion more concrete, it is worth illustrating a range of possible explanations for a particular piece of behavior. The example we choose is due to Hauser and Marler (1992a,b) and is also discussed by Allen and Hauser (1993). Rhesus macaques who discover a pile of food sometimes emit a vocalization that has the effect of attracting other macaques; however, sometimes, after scanning the area, they remain silent and start to eat the food. A silent eater, if detected by another macaque, will be subjected to aggression from the discoverers, regardless of social rank. All those who take a naturalistic approach to animal behavior can agree that this aggressive behavior occurs because neurons transmit impulses from the retina to brains and back out through motor pathways, and this results in muscles' contracting and thus in the animals' behavior. Opinions divide, however, on the means that should be used for describing these internal events, and on the extent to which this sort of description is even necessary for the purposes of psychology.

As we discussed in chapter 4, strict (Skinnerian) behaviorists would deny the necessity for psychologists to concern themselves with processes that are internal to organisms. They would suggest that knowledge of the relationships between previous behaviors and subsequent stimuli (reinforcers) is sufficient to explain, predict, and control all aspects of behavior. A proponent of operant conditioning might attempt to explain the macaque's aggression on the basis of the past consequences of its having behaved in this fashion in similar circumstances.

Other behaviorists, most eliminativists, and cognitive ethologists agree with one another that description of the internal processes is essential to a scientific account, but they disagree about the proper way to characterize these internal events.

From the perspective of folk psychology, one possible explanation of the macaque's aggressive behavior is that it is the result of a belief that the silent feeder was attempting to cheat on a social expectation that the presence of food be signaled to other group members. This explanation imparts considerable sophistication to the macaque—it requires a grasp of a concept of cheating, among other things. We will not debate the specific evidence that might support this particular hypothesis. Rather, our point is that cognitive ethologists believe that empirical investigation can help to answer questions about whether the animal has the requisite concepts and beliefs. Cognitive scientists, and others who are willing to describe internal states in terms of information processing, are also committed to the semantic approach. Alternative theories of information lead to different characterizations of information content (Allen and Hauser 1993). For example, Shannon and Weaver's (1949) conception of information involves probabilities that can be assigned coherently only insofar as information content can be described determinately (in propositional form). Supposing that the informational content can be given a propositional representation, it does not follow that the information must be represented *in* a propositional form by the animal. A macaque may have an internal state that represents the information that *no food call was produced*, where the italicized phrase is a sentence that describes the content of that state, even if the animal itself represents the information in some other way.

Some eliminativists assert that the proper way to characterize internal events is nonintentionally—that is, without regard to the semantic properties of those events. Within a traditional computational perspective one might imagine that a macaque's brain contains states that interact purely according to syntactic rules whose semantics are irrelevant to the interactions (Dennett 1969; Stich 1983). A more connectionist approach might avoid the mention of rules by speaking of vectors of neural activity (as does Churchland (1995), although he may not endorse the abandonment of semantic notions). In the specific example described here, the idea would be that we could explain the macaque's behavior as a vector transformation from the input vector provided at the retina to the output vector defined over the nerve endings in the organism's muscles. Whether one explains the monkey's behavior in terms of vectors of neural activity or in terms of formal tokens manipulated in a rule-governed manner, these structures do not have to be characterized semantically. Eliminativists (see, e.g., Stich 1983) have argued that semantic characterizations should be avoided by cognitive science because they hinder the discovery of scientific generalizations about cognition. A more moderate view, due to Dennett (1983, p. 343), is that the semantic characterizations are heuristically invaluable, enabling ethologists to bridge the gap between "observation of the behavior of, say, primates in the wild to the validation of neurophysiological models of their brain activity."

Our view is that, because both the strict behaviorist view and the eliminativist view ignore content, those views are less suitable for the explanatory purposes of cognitive ethology than are approaches that ascribe content bearing states.

Content and Evolutionary Explanation

We have, to this point, spoken loosely of cognitive ethology's being concerned with the explanation of behavior. But what exactly does this mean? A useful framework for answering this question is provided by Barbara Von Eckardt in her book *What Is Cognitive Science?* Von Eckardt is primarily concerned with human cognitive psychology and artificial intelligence, two areas that aim specifically to provide theories of what she refers to as "adult, normal, typical cognition." She introduces four schemas for the basic research questions of cognitive science. We see no reason in principle why von Eckardt's questions should not be generalized to organisms of any species. Our generalized versions of these questions (adapted from pp. 92–94 of Von Eckardt 1993) are as follows:

Q1   For a normal, typical member of the species, what precisely is the capacity to _____?
Q2   In virtue of what does a normal, typical member of the species have the capacity to _____ such that the capacity is (a) intentional, (b) pragmatically evaluable, (c) coherent, (d) reliable, and (e) productive?
Q3   How does a normal, typical member of the species typically (exercise his or her capacity to) _____?

Q4 How does the capacity to _____ of the normal, typical member of the species interact with the rest of his or her cognitive capacities?

The distinctively cognitive nature of these questions depends on the way in which the capacity filling the blank is characterized. Parts a–e of Q2 indicate Von Eckardt's views about the relevant characteristics of cognitive capacities. Here we briefly illustrate these characteristics in the context of the food-signaling behavior described above and in the context of play-soliciting behavior, leaving a more detailed discussion about a broader range of examples for later chapters.

(a) Intentionality is understood in the sense of involving representational or informational content. Many notions of interest to ethologists involve intentionality in this sense, including communication, kin recognition, and play. For example, the macaque who emits a food call may be described as signaling "food here." Play-soliciting behaviors (such as the canid play bow discussed in chapter 6) may be characterized intentionally— for example, as conveying a message such as "play with me." (We postpone the question of the utility of such a characterization.)

(b) Pragmatic evaluation refers to the possibility of assigning degrees of success or failure to the exercise of the capacity. For example, a macaque's success in conveying the information that food is available may vary, as may a coyote's success in soliciting play. Certainly ethologists are interested in the extent to which this happens.

(c) Coherence is the extent to which the exercise of a capacity is appropriate to the situations in which it is exercised and integrated with other behaviors. Thus, for example, the appropriateness of emitting a food call may vary in different situations, as may the appropriateness of the position of a play bow in a sequence of other behaviors that it precedes or follows.

(d) Reliability is the degree to which capacities are normally exercised successfully—for instance, how often food calls lead to food sharing, or how often play bows lead to the initiation or maintenance of play. It is worth pointing out that Von Eckardt (p. 48) makes what we think is a false albeit common assumption: that cognitive capacities "are *reliable;* that is, typically, they are exercised successfully (at least to some degree) rather than unsuccessfully." Following Millikan (1984) we think that a broader biological perspective shows this view to be untenable. An unreliable signal (i.e. one that is exercised unsuccessfully more often than not) may be selected so long as the cost of the unreliability is not too high. Nonetheless, degree of reliability is certainly a biologically important variable.

(e) Productivity is the extent to which the capacity can be exercised in novel situations. For example, cases of interspecific play provide an interesting starting point for investigating the productivity of a play solicitation, and the ability of monkeys to use a food call to bring other monkeys near for a different purpose could also be investigated.

Von Eckardt's four schemas apply to much of the research in cognitive ethology. However, her framework reflects the fact that it is rare for cognitive psychologists or artificial intelligence researchers to think of cognition in evolutionary terms. *Cognitive ethology is not just cognitive psychology applied to animals.* Cognitive ethologists are additionally concerned with the evolution of cognitive capacities. These concerns generate a set of research questions that can be captured by the addition of a fifth question schema to Von Eckardt's four:

Q5 Why do members of the species typically have the capacity to _____?

"Why" questions of this type are about the biological functions, the selective history, and current adaptiveness of a behavioral trait. They are answered within an evolutionary and comparative framework (Tinbergen 1963; Hinde 1970; Allen and Bekoff 1995a).

Questions about the biological functions of cognitive capacities have been largely ignored by cognitive psychologists and artificial intelligence researchers. But, rather than view Q5 as unique to cognitive ethology, there is good reason to think that cognitive scientists generally should take a more ethological view of their work. For instance, it may be that differences between human performance on social reasoning tasks and formally equivalent nonsocial reasoning tasks are due to selection pressures in the social domain during the evolution of our species (Cummins 1996; Cummins and Allen 1997).

The desire of cognitive ethologists to place cognitive processes in an evolutionary context (Q5) is inherited from the broader field of ethology. Questions about the biological functions and the natural design of behavior are of particular interest to ethologists. These questions may be answered against the background of the history of natural selection for behavioral traits or in the context of assessing behaviors' contributions to the fitness of current organisms (Allen and Bekoff 1995a,b). Answers to questions about biological function require observation in conditions under which selection is operating or has recently operated, and they require inferences drawn by comparing conspecifics and members of other species in similar and different environments. This aspect of cross species comparisons is important for understanding the role of intentional terms in cognitive ethology.

In our view, intentional terms provide a mode of description of animal cognition that is importantly related to the ability of ethologists to describe the adaptive significance of the neural systems that control behavior (Millikan 1984; Bekoff and Allen 1992). In other words, description of internal states as content-bearing corresponds to evolutionary explanations of cognitive states and abilities. Specifically, content-bearing terms provide a functional level of description of cognitive states. This is important because natural selection operates on functional aspects of a trait. Eyes are adaptive because of what they do (allow organisms to see) not because of how they are built (although energetic considerations may be important in favoring some design features over others). Similarly, an explanation of the adaptive value of a particular content-bearing state may apply to animals with rather different neural architectures. If (as seems plausible) the content of a neural state may be independent of its form, content-bearing terms permit generalizations across species that implement them differently, thus enabling comparative claims to be made. For example, aggression by macaques might be seen as an implementation of a general ability to detect cheaters that might evolve in a variety of species for which social cooperation by food sharing is important to survival.

Stich (1983) challenged the idea that representational content has an important role in cognitive science. He proposed a "syntactic theory of mind" that states its generalizations in terms of formal operations computed on cognitive states without any reference to content. According to the syntactic theory, behavior is explained by way of specifying the computations on these formal (syntactically characterized) states. It might seem possible for a defender of the syntactic theory to argue that what is needed for evolutionary explanation is not a notion of content but some alternative theory of interaction between organism and environment. Such a theory might, for instance, explain the appropriateness of the cognitive system by explaining how environmental stimuli affect an organism through its cognitive mechanisms so as to produce behavior that helps the organism survive and reproduce. States would be adaptive insofar as the cognitive computations involving them led to the right kinds of interactions with the environment.

Perhaps there is no irrefutable response to this challenge to the need for semantic characterizations of states. (Note, too, its similarity to the behaviorist hope of correlating behavior with a diverse range of neutrally characterized stimuli.) But given a syntactic theory, one is deprived of an obvious way of explaining how these states function to produce the appropriate behavioral responses. A theory that describes the internal states of organisms in terms of content seems better equipped to provide explanations. That is, the explanation of why certain cognitive states are adaptive is more complete if those states are understood to have content relating them to the environment of the organism. Of course, it might be argued that this extra explanatory value is illusory, and that it only seems as though ascribing content gives us better explanations because, for example, it makes talking about the cognitive states easier. However, if content-based descriptions are in fact less cumbersome than syntactic or behavioristic alternatives, this provides them with a *prima facie* edge. Thus, all other things being equal, cognitive ethologists have an interest in making use of intentional notions.

From Folk Psychology to Science

Cognitive ethologists begin their investigations with questions about the mental capacities of animals—questions typically framed in the naive vocabulary of folk psychology. The categories of folk psychology are ancient relics of human discourse. This fact is sometimes taken to support the eliminativist view that such ancient ideas are very unlikely to have a useful scientific life. But this longevity can be taken either as a fact against folk psychology or as a fact in its favor. Ultimately, cognitive ethologists want to describe and explain the phylogenetic distribution of mental phenomena. But the role of folk-psychological notions in getting from initial questions to scientifically credible answers is far from clear.

As a science evolves, different things can happen to the naive questions with which it began. Some questions persist; others are abandoned. Thus, for example, physical scientists still address the ancient question "What are the basic materials of the universe?" but no longer consider the categories of earth, air, fire, and water as basic. Consequently, questions such as "What is the ratio of earth to fire in gold?" have fallen by the wayside. It is likewise conceivable that some questions such as "Do animals have beliefs?" and some specific questions framed in folk-psychological terms, may fall by the wayside. In the extreme case, this would require some way of characterizing mental capacities in non-folk-psychological terms. In a less extreme case one might characterize the capacities folk-psychologically, but aim to explain them in some other terms. And in the most conservative case one might both pose and answer questions using the conceptual framework provided by folk psychology.

Alternatively, as a science evolves, it may coopt the terms of ordinary language and provide them with more specific definitions. For example, the physical concept of work diverges from the concept embodied in ordinary language. A human who stands still holding a heavy weight at an even height will feel as though he is doing work, but no work is being done in the physical sense. It is conceivable, too, that folk-psychological terms might be coopted into the cognitive sciences but given different meanings. Thus, questions about the beliefs of animals may come to be redefined and answered accordingly. We are still postponing our discussion of consciousness; however, it might be thought that, if the notion of belief is redefined in such a way that consciousness is not entailed, then the folk-psychological notion has been abandoned. Ultimately, however, we believe that this is a terminological issue that obscures the real possibility that human mental states paradigmatically have two features—intentionality and consciousness—that need not be considered inseparable. In trying to understand the evolution of these states, it is important to consider the extent to which these two features of belief may be independent.

Although some comparative psychologists, including Heyes and Dickinson (1990), have attempted to bring folk-psychological notions of belief and desire within the purview of a Skinner box, most comparative psychologists avoid obviously mentalistic terms. Nevertheless, many are comfortable with more apparently technical notions borrowed from cognitive psychology and artificial intelligence, such as cognitive maps, schemas, and scripts even though at least some of these information-processing notions preserve one of the core elements of folk psychology: commitment to propositional content. Even those notions whose content is not obviously propositional (such as maps) are intentional in Brentano's sense because they are representational. Thus, although these technical notions may avoid issues of consciousness, they do not avoid issues of content. Successful deployment of these technical notions would represent precisely the kind of outgrowth and development of folk-psychological notions that many would regard as vindicating the view that folk psychology is a prototheory of behavior.

Furthermore, whether one theorizes about beliefs or other representational states in nonhuman animals, one is faced with criticisms that focus on the alleged impossibility of specifying the contents of those states.

The Case Against Belief

Stich (1983) presents a sustained attack on the role of folk-psychological notions in cognitive science. His general strategy is to argue that the intentional states of folk psychology are not well suited for the purposes of cognitive science. This is an instance of a more generic argument against folk-psychological notions that can be outlined as follows:

(1) An aim of cognitive science is G.
(2) Folk-psychological concepts are unsuitable for G.
So, (3) Cognitive science should abandon folk-psychological concepts for purpose G.

Although this argument scheme is directed at cognitive science generally, we are ultimately interested in arguments that apply to cognitive ethology specifically. Explicit attention to the role of folk-psychological notions in cognitive ethology is rare (but see Dennett 1983; Allen 1992b). Philosophers who have addressed the role of folk-psychological terms have usually focused on the more central parts of cognitive science. To evaluate their arguments from the perspective of cognitive ethology may be unjust to the intentions of these authors. Nonetheless, the exercise is justified by what is learned about cognitive ethology in the process.

Dennett (1969, 1996) and Stich (1983) have argued independently but similarly that the contents of nonhuman mental states cannot be specified precisely enough for the purposes of scientific prediction and explanation of behavior (see also Rosenberg 1988, 1990). Their arguments, if correct, would have obvious significance for cognitive ethology. Although Dennett later argued (1983) that folk-psychological notions may play a useful heuristic role for cognitive ethologists, his earlier work argues that there are severe limits on their utility for the explanation of animal behavior.

To focus the discussion, we present the following argument, which we call DS. This argument cannot be directly attributed to either Dennett or Stich, but it is easily extrapolated from their work. (See also Rosenberg 1988.)

(1) An aim of cognitive ethology is the prediction and explanation of non-human animal behavior.

(2) Folk-psychological notions are unsuitable for the prediction and explanation of nonhuman animal behavior because

(a) animal behavior can be predicted and explained with scientific precision using folk-psychological notions only if mental content can be determinately specified for nonhuman subjects; but,

(b) mental content cannot be determinately specified for nonhuman animal subjects.

So, (3) Cognitive ethology should abandon folk psychology for the purposes of predicting and explaining nonhuman animal behavior.

DS-1: Explaining and Predicting Behavior

Our earlier discussion of the nature of cognitive ethology has put us in a position to reject a common but incorrect interpretation of the first premise of DS. It is natural from a naive perspective to think that cognitive scientists must explain and predict specific behavioral acts. Why did the antelope freeze on this occasion? Will the dog perform a play bow in exactly 45 seconds? Will this hare stand erect when it sees that fox, or will it run? As we shall see, this is the interpretation that Dennett and Stich seem to force upon the premise.

This interpretation is not reasonable. Take prediction first. The inability of a science to predict specific events with complete precision need not provide a measure of its scientific status. Recent developments in the theory of complexity suggest that exact predictions of specific earthquakes, tornadoes, or hurricanes may be computationally intractable over extended time spans. Even if this is true, there is still much left for seismologists or meteorologists to do. In particular, it is important for them to characterize the general conditions that allow these phenomena to form and to provide probabilistic predictions of their occurrence.

The bases of organismic behavior are at least as complex as the atmospheric conditions that lead to the formation of vortices, so it would not be at all surprising to find out that the specific prediction of behavioral events is every bit as intractable as the forecasting of storms. Nevertheless, it is still possible to characterize the processes that enable organisms to express certain behaviors. A particular issue here is an organism's capacity to register information from a variety of sources and to compute solutions to problems on the basis of the information that is at its disposal—these are the organism's cognitive capacities, in von Eckardt's terms.

It is important not to set a higher standard for the prediction of non-human behavior than for the prediction of human behavior. Neither behavioristic nor cognitive approaches to psychology are particularly good at predicting the precise moment-to-moment behaviors of individual humans. In view of the discussion above, this is hardly surprising. If, as premise DS-1 states, prediction of animal behavior is an aim of cognitive ethology, there are no grounds for thinking that cognitive ethology should do any better at this task than psychology can do with respect to human behavior.

The other part of DS-1 concerns the explanation of behavior. This too can be interpreted as the explanation of specific behavioral acts, and to a certain extent this is a more reasonable requirement than the prediction of those acts. A tornado specialist may be able to say in retrospect what caused a particular storm to follow a given trajectory, even though the trajectory could not have been predicted with much accuracy. Likewise, it may be possible to explain retroactively why a hare stood erect when it saw a fox, although it could not have been precisely predicted that the hare would have done this rather than run (although standing or running might have been judged more or less likely). We do not deny that there may be precise causes for the behavior; rather, we maintain that as systems become more complex, the prospect of precise moment-to-moment prediction of their behavior becomes less likely, especially if the behavior of the system is nonlinear.

In circumstances where precise prediction is not feasible, a measure of a successful explanatory theory is its ability to produce similar phenomena in simulation. One may be impressed by a computer simulation of a tornado because of the level of detail, corresponding to features of real storms, that it reproduces. This is the respect in which artificial intelligence and artificial life projects may be (or fail to be) impressive. We don't expect any particular chess-playing program (such as IBM's "Deep Blue") to be able to predict or even reproduce the behavior of any specific chess player. Rather, we look for it to play chess in a way that is qualitatively similar to a good chess player. Folk-psychological (intentional) models may well be better at producing qualitatively realistic simulations of animal behavior than other approaches.

In addition, cognitive or mentalistic explanations may provide a *metacausal* explanation of behavior that accounts for why certain causal relations between neural states and behavior are maintained in an organism (Dretske 1988). Allen (1995a) argues that this provides a causal role for intentional properties even if the intentional properties of any particular instance of a neural state are entirely irrelevant to its effects on immediate behavior. Such accounts are metacausal because they implicate a role for mental properties in preserving other causal relationships. The representational properties of a state may, for example, account for the origin and preservation of a particular neural pathway. These kinds of considerations are entirely consistent with normal ethological practice in seeking both proximate and ultimate (functional) explanations of behavior. Ethologists and behavioral ecologists alike are much more concerned with explaining the qualitative aspects of behavioral repertoires than with predicting specific actions by individual organisms.

In evaluating the remainder of DS, it is important to bear in mind that the most reasonable interpretation of DS-1 may not be concerned with the explanation of specific behavioral events.

DS-2: The Suitability of Intentional Notions for the Purposes of Explaining Behavior

The second premise of DS insists that folk-psychological notions are not suitable for the purposes of explaining behavior. The subsidiary argument for this has two premises: that one needs a certain level of precision to do the work and that folk psychology cannot provide this level of precision.

Allen (1992a) provides a detailed critique of this subsidiary argument as it is presented by Dennett (1969) and Stich (1983). We excerpt that discussion here, while still, we hope, providing enough detail to make it clear that the arguments presented by Dennett and Stich are not strong enough to support the assertion of DS-2. If one grants (2a), that precise content specification is a desideratum, it is still possible to defeat the argument if one can show that sufficient precision is available. This is the approach that we shall explore.

Both Dennett and Stich use thought experiments about dogs named Fido (a coincidence, perhaps, of imaginative failure). Dennett asks his readers to imagine a scientist of the future who has detailed knowledge of the neural states and events of Fido's brain. Fido is observed, and when presented with a piece of steak located in the middle of a frozen pond he does not go out across the ice to retrieve the steak. The scientist, monitoring Fido's brain, detects neural states that normally occur when Fido sees a steak; thus he has every reason to believe that Fido has detected a steak's presence. In addition, Dennett's story (1969, p. 84) goes, the scientist detects that Fido's normal retrieval behavior is being inhibited by "signals with a source traceable to a previous experience when he fell through thin ice." Dennett says:

> . . . the [hypothetical scientist] has information regarding neural functioning that puts him in a strong position to say that Fido's behavior is determined in this case by the stored information that it is dangerous to walk on thin ice. . . . On the basis of his past knowledge of the functional interrelations in Fido's nervous system, the [scientist] assigns certain contents to certain events and structures. Roughly, one afferent signal means "Get the steak," its continuation means "Get the steak," some structure or state stores "Thin ice is dangerous" and produces, when operated on by a signal meaning "This is thin ice," another signal meaning "Stop; do not walk on the ice."

But, Dennett asks, are these content ascriptions accurate? He points out that it seems unlikely that we should use the word "steak," because it is far too specific. Under the circumstances, Fido would probably react no differently if the object was a pork chop. Even "meat" would be too specific, because "the dog does not recognize the object as a butchered animal part, which is what the word meat connotes" (ibid.). "Food" would not be specific enough, because the dog would have shown less interest in dog biscuits. Dennett claims (p. 85) that "what the dog recognizes this object as is something for which there is no English word."

Stich (1983, pp. 104–105) raises similar concerns about *alter* Fido, who having chased a squirrel to the base of a tree, stands there barking up at the tree:

> To explain Fido's behavior it would be perfectly natural to say he believes that the squirrel is up in the oak tree. But suppose now that some skeptic challenges our claim by focusing attention on the differences separating Fido's belief from ours. "Does Fido really believe it is a squirrel up in the oak tree? Are there not indefinitely many logically possible creatures which are not squirrels but which Fido would treat indistinguishably from the way he treats real squirrels? Indeed does he believe, or even care, that the thing up the tree is an *animal*? Would it not be quite the same to Fido if he had been chasing some bit of squirrel-shaped and squirrel-smelling machinery, like the mechanical rabbits used at dog-racing tracks? The concept of animal is tied to the distinction between living and nonliving, as well as to the distinction between animals and plants. But Fido has little grasp of these distinctions. How can you say that he believes it is a squirrel if he doesn't know that squirrels are animals?" Confronted with the challenge, which focuses attention on the ideological gap that separates us from Fido, intuition begins to waiver [*sic*]. It no longer sounds quite right to say that Fido believes there is a *squirrel* up in the oak tree.

(This is reminiscent of an example given in Malcolm 1973.)

The strategy in both these cases is to call attention to a conceptual divide between dogs and normal speakers of English (or, *mutatis mutandis*, speakers of other human languages). This divide makes it difficult to use our concepts to describe the dogs' concepts. But the fact that it is difficult to express the content of an animal's belief does not entail that it is impossible to do so. In the absence of a principle to explain why no sentence will do, the possibility remains that there is some suitably complex sentence which we lack enough ingenuity (or patience) to discover. Dennett (1969, p. 85) considers this possibility:

> It might seem that we could get at the precise content of the signal by starting with an overly general term, such as "food," and adding qualifications to it until it matches the dog's differentiations, but this would still impart sophistications to the description that do not belong to the

dog. Does the dog have the concept of nourishment that is involved in the concept of food? What could the dog do that would indicate this? Wanting to get and eat x is to be distinguished from recognizing x as food.

There are two points to be distinguished in this passage. First, there is the claim that even with qualifications added the description would be too sophisticated. Second, there is the point about relating behavioral evidence to ascriptions of content.

With respect to the first point: There is still no argument to justify the claim that no appropriately qualified sentence would do. Dennett asks whether the dog has the concept of nourishment associated with the concept of food—implying that, since the dog does not, to use the word "food" at all would be incorrect. But precisely the point of adding qualifications would seem to be the removal of connotations which the word "food" might normally bear. We can well imagine a person who distinguishes food in the sense of being able to choose the things that are desirable to eat, but who does not know anything about nourishment—e.g., does not understand why he has to eat food. With these qualifications, one might think that it is correct to say that our hypothetical person believes of a piece of fruit that is it food. In view of the list of concepts (such as nourishment and edibility) that are related to the concept of food, it might then be possible to specify the deletion or addition of links to specific concepts from or to this list and thereby to end up with a concept that does match the dog's. Although Dennett (1969, p. 85) is undoubtedly right that "the differentiations of a dog's brain" do not "match the differentiations of ordinary English," it does not follow that the differentiations of dictionary English cannot be manipulated so as to delineate the contents of the dog's brain. Thus far, it does not seem that Dennett has given us a principled reason for thinking that these manipulations are not possible.

With respect to the second point: If Dennett's claim is just that we may have *difficulty* making the observations that would enable us to determine the content of a particular state, this seems true, but it does not seem to show that there is no correct ascription that can be made. If Dennett is saying that in fact there will be no behavior in any circumstances from the dog that would lead us to say that the dog has the concept of nourishment, then maybe we should infer that the dog does not have this concept. From that we could infer that the dog does not exactly have our concept of food (if our concept of food involves the concept of nourishment). But even these circumstances do not rule out the possibility that we could specify the dog's concept by claiming it to be like our concept of food but without any connotations about food having nutritional value. Indeed, there must have been a time when humans had a concept of things that were good to eat without having any concept of nutrition. There may even still be humans in this position. Thus, the argument may apply equally (well or poorly) to humans and other animals. There is still no reason to think that we cannot manipulate English so as to explain what the dog's concepts are.

Stich (1983) makes a similar point about behavior and content ascription when his skeptic says that, because there are an indefinite number of logically possible objects that Fido would treat indistinguishably from a squirrel, it is not correct to say that Fido's belief is a belief about a squirrel. If Stich or Dennett is basing his case on the existence of objects that Fido would treat indistinguishably from squirrels in all circumstances, the conclusion is unwarranted. One can also imagine an indefinite number of logically possible objects that humans would find to be indistinguishable from squirrels; it does not follow that humans have no beliefs about squirrels.

This issue is closely related to the much discussed "disjunction problem" according to which it is difficult for naturalistic theories of mental content to distinguish the external causes of mental states which fix their content from those that don't. What, besides the presence or absence of a squirrel, distinguishes those occasions when a squirrel causes a particular internal state from other occasions when the same internal state is caused by something other than a squirrel? Unless this question can be answered in a noncircular fashion that does not appeal to a prior conception of intentionality, there is no naturalistic theory to explain why the internal state represents squirrels rather than all of its various causes. There is much disagreement as to whether the disjunction problem can be resolved. (For discussion see Shapiro 1992; Clark 1993; Millikan 1993; Fodor 1995.) However, the present point to recognize is that insofar as this presents a problem at all for ascribing beliefs to animals, it presents a corresponding problem for the ascription of beliefs to humans. Thus, any conclusion to the effect that the folk-psychological notion of belief is *especially* unsuited for use with regard to nonhuman animals would be unwarranted.

Perhaps, though, Stich and Dennett have less arcane possibilities in mind. Stich asks whether it would make any difference to Fido if he were chasing a mechanical squirrel. He suggests that Fido might be fooled by such a device, just as racing greyhounds are (he alleges) fooled by mechanical rabbits. But in this case it is simply not true that the mechanical substitute is completely indistinguishable to the dog—we would wager that Stich's Fido would behave somewhat differently if he managed to sink his teeth into the mechanical substitute than if he was able to get his teeth into the real thing. And Dennett's Fido might well show a preference for pork chops over steak. But if Stich means only that Fido would treat these things indistinguishably in certain circumstances (e.g., chasing, but not sinking teeth into), once again it does not seem that there is any special question, arising from the fact that Fido is not human, to be raised about the content of Fido's beliefs. As before, there is symmetry between Fido and humans. In certain circumstances people will treat iron pyrites (fool's gold) indistinguishably from gold, yet we ordinarily would not have conflicting intuitions about the content of their beliefs in such circumstances. Gold miners who thought they had struck it rich when really all they had found was a vein of iron pyrites nonetheless believed that they had *gold* in their possession. If Stich means only that Fido will treat two or more things the same in some circumstances, this does not seem relevant to the content of Fido's beliefs, provided that he does distinguish between those things in some other situations. In some circumstances we may treat things that fall under different concepts identically. Nonetheless, in those circumstances our beliefs will be different according to which concept the things fall under. Considerations about indistinguishability do not, therefore, help to provide a principled reason for why English sentences cannot be used to give the contents of animals' beliefs.

The crux of the matter is reached when we consider Stich's and Dennett's views on why precise content specification is a desideratum. Both Stich and Dennett harp on the inability of folk psychology to provide accurate prediction of specific behavioral events. Dennett (1969, p. 85) writes that "precision would be a desideratum if it allowed safe inferences to be drawn from particular ascriptions of content to subsequent ascriptions of content and eventual behavior, but in fact no such inferences at all can be drawn from a particular ascription." But if we are right that cognitive ethologists should be more concerned with the explanation of capacities than with the specific prediction of specific movements or actions, then this point is not particularly telling. The interesting question about Fido is whether any of the behaviors of which he shows himself capable depend on a capacity for using memories of past incidents (involving ice) as informational inputs to the present situation, and if some do, what information is needed to explain the capacity.

Stich (1983, p. 106) takes a slightly different tack and claims that "belief ascriptions are similarity claims, and similarity claims are context dependent." His view is that ascription of content to beliefs of a subject gives us information about how the subject is likely to behave. This information is derived from our knowledge of how we would behave if we held the same belief. In some contexts it is all right to say that the dog believes that it is chasing a squirrel because in that context the dog will behave similarly to a normal English speaker who is chasing a squirrel. In other contexts, the dog would not behave similarly at all, so it would be inappropriate to say that the dog believes it is chasing a squirrel. In cases where precision in predicting a specific behavioral outcome is a desideratum, Stich claims that the tendency is to deny that English sentences accurately capture the content of the animal beliefs. As before, there are grounds for disputing the presumption that accuracy in predicting specific actions is the correct standard to apply.

DS-3: The Conclusion

Our evaluation of the argument we call DS has turned out to be rather complicated. The claims made by Dennett and Stich have some intuitive plausibility when applied to the explanation or prediction of specific motor patterns. How could one ever have enough information about the content of an animal's mental states to be able to predict specific behavioral outcomes? But there are several points to notice about this:

Behavioristic and neurological approaches are no better than folk-psychological or intentional accounts at predicting specific outcomes because the complexity of the systems involved militate against the kind of accuracy that is being demanded of folk-psychological or intentional accounts.

The application of folk-psychological notions to human behavior is no better off than other approaches. One might conclude "So much the worse for mentalistic explanations of *human* behavior." Fair enough for now. Our point here is that there is nothing that is specially problematic for cognitive ethology and the use of mentalistic explanations to explain *animal* behavior.

Ethologists may be as interested in general patterns as in specific behaviors. If certain kinds of behaviors are best understood in terms of interactions between representational states, the attribution of such states to the organisms involved would be vindicated whether or not such attributions enable specific predictions to be made.

For all these reasons we reject the idea that the argument DS establishes its conclusion.

Concluding Remarks

We have argued that a notion of content is essential to the explanatory project of cognitive ethology by providing a level of abstraction that is important for comparative accounts of behavior. A common objection to the use of mentalistic terms to explain animal behavior involves both a mistaken understanding of what such terms are best at explaining and an overoptimistic assessment of what can be achieved by nonmentalistic explanations behavior.

We have also argued that there is less ground for pessimism about the precise specification of the contents of animal beliefs than critics have supposed. We have left unresolved the question of just how much precision is required for the objectives of cognitive ethology. However, we do not think that this question can be resolved in an *a priori* fashion. The application of the cognitive approach to specific examples of animal behavior will lead to the development of more informed theories of content specification.

6

Intentionality, Social Play, and Communication

To return to our immediate subject: the lower animals, like man, manifestly feel pleasure and pain, happiness and misery. Happiness is never better exhibited than by young animals, such as puppies, kittens, lambs, &c., when playing together, like our own children. Even insects play together, as has been described by that excellent observer, P. Huber, who saw ants chasing and pretending to bite each other, like so many puppies.

—Charles Darwin (1871, p. 448)

After all, from an evolutionary point of view, there ought to be a high premium on the veridicality of cognitive processes. The perceiving, thinking organism ought, as far as possible, to get things right. Yet pretense flies in the face of this fundamental principle. In pretense we deliberately distort reality. How odd then that this ability is not the sober culmination of intellectual development but instead makes its appearance playfully and precociously at the very beginning of childhood.

—Alan Leslie (1987, p. 412)

In his book about the behavior of ants, Pierre Huber (1810, p. 148) claims that if one were not accustomed to treating insects as machines one would have trouble explaining the social behavior of ants and bees without attributing emotions to them. But even if the issue of emotions is set aside, readers conditioned by the scruples of modern psychology are likely to be skeptical of Darwin's ready acceptance that Huber observed ants playing with each other. Hölldobler and Wilson (1990) have suggested that ants engage in a form of nonsocial "antennal play" that functions to dishabituate antennal neurons, but they do not believe that ants engage in social play. Social play, as both of the quotations above indicate, seems to involve pretense, and pretense is commonly thought to require more sophisticated intentions than are usually attributed to ants. How could Huber have seen or inferred pretense from the behavior of the ants? And how could he be sure that the observed behavior was not, in fact, directed toward some very specific and immediate function? These questions raise the difficult issue of what play is (or, as biologists are wont to put it, how to define "play"). This issue has proven to be a great challenge to ethologists and philosophers, alike.

Although there are many areas of research in which cognitive-ethological approaches have been or could be useful in gaining an understanding of the behavior of diverse animals, we choose to use play, particularly social play, for our first case study. We do so for several reasons. First, social play exemplifies many of the theoretical issues faced by cognitive ethologists. Second, empirical research on social play has benefited and will further benefit from a cognitive approach, because play involves communication, intention, role playing and cooperation. Third, many believe that detailed analysis of social play may provide more promising evidence of animal minds than research in many other areas, for it may yield clues about the ability of animals to understand one another's intentions. Fourth, play occurs in a wide range of mammalian species and in a number of avian species, and thus it affords the opportunity for a comparative investigation of cognitive abilities extending beyond the narrow focus on primates that often dominates discussions of nonhuman cognition. Our choice of social play is also in keeping with one of our major goals for these case studies: to argue that there are behavior patterns—tractable, evolved behavioral phenotypes—that lend themselves to detailed empirical study by cognitive ethologists.

One of our major examples of intentional behavior presented in this chapter comes from detailed observations of the social play of various canids (domestic dogs, coyotes, and wolves). Niko Tinbergen and others have claimed that we may learn at least as much about human social behavior by studying social carnivores as by studying nonhuman primates. Byrne, who otherwise takes a strongly primatocentric view of animal cognition, notes that we really know little of the "intellectual skills" used by carnivores when they hunt (1995, p. 184) and implies that we might learn more about the phylogenetic distribution of what he calls "intelligence" by doing comparative research. Furthermore, Povinelli and Cant (1995, p. 400) suggest that the performance by arboreal ancestors of the great ape/human clade of "unusual locomotor solutions . . . drove the evolution of self-conception." Many nonprimate mammals also perform complex, flexible, and unusual acrobatic motor patterns (locomotor-rotational movements) during social play, and it would be premature to rule out the possibility that the performance of these behavior patterns might also be important in the evolution of self-conception in nonprimates. In some instances it is difficult to know whether arboreal clambering or the performance of various acrobatic movements during play may be related more to the evolution of mere body awareness (e.g., knowing one's place in space) than to a concept of self.

What Is Play?

The term "play" covers a wide range of behavior patterns. In this respect it is no different from "feeding" or "mating," each of which may encompass a variety of quite different behaviors both when used to compare members of the same species and when used to compare members of different species. Unlike play, however, feeding and mating correspond to easily identified biological functions. Feeding behaviors are normally proximally related to an organism's ingestion of nutrients, mating behaviors are normally proximally related to an organism's contribution to the merging of male and female gametes. Following Millikan (1984), we place a particular interpretation on the word "normally" in these statements. The claim is not that conception or improved nutrition must be statistically likely to follow from the behaviors. Instead, "normal" outcomes of behavioral traits are those that, when they occurred during the phylogenetic history of the species, increased the likelihood that these traits would be passed on to descendants.

Play is not easily defined. Fagen (1981) lists 39 definitions that have been proposed over the years. Functional definitions of play are difficult to formulate because it is not obvious that play serves any particular function, either at the time it is performed or later in life. Indeed, several authors have been tempted into defining play as functionless behavior. Alternatively, it has sometimes been suggested that play improves some of the general abilities of young animals (e.g., the improvement of motor and cognitive skills), resulting in possible payoffs for these animals through their entire lifespans (e.g., in their hunting, foraging, or social abilities). Even if this is correct, the reproductive-fitness consequences of play may typically be so far removed in the lifetimes of the organisms involved that it would be very difficult to collect data to support the assertion that play increases fitness; there is an "ontogenetic gap" between early play and reproductive activity. Consequently, it is difficult to design experiments to test hypotheses about functions of play that are both practicable (Burghardt 1996) and ethical. Furthermore, play may have different evolved functions in different species and it may have different consequences for individuals of different ages and sexes.

Considerations such as these led Bekoff and Byers (1981, pp. 300–301; see also Martin and Caro 1985) to eschew a functional characterization of play by offering the following definition: "*Play* is all motor activity performed postnatally that *appears* [our emphasis] to be purposeless, in which motor patterns from other contexts may often be used in modified forms and altered temporal sequencing. If the activity is directed toward another living being it is called *social play.*" This definition centers on the structure of play sequences—what animals do when they play—and not on possible functions of play. Nonetheless the definition is not without problems. For example, it would seem to apply to stereotypical behaviors, such as the repetitive pacing and the excessive self-grooming sometimes evinced by caged animals. It is difficult to see how to state a non-arbitrary restriction on the range of behaviors that may constitute play.

Because it is not easily defined, play (both social and nonsocial) has been a very difficult behavioral phenotype with which to deal rigorously. A few people would claim that only humans engage in play, but most agree that nonhumans play despite the difficulty of offering an exceptionless definition. The lack of a comprehensive definition need not be an impediment to solid research, however.

Some scientific readers are likely to be made uneasy by our unwillingness to provide a specific definition of play at this point in our discussion. We think, however, that it would be premature to do so. Besides, to demand such a definition is to be mistaken about appropriate scientific method. Satisfactory definition is an endpoint of scientific investigation, and does not have to be a starting point. Early chemists could not have defined gold correctly. They started with putative examples of gold. These examples were initially identified according to a "working definition" that made use of their appearance as a soft, yellow, metallic substance. Investigations revealed a common atomic structure for many of the samples identified in this way. Only after extensive comparative work could chemists define gold in terms of its position in the periodic table of the elements.

Even a useful working definition may be hard to provide at the very early stages of a scientific investigation, particularly when the topic of the investigation may have many forms. (Compare the task of trying to provide a working definition of carbon that would have correctly picked out the various forms in which it appears without referring to atomic structure.) Whether it is useful to recognize a category of behavior such as play is a question of theoretical usefulness: Are there useful generalizations to be made about the behaviors if they are lumped together in this way? Our view, described in more detail in Allen and Bekoff 1994, is that the study of play ought to be approached like the study of any other putative natural kind. To study play, one ought to start with examples of behaviors that superficially appear to form a single category—those that would be initially agreed upon as play—and look for similarities among these examples. If similarities are found, *then* we can ask whether they provide a basis for useful generalizations. We therefore propose to proceed on the basis of an intuitive understanding of play, guided to some extent by Bekoff and Byers's attempt to define it, but without the view that this or any other currently available definition strictly includes or excludes any specific behaviors.

The great variety of forms in which social play occurs, both within and between species, makes it a good candidate for what we have been calling stimulus-free behavior patterns. The next action in a play sequence can rarely be predicted with confidence although the degree of variability can be affected by the ages of the participants, their sexes, their social ranks, their social experience, their energy levels, and their habitat (Berger 1991; Bekoff and Byers 1998). The flexibility and the versatility of social play make it a good candidate for comparative and evolutionary cognitive studies.

Can There Be an Evolutionary Biology of Play?

Alexander Rosenberg (1990) provided several challenges to evolutionary approaches to social play. Our responses to these challenges are excerpted here from Allen and Bekoff 1994. One of Rosenberg's concerns hinges on his claim that play is an intentional activity. For reasons similar to those of Dennett (1969) and Stich (1983)—reasons we rejected in chapter 5 above—Rosenberg believes that intentional explanations are not suitable for scientific explanations of behavior. He suggests, for instance, that it might be inappropriate to attribute the concept of mouse-catching to a cat because one must give a negative answer to the question "Does it have the concept of mouse, *Mus musculus* in Linnaean terms?" (p. 184). Possession of the Linnaean concept of a mouse is not a reasonable requirement to place on the attribution of beliefs about mouse catching.

Another of Rosenberg's concerns is that there can be no unified evolutionary account of play. Because actual cases of play have heterogeneous causes and effects and different underlying mechanisms, Rosenberg draws an analogy between play and clocks, pointing out that because there are so many different mechanisms that constitute clocks there is no "single general explanatory theory that really explains what clocks do, how and why they do it" (p. 180). The problem with this argument is that the kind of "single general explanatory theory" referred to is not (and should not be) the kind of thing evolutionary biology is concerned with. Though it is the concern of some branches of biology (particularly molecular and cellular) to explain *how* certain organs do what they do, other branches of evolutionary theory are concerned with *what* organs do and *why* they do it. Thus, whereas it would be foolish to expect a singular molecular or cellular account of light-sensing capabilities across species, it would not be foolish to expect unity in some aspects of the evolutionary explanations of the development of such organs (although, of course, there will be differences in the evolutionary histories across species). If Rosenberg were right, there could be no general evolutionary theory of predation or sexual selection by mate choice, for these phenomena too depend on a very heterogeneous set of mechanisms. Play, we submit, is in no worse shape than these well-entrenched targets of biological explanation.

Play, Pretense, and Intentionality

As we have already noted, discussions of play commonly refer to the concept of pretense. Because pretense seems to be a fairly sophisticated cognitive ability, it has led some authors to deny that nonhuman animals can be said to engage in play. Rosenberg (1990) associates pretense with "third-order" intentionality (Grice 1957; Dennett 1983, 1987). Specifically, according to Rosenberg (1990, p. 184), for animal *a* truly to be playing with animal *b*, it must be that "*a* does *d* [the playful act] with the intention of *b*'s recognizing that *a* is doing *d* not seriously but playfully. So, *a* wants *b* to believe that *a* wants to do *d* not seriously but with other goals or aims." This is third-order because there are three levels of mental-state attribution involved: *a* believes that *b* believes something about *a*'s desires. This degree of sophistication seems to us to rule out play not only in nonhuman animals but also in human infants.

In contrast to this approach, the Bekoff-Byers characterization of play is neutral about the intentionality of play behavior. Ultimately it might be found that play is an intentional activity; however, to include this in the definition of play would be premature, in our view, in the same way that it would have been premature of early chemists to include or specifically exclude atomic structure in the definitions of the elements. The relevance of intentionality to play is a matter for empirical investigation not *a priori* definition, and we urge its investigation as such.

Any empirical investigation of the connection between play and intentionality will be shaped by the account of intentionality that is provided. To illustrate the different consequences of different accounts, we will contrast Dennett's intentional stance with Millikan's biofunctional account of intentionality. According to Dennett (1987), the attribution of intentional states to an organism is a "stance" taken to enable prediction of the organism's behavior. The effectiveness of the stance depends on how closely the organism conforms to Dennett's conception of ideal rationality. According to Dennett, because no organism is ever perfectly rational, the intentional stance can, at best, provide only approximate predictions of an organism's behavior.

In chapter 5 we critiqued the claim that prediction of the behavior of individual organisms is the proper target of cognitive ethology. If we set this objective aside, Dennett's intentional stance is of interest because it also provides a way of characterizing the "competence" of an organism. For example, one might discover that to perform a particular task an organism would need access to a particular piece of information about the inanimate environment, or about other organisms in the environment. The intentional stance suggests that we can model organisms as representing various aspects of their environments and their actions as guided by those representations. For some organisms, these representations may themselves contain information about how other organisms represent their environments. In Dennett's scheme, such a representation of a representation is a case of second-order intentionality. Dennett treats higher-order intentionality as cognitively more sophisticated (and therefore more recently evolved) than first-order intentionality (which, in turn, is more sophisticated than zero-order intentionality—i.e., nonintentionality). Thus, to place cognitive capacities into an evolutionary framework, Dennett thinks it is important to identify the distribution of higher-order intentionality among animals.

Millikan (1984) provides a contrasting approach to intentionality. According to her account, intentionality is a functional property—attributions of intentionality provide information about the historical role of a particular trait but do not directly explain or predict the operations of that trait. To understand this, it is useful to consider a non-intentional example of a functional property: the function of a sperm to penetrate an egg. Even knowing this function, one cannot predict that any particular sperm will penetrate an egg—it is far more likely that it will not. Likewise, in intentional cases, one cannot predict that any particular organism will act in a way that is rationally predicted by attributing a state with intentional content. Though it may be a function of that intentional state to produce the behavior, there is no more guarantee that a state such as a belief or a desire will fulfill its function than there is that a sperm will penetrate an egg.

Millikan's theory seems useful for informing and motivating studies in cognitive ethology for a number of reasons:

It presents new ways of thinking about biological function and new ways of thinking about relationships between function and structure. These new perspectives should motivate ethologists and other students of behavior to look at old data in innovative ways.

It is strongly grounded in evolutionary theory and has the potential for stimulating much-needed comparative research concerned with the nature of animal minds and mentation.

It "looks to history rather than merely to present properties or dispositions to determine function" (Millikan 1989, p. 289).

It forces one to recognize the strong probability of the existence of intentional behavior among diverse animals.

Unlike Dennett's intentional stance, Millikan's naturalistic theory of intentionality (1984, 1986) does not require the implausible assumption of perfect rationality.

It considers intentionality as a precursor for cognition rather than a defining characteristic (Brentano 1874).

Millikan (1984, pp. 95ff.) introduces the idea of "intentional icons" as "devices" that stand as intermediaries between two other cooperating devices. Cooperating devices are coevolved systems, designed by evolution to cooperate. Cooperating devices may be internal to a single organism, such as the cooperation between heart and lungs to oxygenate blood. (Not all cooperating devices make use of intentional icons.) Or the cooperating devices may be distinct organisms, as when two organisms communicate to achieve a mutual goal in a specific behavioral context. The notion of an intentional icon can usefully be compared with classical ethological notions, such as "releaser" and "sign-stimulus," which often involve cooperation (e.g., between parents and offspring, or between an animal and its mate). When cooperating devices interact via some intermediary device (such as an auditory, visual, or chemical cue), the intermediate device counts as an intentional icon.

Intentional icons are supposed to work because they map onto the world in a particular way, and this gives them what Millikan (1984, pp. 95–96) calls "a sort of 'ofness' or 'aboutness' that one usually associates with intentionality." On her view, the presence of both producing and receiving cooperative devices is necessary to explain the production of intentional icons. When the producing and receiving cooperative devices are internal to a single nervous system, there may be a neural state that serves as an intentional icon. For example, a neural state that is intermediate between a perceptual system and a motor system will count as an intentional icon if its function is to adapt the motor system to a specific state of affairs in the organism's environment.

The different theories of intentionality have different consequences for specifying the contents of intentional states. Take Dennett's intentional stance first. Consider a subject who can be said to have a belief whose content is about a conjunction of environmental conditions, which we shall represent arbitrarily as P and Q. Because it would, by Dennett's lights, be irrational for a subject to fail to infer Q from the conjunction of P and Q, it is a consequence of his theory that the subject must also be capable of having the belief that Q alone. In other words, this rather minimal notion of rationality entails that any subject capable of believing a conjunction must also be capable of believing each conjunct separately. But in Millikan's framework it is quite possible to have an intentional icon whose function it is to map onto the conjunction of P and Q without the system's having either the ability or the tendency to represent the singular Q. Imagine, for example, a system whose Q-detector only becomes operative once its P-detector registers an occurrence of P. Such a system would be capable of representing the conjunction of P and Q without being able to represent Q alone. Perhaps, because Q rarely occurs in isolation, or because when it does its occurrence is normally irrelevant to the organism, it was never important for the members of the species to have evolved isolated Q-detectors or the capacity for representing Q alone. Under this proposal, the semantic interpretation of the conjunction P and Q is not "compositional" (Fodor 1987), meaning that the whole meaning is not composed directly from independently meaningful parts.

It may seem that, because Dennett is concerned primarily with beliefs and desires, he is talking about much higher-level cognition than Millikan. However, it is Millikan's (1984) view that belief and desire can be analyzed in terms of simpler intentional systems. The kind of sophistication that might be required before one would say that an organism has beliefs and desires includes the capacity to integrate information obtained from various sources in ways that may produce something like a compositional semantics, but that's not what is important here. Rather, our point here is that Millikan's analysis of intentionality does not require compositionality. And because her analysis of intentionality does not require compositionality, it does not conform to Dennett's assumption of ideal rationality.

Each of these different conceptions of intentionality provides a framework within which one may ask different kinds of questions about the behavior of animals; thus, each provides opportunities for research. Dennett's framework emphasizes order of intentionality as a significant evolutionary variable, and Dennett (1983) suggests experiments that might be performed with vervet monkeys to test his ideas. Dennett is also concerned to explain how animals may sometimes show evidence of higher-order capabilities but at other times or in other contexts show a lack of ability to reason at a similarly high level—a phenomenon that would be puzzling if the animals were ideally rational. But from within Millikan's perspective this puzzle does not arise, because intentional states which are supposed (evolutionarily) to correspond to the intentional states of other organisms (second-order content) need not be related by inference to any general ability to form states with second-order intentional content. An animal may have very specific cognitive abilities with respect to particular intentional states of other organisms without having the general ability to attribute intentional states to those organisms.

Returning to Rosenberg's third-order account of pretense we see that whether one regards it as plausibly attributed to nonhuman animals depends on the general account of intentionality that one adopts. From the intentional stance, if a has the third-order belief that b believes that a desires to play, it would seem that ideal rationality would also require that a has the second-order belief that b has a belief. From a Millikanian perspective, however, this more general second-order belief, if it requires a to have a general detector for beliefs, may actually be more sophisticated than the third-order belief that supposedly entails it. A general detector for beliefs may be much more difficult to evolve than a detector for a specific belief, for the detection of specific beliefs may be accomplished by the detection of correspondingly specific cues. In other words, just as the ability to represent the conjunction of P and Q might not entail the ability to represent the simplified Q alone, the capacity for a specific third-order intentional state need not entail a general capacity for putatively simpler second-order states. If this is correct, then on Millikan's account Jethro (Marc's dog) may be capable of the third-order belief that (or, at least, a state with the intentional content that) Sukie (Jethro's favorite canid play pal) wants Jethro to believe that her bite was playful and not aggressive, even though Jethro is perhaps limited in his ability to represent and hence think about Sukie's second-order desires in general.

Relative to Dennettian third-order intentionality, Rosenberg's third-order analysis of pretense seems over-inflated. It is doubtful that many animals could make the general inferences that the rationality assumption seems to require them to be capable of making from any specific third-order belief. A particular behavioral sequence in social play may involve pretense even though neither participant has a general conception of pretense. In social play, an animal *a* may, for example, bare its teeth in a gesture that might also occur during or as a prelude to a fight. The playmate *b* may respond by growling—another behavior that might occur during a fight. Animal *a* may then pounce on animal *b* and grasp some portion of *b*'s body between its teeth. This sequence involves motor patterns found in fighting, yet the animals are not fighting. What cognitive abilities must *a* and *b* possess for this to be possible? They must be capable of discriminating occasions when a behavior is genuinely aggressive from those when it is playful. This could be achieved by detecting subtle differences between, for example, aggressive teeth baring and playful teeth baring—if such differences exist. (In the only study of its type of which we are aware, Hill and Bekoff (1977) found that bites directed toward the tail, a flank, a leg, the abdomen, or the back lasted a significantly shorter time and were more stereotyped during social play than during aggression in eastern coyotes.) Alternatively, the discrimination could be achieved by providing contextual cues that inform players about the difference between aggression and play. In many species, signals have evolved to support the second approach. Such signals may be understood as intentional icons that convey messages about the intentions of participants in play. Thus, we believe, empirical results gathered so far seem to favor Millikan's approach to intentionality over Dennett's, although we would reemphasize that both require further empirical investigation.

Play Signals

When animals play, they typically use action patterns that are also used in other contexts, such as predatory behavior, antipredatory behavior, and mating. These action patterns may not be intrinsically different across different contexts, or they may be hard to discriminate even for the participants. To solve the problems that might be caused by, for example,

Figure 6.1
Typical play bow.

confusing play for mating or fighting, many species have evolved signals that function to establish and maintain a "mood" or context for play. In most species in which play has been described, play-soliciting signals appear to foster some sort of cooperation between players so that each responds to the other in a way consistent with play and different from the responses the same actions would elicit in other contexts (Bekoff 1975, 1978b, 1995b; Bekoff and Byers 1981; Fagen 1981; Thompson 1996). Play-soliciting signals also aid in the interpretation of other signals by the receiver (Hailman 1977, p. 266). Coyotes, for example, respond differently to threat gestures in the absence of any preceding play signal than to threat gestures that are immediately preceded by a play signal or in the middle of sequence that was preceded by a play signal (Bekoff 1975). In view of the possible risks that are attendant on mistaking play for another form of activity, it is hardly surprising that animals should have evolved clear and unambiguous signals to solicit and maintain play.

The canid "play bow" (figure 6.1), a highly ritualized and stereotyped movement that seems to function to stimulate recipients to engage (or to continue to engage) in social play (Bekoff 1977a), provides an excellent example of what we are calling a play signal and has been extensively studied in this context. That play bows are important for initiating play is illustrated by the example of a dominant female coyote pup who was successful in initiating chase play with her subordinate brother on only one of 40 occasions. Her success occurred on the only occasion in which she had signaled previously with a bow, although on the other occasions she engaged in a variety of behaviors that are sometimes successful in initiating play, such as rapid approach and withdrawal, exaggerated pawing toward the sibling's face, and head waving and low grunting (Bekoff 1975).

To say that play bows are stereotyped is to say that their form is highly uniform, but it does not imply anything about their contextual versatility. When performing a bow, an individual crouches on its forelimbs, remains standing on its hind legs, and may wag its tail and bark. The bow is a stable posture from which the animal can move easily in many directions; it also allows the individual to stretch its muscles before and while engaging in play, and it places the head of the bower below the head of another animal in an unthreatening position. Play-soliciting signals show little (but some) variability in form or temporal characteristics (Bekoff 1977a). The first play bows that very young canids have been observed to perform are highly stereotyped, and learning seems to be relatively unimportant in their development. The stereotyped nature of the play bow is probably important for avoiding ambiguity.

Play bows occur throughout play sequences, but most commonly at the beginning or toward the middle of playful encounters. In a detailed analysis of the form and duration of play bows, Bekoff (1977a) found that duration was more variable than form, and that play bows were always less variable at the beginning than in the middle of a play sequence. Three possible (and not mutually exclusive) explanations for this change in variability are fatigue, the fact a play bow can be preceded by any of a wide variety of postures, and the fact that there is less of a need to communicate the continuation of play than there is to communicate its initiation.

The Meanings of Play Bows

Play bows occur almost exclusively in the context of play, and it is common for scientists to gloss play-soliciting signals with the message "What follows

Figure 6.2
Growl and play (play solicitation).

is play" or "This is still play." What is the significance of these interpretations for the players? Are they in any way aware of the meaning of the play bows, or are they simply conditioned to respond differently (e.g., less aggressively or less sexually) when a specific action such as a bite or a mount is preceded by a play bow?

One way to approach this question is to ask whether play signals such as bows are used to maintain social play in situations where the performance of a specific behavior during play could be misinterpreted. A recent study of the structure of play sequences (Bekoff 1995b) showed that infant and adult domestic dogs, infant coyotes, and infant wolves often bow immediately before and immediately after an action that might otherwise be misinterpreted and disrupt ongoing social play. Recall that the social play of canids and of other mammals contains actions that are used in other contexts (figures 6.2, 6.3) that do not contain bows (e.g., agonistic, predatory, or antipredatory behavior). Biting accompanied by rapid side-to-side shaking of the head is used in aggressive interactions and also during predation, and could be misinterpreted when used in play.

Bekoff asked the following questions:

What proportion of bites directed to the head, neck, or body of a play partner and accompanied by rapid side-to-side shaking of the head are immediately preceded or followed by a bow?

Figure 6.3
Mounting during play.

What proportion of behavior patterns other than bites accompanied by rapid side-to-side shaking of the head are immediately preceded or followed by a bow? Actions considered here were mouthing (gentle biting during which the mouth is not closed tightly and rapid side-to-side shaking of the head is not performed), biting without rapid side-to-side shaking of the head, chin-resting, mounting from behind (as in sexual encounters), hip-slamming, assertive standing-over, incomplete standing-over, and aggressive vocalizing. (For descriptions see Bekoff 1974; Hill and Bekoff 1977.)

It was rare for an animal to bow immediately before or immediately after its partner performed an action that could have appeared in a different context (e.g., a bite accompanied by rapid side-to-side shaking of the head). Bekoff hypothesized that if such actions could be misread by their recipients and thereby result in inappropriate responses (e.g., fighting or mating), then animals who performed misinterpretable actions might have to communicate to their partners that the actions were performed in the context of play and were not meant to be taken as aggressive, predatory, or sexual moves. On this view, bows would not occur randomly in play

Table 6.1

Proportions of various behavior patters that were immediately preceded of immediately followed by bows in adult and infant dogs (649 sequences), in infant wolves (215 sequences), and in infant coyotes (292 sequences). BHSS: biting directed to head, neck, or body of play partner, accompanied by rapid side-to-side shaking of of head. B/NOHSH: biting in absence of side-to-side shaking of of head. Mouthing: chewing or gentle biting without tight closing of mouth. For each action, differences in percentages between numbers labeled * or + are not statistically significantly different ($z \leq 1.96$, $p > 0.05$); numbers labeled ** or ++ are statistically significantly different from numbers labeled * or + respectively ($z > 1.96$, $p < 0.05$). Reprinted from Bekoff 1995a.

Action	Species	Preceding action	Following action
BSSH	Dogs	4.9*	11.0*
	Wolves	7.0*	16.0*
	Coyotes	13.0**	27.0++
B/NOHSH	Dogs	1.8*	1.4+
	Wolves	3.1*	2.6+
	Coyotes	6.8**	7.2++
Mouthing	Dogs	1.3*	1.5*
	Wolves	2.8*	2.3*
	Coyotes	3.4*	4.2*
Standing over	Dogs	1.5*	1.8+
	Wolves	2.3*	1.9+
	Coyotes	4.8*	9.9++

sequences; the play atmosphere would be reinforced and maintained by means of bows immediately before or after misinterpretable actions.

The results of Bekoff's study (table 6.1) support the inference that bows may serve to provide information about other actions that follow or precede them. In addition to sending the message "I want to play" when they are performed at the beginning of play, bows performed in a different context, namely during social play, might also carry the message "I want to play despite what I am going to do or just did—I still want to play." This message would be useful when it might otherwise be difficult to share this information between the interacting animals. Bekoff (1974; see also Feddersen-Petersen 1991) also found interspecies differences among canids that can be interpreted in the light of the known variations in their early social development and which are related to the question at hand. For example, the infant coyotes were much more aggressive and engaged in significantly more rank-related dominance fights than the infant dogs, the adult dogs, or the infant wolves studied. During the course of Bekoff's study, no consistent dominance relations were established in either the dogs or the wolves, and no large individual differences among the play patterns. Social play in coyotes typically is observed only after dominance relationships have been established in paired interactions. Coyotes appear to need to do more to maintain a play atmosphere, and seem to need to communicate their intentions to play *before* play begins more clearly, than dogs or wolves (Bekoff 1975, 1977a). Subordinate coyote infants are more solicitous and perform more play signals later in play bouts than dominant individuals. These data suggest that bows are not repeated randomly or when individuals merely want to increase their range of movement or stretch their muscles. However, because the head of the bowing individual is usually below that of the recipient, and for other reasons, bowing may place the individual in an unthreatening, self-handicapping posture.

Standing over, which usually is an assertion of dominance in infant coyotes (Bekoff 1974) but not in infant beagles or wolves, was followed by bows significantly more frequently in infant coyotes than in dogs or infant wolves. Because bows embedded within play sequences were followed significantly more often by playing than by fighting after misinterpretable actions were performed (Bekoff, unpublished data), it does not seem likely that bows allow coyotes (or other canids) more readily to engage in combat, rather than play, by increasing their range of movement, although this possibility cannot presently be ruled out in specific instances.

Play Signals as Intentional Icons

The idea that senders and receivers are cooperating, interacting units has been important in furthering understanding of the evolution of a wide variety of social signals. Play signals, too, lend themselves to this kind of analysis, and it is especially useful to relate their evolution to Millikan's ideas about intentional icons. Millikan (1984) lists four criteria defining the paradigm of intentional icons and illustrates their application to bee dances. In this section we discuss these criteria, illustrate their application to play bows, and discuss the utility of this approach. It should be emphasized that we think it is appropriate to explore the application of Millikan's theory without being committed to its complete adequacy.

(1) "An intentional icon is a member of a reproductively established family having direct proper functions." (Millikan 1984, p. 97)

According to Millikan (ibid., p. 17), "having a proper function is a matter of having been 'designed to' or of being 'supposed to' (impersonal) perform a certain function." A device (e.g., an evolved system or organ) has a proper function when it belongs to a lineage of similar devices in which the performance of these functions by ancestral members of the lineage helps to account for their survival and proliferation (see Millikan 1986, p. 52). Our view, described in detail in Bekoff and Allen 1992, is that the proper functions of play bows include initiating and maintaining social play by modifying the behavior of the recipient. Millikan's notion of proper function is useful because it allows that play bows did not and do not always function properly. This does not matter, for play bows need only fulfill their proper function enough so that they will be maintained in the behavioral repertoire of a species.

(2) "An intentional icon Normally stands midway between two cooperating devices, a producer device and an interpreting device, which are designed or standardized to fit one another, the presence and cooperation of each being a Normal condition for the proper performance of the other." (Millikan 1984, p. 98)

Here, in order for a play bow to function properly, the disposition to produce a play bow and the disposition to respond are linked evolutionarily. Both dispositions are necessary for cooperation to evolve—neither alone is sufficient. How the proper performance of play bow producers might depend on the presence and cooperation of interpreters, and vice versa, is a question for empirical research. Several tempting testable hypotheses are available. Developmental studies would be especially important. For example, social situations could be experimentally set up in which the presence and the responsiveness of recipients of play signals vary (e.g., recipients may be cooperative, passive, or aggressive) and the signaler's attempts to solicit play are differentially reinforced. It has been proposed that individuals who are unsuccessful in soliciting play from other group members would engage in more self-directed play (Bekoff 1972) and also that an individual's dominance rank within his group influences that individual's success in soliciting play from other group members (Bekoff 1977b). The absence of cooperation in play might have long-term consequences due to its effect on individual dispersal tendencies. Although data are lacking, our point here is that Millikan's framework is useful if it stimulates empirical research. It should be possible to integrate her framework with several of the ideas about the empirical study of play already in the literature (see, for example, Bekoff and Byers 1981; Fagen 1981; Tomasello et al. 1985, 1989; Bekoff 1995a,b).

(3) "Normally an intentional icon serves to adapt the cooperating interpreter device to conditions such that proper functions of that device can be performed under those conditions." (Millikan 1984, p. 98)

The application of this idea to play bows entails that the recipient of the bow is adapted to the disposition of the sender, who instructs or requests the recipient to engage in play. Thus, when the play signaler bites or mounts the recipient, the recipient is not disposed to injure or to mate with the signaler. Applying this criterion to play bows suggests that, if play bows are to count as intentional icons, it is necessary to explain how they adapt the recipient in such a way that the recipient's subsequent behavior fulfills (at least sometimes) a proper function for the recipient. This may appear problematic since it is initially more appealing to see play bows as supporting a proper function of the sender by making the recipient less disposed to injure or attempt to mate with the signaler. This perspective is consistent with viewing communication primarily as a means by which actors (signalers) exploit the muscle power of reactors to the actor's own ends (Dawkins and Krebs 1978; Krebs and Dawkins 1984). An alternative view of communication is that it is a cooperative venture providing benefits to both participants (Tinbergen 1963; Marler 1968; Smith 1977).

Our view is that whether the adaptive benefit(s) of communication favors only the actor or is shared between the actor and the reactor should be decided empirically rather than definitionally. Despite this, Millikan's framework is useful, since it suggests a distinction that many biologists do not always make. For example, on the "exploitative" conception of communication, an angler fish's moving its lure appendage counts as communication in exactly the same sense as behavior patterns such as play bows.

In the former kinds of cases, "deception," such as it is, relies on the inability of a reactor's perceptual system to discriminate the actor's "signal" from the real thing, and the expectation is for increased perceptual discriminatory ability to evolve. In the latter kinds of cases the expectation is for evolution toward generally increased responsiveness to signaling and toward signals that are more detectable (Guilford and Dawkins 1991). Deception, where it occurs, may more likely be due to the withholding of information than to active signaling (Hauser and Nelson 1991). The ability to withhold information selectively requires different cognitive abilities than perceptual discrimination requires.

The apparent difference between selective pressures and cognitive requirements suggests that it may be useful to distinguish the two types of communication. Furthermore, the applicability of Millikan's framework for intentionality to the latter rather than the former type of communication supports the idea that mentalistic attributions may be more reasonable in cases like play bows than in cases like lure jiggling by angler fish. We emphasize, again, that our intention here is not to adopt Millikan's framework as the last word on these matters, but to show how it is a useful tool for thinking about these issues.

(4a) "In the case of imperative intentional icons, it is a proper function of the interpreter device, as adapted to the icon, to produce something onto which the icon will map in accordance with a specific mapping function. . . ." (Millikan 1984, p. 99)

The normal function of imperative intentional icons is to get the interpreter to bring about a certain state of affairs. Play bows may be imperative intentional icons, because their proper function appears to be to produce play between two individuals through a change in the reaction of the recipient.

(4b) "In the case of indicative intentional icons, the Normal explanation of how the icon adapts the interpreter device such that it can perform its proper functions makes reference to the fact that the icon maps onto something else in accordance with a specific mapping function. . . ." (ibid., p. 99)

Indicative intentional icons are supposed to influence the interpreter "in such a way that the interpreter's functions . . . are only more likely to be performed Normally if a certain state of affairs obtains in the environment" (Godfrey-Smith 1988, p. 26). Play bows may also be indicative intentional icons, because they function to stimulate other individuals to engage in play, and they cause the cooperating interpreter (recipient) to map its own behavior onto the "rules" of play. Play generally seems to be intentionally directed toward this end (Mitchell 1990).

In view of what is currently known about play bows, it probably is more correct to view them as intentional signals, a limiting case of intentional icons (Millikan 1984, pp. 116–118, and personal communication), because play bows simply function in the "here and now." The time and place of bows correspond to the time and place of the disposition to play. This is in contrast to bee dances, which, as intentional icons, are more complex than intentional signals—they can transcend the here and now, and they can make reference to distant temporal and spatial variables in the environment rather than only to the immediate surroundings of the signaler.

In addition to the use of signals such as bows, it is possible that the greater variability of play sequences when compared to sequences of agonistic behavior (Bekoff and Byers 1981) allows animals to use the more varied sequences of play as a composite play signal that helps to maintain the play mood; not only do bows have signal value, but so also do play sequences (Bekoff 1976, 1977a, 1995b). Self-handicapping (Altmann 1962; Parker and Milbrath 1994), such as occurs when a dominant individual allows itself to be dominated by a subordinate one, also might be important in maintaining on-going social play. Watson and Croft (1996) found that red-neck wallabies (*Macropus rufogriseus banksianus*) adjusted their play to the age of their partner. When a partner was younger, the older animal adopted a defensive, flat-footed posture, and pawing rather than sparring occurred. In addition, the older player was more tolerant of its partner's tactics and took the initiative in prolonging interactions. While more data are needed, this study also suggests that the benefits of play may vary according to the age of the player.

Putting Play in a Broader Cognitive Context

Bekoff's data, presented above, suggest that at least some canids cooperate when they engage in social play, and that they may negotiate these cooperative ventures by sharing their intentions. Fagen (1993, p. 192) also has noted that "levels of cooperation in play of juvenile primates may exceed those predicted by simple evolutionary arguments." In general, animals engaged in social play use specific signals to modulate the effects of behavior patterns that are typically performed in other contexts and whose meaning is changed in the context of play. These signals are often flexibly related to the occurrence of events in a play sequence that might violate expectations within that sequence. Furthermore, the relation of play to a cognitive appreciation of the distinction between reality and pretense provides an important link to other cognitive abilities, such as the ability to detect deception or to detect sensory error. In view of these connections, a detailed consideration of some selected aspects of social play might help promote the development of more sophisticated theories of consciousness, intentionality, representation, and communication.

The ability to engage in pretend play (e.g., to manipulate an object as if it is something else) normally first appears in human children around 12 months of age (Flavell et al. 1987). This is well before children appear to be capable of attributing mental states to others. Human children also seem capable of engaging in social play before they have a developed theory of mind. Leslie, in the quotation at the beginning of this chapter, expresses surprise about the distortion of reality implied by pretense. We, however, are inclined to suggest that play is one way that an animal may learn to discriminate between its perceptions of a given situation and reality (learning, for example to differentiate a true threat from a pretend threat). From this perspective it would be perhaps more surprising if cognitively sophisticated creatures could get to this point without the experiences afforded by play.

It is also possible that experiences with play promote learning about the intentions of others. Even if the general capacity for understanding the mental states of others is a specifically human trait, many other species may be able to share information about particular intentions, desires, and beliefs. How might a play bow serve to provide information to its recipient about the sender's intentional state? It is possible that the recipient shares the sender's intentions, beliefs, or desires as a result of prior experiences of situations in which the recipient performed bows. In light of our earlier discussion of specialized mechanisms, it may be reasonable to attribute a very specific second-order inference of the form "When I bow

I want to play, so when you bow you want also to play" without being committed to a general capacity for the possession of second-order mental states in these animals.

In a recent paper on human behavior that has yet to find its way into comparative ethology circles, Alison Gopnik (1993, p. 275) argues as follows: ". . . certain kinds of information that comes, literally, from inside ourselves is coded in the same way as information that comes observing the behavior of others. There is a fundamental cross-modal representational system that connects self and other." Gopnik (see also Meltzoff and Gopnik 1993) claims that others' body movements are mapped onto one's own kinesthetic sensations, on the basis of one's prior experience, and she supports her claims with discussions of imitation in human newborns.

For example, Gopnik (1993, p. 276) wants to know if there is an equivalence between the acts that infants see others do and the acts they perform themselves. She imagines that "there is a very primitive and foundational 'body scheme' that allows the infant to unify the seen acts of others and their own felt acts into one framework." If by "primitive and foundational" Gopnik means phylogenetically old, then it would seem reasonable to search for examples or, at least, precursors of this ability in other animals. Gopnik and her colleague Andrew Meltzoff also consider the possibility that there is "an innate mapping from certain kinds of perceptions of our own internal states." "In particular," they continue, "we innately map the body movements of others onto our own kinesthetic sensations. This initial bridge between the inside and the outside, the self and other, underlies our later conviction that all mental states are things both we and others share." (Gopnik 1993, p. 275) Flanagan (1992, pp. 102ff.), who also is interested in ways in which mental states can be shared, introduces the notion of a "mental detector" that is used to detect others' invisible mental states.

How these ideas might apply to nonhuman animals awaits further study. There are preliminary suggestions that Gopnik's ideas might enjoy some support from comparative research on animal cognition. For example, Savage-Rumbaugh (1990, p. 59) notes: "If Sherman screams when he is upset or hurt, Sherman may deduce that Austin is experiencing similar feelings when he hears Austin screams. This view is supported by the observation that Sherman, upon hearing Austin scream, does not just react, but searches for the cause of Austin's distress." This cause-effect relationship is generated after sufficient experience—if an animal screams when upset or hurt, that animal may deduce that another is experiencing similar feelings when it hears a scream. Tomasello et al. (1989, p. 35) also note that some gestures in chimpanzees may be learned by "second-person imitation"— "an individual copying a behavior directed to it by another individual." They conclude (p. 45) that chimpanzees "rely on the sophisticated powers of social cognition they employ in determining what is perceived by a conspecific and how that conspecific is likely to react to various types of information." Questions about the role of such mechanisms might also be further studied in canids, by addressing questions such as whether viewing a play bow induces a play mood in the recipient because of kinesthetic mapping, and whether viewing a play bow induces knowledge in the recipient of how the actor feels.

A cognitive perspective will be very useful in future analyses of social play. Some thoughts on the direction of empirical research center on learning more about what a bowing (or soliciting) dog, for example, expects to happen after (or even as) it performs a play-soliciting signal. Comparative observations strongly suggest that a dog expects that play will ensue if it performs a bow; it acts as if it wants play to occur. On what sort of grounds is this claim based? Specifically, it looks as if a dog is frustrated or surprised when its bow is not reciprocated in a way that is consistent with its belief about what is most likely to occur (social play). Dogs and other canids are extremely persistent in their attempts to get others to play with them; their persistence suggests a strong desire to engage in some sort of activity. Frustration may be inferred from the common observation that canids and other mammals often engage in self-play (e.g., tail chasing) after a bow or some other play invitation signal to another animal is ignored, or they rapidly run over to a third individual try to get it to play. Surprise is more difficult to deal with, but many observers of Bekoff's filmed play sequences agree that a dog or coyote looked surprised when, on the very rare occasion, a bow was followed by the recipient's attacking the signaler. The soliciting animal's eyes opened widely, its tail dropped, and it rapidly turned away from the noncooperating animal, as if what had happened was totally unexpected and perhaps confusing. (See also Tinklepaugh's (1928) observation of surprise in monkeys when an expected and favored piece of food was replaced with lettuce.) After moving away the surprised animal often looked at the other individual, cocked its head to one side, squinted, and furrowed its brow.

With respect to the solicitor's beliefs about the future, detailed analyses of films also show that on some occasions a soliciting animal begins to perform another behavior before the other animal commits itself. The solicitor behaves as if it expects that something specific will happen, and commits itself to this course of action. The major question, then, is how to operationalize these questions. What would be convincing data? How do we know when we have an instance of a given behavior? Thus, we need to consider what is frustrated, what the goal is, what the belief is about, and how we could study these questions. There simply is no substitute for detailed descriptions of subtle behavior patterns that might indicate surprise—facial expressions, eye movements, and body postures. Studies of social play are challenging and fascinating, and for many questions there is a disturbing lack of detailed answers based on empirical research. The cognitive approach is helpful for coming to terms with old data and for raising new questions.

Concluding Remarks

Darwin thought that playful behavior indicated pleasure. Although we have skirted the issue of emotion, many observers would agree that animals play because it is fun for them to do so. That aside, there is much of directly cognitive interest in the study of play, including the requirement for animals to communicate their intentions and the role of context in the capacity of animals to distinguish playful actions from their nonplayful counterparts. It has even been suggested that for the reasons of communication and context a proper understanding of play is essential to the development of androids (Caudill 1992, p. 5).

Primatologists are often convinced that theirs are the only subjects who are capable of recognizing the intentions of others. To dismiss the possibility that nonprimates are capable of having a theory of mind, much more data need to be collected. Byrne (1995, p. 146) writes: ". . . great apes are certainly 'special' in some way to do with mentally representing the minds of others. It seems that the great apes, especially the common chimpanzee, can attribute mental states to other individuals; but no other group of animals can do so—apart from ourselves, and perhaps cetaceans." His claim is premature because there are very few comparative data on nonprimates. (See also Beck 1982, who labels such narrow views "chimpocentric.") Furthermore, this claim is based on very few comparative data derived from tests on very small numbers of nonhuman primates who might not be entirely representative of their species. The range of the tests that have been used to obtain evidence of intentional attributions is very narrow, and such tests are often biased toward activities that may favor apes over monkeys or members of other species. Also, as we mentioned in chapter 2, there is evidence (Whiten and Ham 1992) that mice can outperform apes on some imitation tasks. These data do not make mice "special"; rather, they suggest that it is important to investigate the abilities of various organisms in respect to their normal living conditions. Because social play is a widespread phenomenon, especially among mammals, it offers the opportunity for much more truly comparative work on intentionality, communication, and information sharing.

7

Antipredatory Behavior: From Vigilance to Recognition to Action

Researchers have only just begun to plumb the cognitive abilities of birds in this area [predator recognition]; a marriage of psychology and ethology might help to point the way forward.
—Ian McLean and Gillian Rhodes (1991, p. 205)

. . . little is known about the perceptions of the animals being studied, thus our models [of vigilance] reflect mainly the perceptions of the modelers themselves.
—Steven Lima (1996, p. 213)

Antipredatory behavior, even more so than play, lends itself to broad taxonomic comparisons. The danger of being eaten is a daily fact of life for vertebrates, invertebrates, and plants, and the range of adaptations to counter predation is wide. Adaptive responses to predation are found in plants: for example, some close their leaves in response to touch, and others respond by raising their tannin levels so they taste bad to herbivores, and others may even signal nearby conspecifics when predation occurs (Hughes 1990). Whereas the ability of plants to detect and escape predation is somewhat limited, animals exploit various capacities, including individual and group vigilance, predator recognition and classification, and the selection of appropriate behavioral responses. Individual animals show minute-by-minute, daily, and seasonal changes in their vigilance behavior and their antipredatory responses. The causes of these changes are often not amenable to simple, single-factor explanations (Triesman 1975a,b; Elgar 1989; Lima 1996); they may be constrained by evolutionary conservativism of perceptual mechanisms found in diverse animal taxa

(Gerstner and Fazio 1995), they often involve learning, and sometimes they lend themselves to cognitive analysis. Studying antipredatory behaviors might allow cognitive ethologists to break the mold of appealing to studies and techniques that are not easily generalized because they focus on a few individuals representing limited taxa. In short, such studies might allow cognitive ethologists to escape the primatocentrism that plagues much of comparative psychology by conducting comparative studies in a variety of taxonomic groups.

In this chapter we illustrate the application of cognitive approaches to three stages of antipredator capacity: vigilance, predator classification, and choice of response. Vigilance is of evolutionary interest because the benefits of increased predator detection may also have their costs to the vigilant organism: time spent monitoring surroundings is time away from other activities, such as feeding and attending to mates and young. Vigilance in many species is of cognitive interest because it appears to involve a complex combination of monitoring the behavior of conspecifics and monitoring for predators. Predator recognition is of evolutionary and cognitive interest because the cost of having the more complex neural machinery necessary to implement more sophisticated discriminatory capacities may outweigh the benefits of more precise predator identification. Also of interest for understanding the cognitive bases of predator classification is the relative importance of predator morphology, predator behavior, and previous experience of the potential prey with predators. Response strategies to predator detection may involve fleeing, hiding, fighting, signaling conspecifics of the danger, performing distraction displays to draw predators away from more vulnerable individuals such as the young, and engaging in attention displays that seem to function to inform the predator that it has been detected. These responses may carry different costs and benefits, and the extent to which prey species can effectively choose between different responses in different circumstances has the potential to reveal much about their cognitive abilities. A further reason for interest in antipredatory behavior is that it may shed light on the evolution of sociality because of the social aspects of predator detection, deterrence, evasion, and signaling. It is also possible that the evolution of communication has been strongly influenced by the function of alarm signals (Macedonia and Evans 1993; Allen and Saidel 1997).

We consider the three stages of antipredatory capacities in the order *response, classification, vigilance*. This is the reverse of temporal order; however, it is a useful approach, because by understanding the range of antipredatory responses available to an organism one learns which capacities are required to implement those responses.

Flee, Fight, or Shout?

An organism confronted by a predator can take actions to maximize the chances of its own survival and can also take actions to increase the survival of other members of its group. From a theoretical standpoint, one can imagine varying degrees of sophistication in antipredatory responsiveness, ranging from no response (as in most plants) to a uniform response to all predators (such as withdrawal into a shell) to multiple and flexible responses to different predators (such as the varying responses of vervet monkeys to snakes, eagles, leopards, and baboons or humans). In organisms who have multiple responses there are also varying degrees of sophistication. For example, Mary Wicksten (1980; personal communication) reports that decorator crabs have several different antipredatory responses but that during a prolonged harassment they will cycle through their entire repertoire, the final response being to freeze. Other animals seem more flexible in choosing appropriate strategies for different predators. This flexibility depends on the capacity to recognize and classify predators. Additionally, social organisms can perform actions that serve to alert others to the presence of a predator, they can initiate or participate in cooperative activities such as predator mobbing, or they can attempt to lead a predator away from more vulnerable group members (e.g., young animals who are unable to engage in antipredatory maneuvers for themselves). In addition, an animal who monitors the behavior of predators may be able to learn which actions are most effective and apply this knowledge to future encounters.

In some organisms defensive responses are triggered by stimuli that allow little differentiation. For example, an abalone clamping down on a rock in response to a sudden change in the amount of light reaching its photoreceptors has little capacity for discriminating human predators from sea otters. Conditioning of similar responses has been shown to be possible for other marine invertebrates (Kandel et al. 1991), but with such a simple scheme there is little potential for selecting alternate responses to different predatory techniques. In contrast, a number of species have antipredatory responses that are geared to specific predators. Vervet monkeys, for instance, seek cover in trees when confronted by leopards but behave differently when confronted by other predators. Furthermore, experiments using playbacks of recorded alarm calls have shown that vervets have alarm calls for different predators that produce the appropriate responses from conspecifics: a "leopard" alarm call sends those who hear it to the trees; an "eagle" alarm call results in increased vigilance toward the sky; a "snake" alarm call results in the vervets' standing bipedally and searching the ground (Cheney and Seyfarth 1990). Systems of alarm calls are not restricted to primates, or even to mammals; some birds have them too. Evans and Marler (1995) have shown that domesticated chickens give distinct alarm calls for aerial predators and terrestrial predators and that these calls evoke different responses.

The emission of alarm calls is affected by social context. A lone male vervet monkey confronted by a predator does not emit an alarm call (Cheney and Seyfarth 1990). A male cockerel is more likely to give an alarm call when in the presence of a female conspecific (Marler et al. 1991). Besides alarm calling, other social responses to predation are important. Some theorists have argued that group living might itself be an adaptation to predation, because being part of a crowd automatically lowers the probability that a particular individual will be taken. Furthermore, animals in groups may benefit from the enhanced vigilance that more eyes and ears make possible. Group responses are also important. Groups of birds are commonly observed mobbing hawks and ravens (Curio 1976). McLean and Rhodes (1991) argue that mobbing involves reciprocal altruism: animals will assume a risk that provides a benefit to others, while sometimes receiving the benefit of actions of those previous aided. They suggest that such altruism is possible without individuals keeping score of the contributions of others. However, in some species cooperative responses to potential threats may depend on individuals' assessments of the contributions of other members of their group, and the capacity to keep score is itself of cognitive interest. In a study of a group of female lions (*Panthera leo*), Heinsohn and Packer (1995) showed that some females consistently led approaches to simulated threats, but that a lead female "stopped more often to look behind at her companion when she was paired with a laggard" (p. 1261) and continued to approach the threat anyway. They speculate that the tit-for-tat strategy (doing what was just done to you), which dominates reciprocal altruism in computer simulations, is not adequate to explain the continued leading behavior, because it would predict that a leading animal should lag the next time she is partnered with a laggard. Heinsohn and Packer suggest that there are many behaviors other than approaching threats (e.g., taking care of infants) where some form of payback may be possible. Sophisticated monitoring of cooperative efforts allows animals to represent the behavior of others and to adjust their present and future behavior accordingly in a variety of behavioral domains.

Some animals harass potential predators. Others try to bluff them. Ristau (1991) has shown that the antipredatory repertoire of piping plovers includes displays that seem designed to distract predators and other potential agents of harm away from a nest. The most famous of these is the broken-wing display, but plovers also sometimes fly conspicuously in front of a trespasser, vocalize toward an invader, and engage in "false brooding" on a site that is not a nest. Ristau framed her hypotheses for a study of the broken-wing display by viewing it as an intentional or purposeful behavior ("the plover wants to lead the intruder away from her nest or young") rather than a hard-wired reflexive response to the presence of a particular stimulus (an intruding potential predator). This led her to investigate carefully the direction in which birds moved during the broken-wing display, how they monitored the location of the predator, and the flexibility of the response. Ristau found that in 44 out of 45 cases birds performed the display in the direction that would lead an intruder further away from the threatened nest or young, and also that birds monitored the intruder's approach and modified their behavior in response to variations in the intruder's movements.

Ristau also observed that the plovers selected different behaviors according to the type of threat posed by different classes of invaders. For example, a cow near a nest is not a predator per se, but it is quite likely to step on the nest inadvertently. A prominent display directly between the trespassing animal and the nest functions to turn the trespasser away. Most predators need to be led away from the nest, so plovers display conspicuously in a direction that leads away from the nest. Additionally, Ristau found that plovers selected different strategies for specific individuals on the basis of prior experience with those individuals. For example, a human who had previously behaved in a way that plovers perceived as threatening was treated differently from a human who had merely walked past the nest while looking in the opposite direction. The plovers were capable of learning about these difference in individual behavior from just a single exposure. Ristau states that her investigations are "only a beginning in the exploration of whether and to what extent plovers are intentional creatures" (p. 124). She carefully distinguishes the philosophical sense of "intentional" from the ordinary sense of purposefulness (see chapter 1 above) and argues for consideration of hypotheses that attribute mental states with intentional content. The capacities of the plovers obviously depend on the ability to classify predators and to discriminate individuals. As Ristau verifies, the frustrations of fieldwork make it extremely unlikely that *all* the interesting questions will ever be answered. *Some* of them can be answered, however, and this makes it worthwhile to endure the frustrations of fieldwork.

Among the other forms of prey-predator communication are the high bounding gait of antelopes called "stotting" (Caro 1986) and the bipedal standing of hares (Holley 1993). In each of these cases, the behavior makes the animal more visible to predators; however, the function of the behavior seems to be to indicate to the predator that the potential prey knows that the predator is present and is prepared to flee, which makes it less likely to be caught and thus a potential waste of effort on the part of the predator (Berger 1979; Lipetz and Bekoff 1980). The effectiveness of this strategy item depends on correctly locating the predator and determining what kind of threat it poses. There is also evidence that prey animals detect minor indications of when a predator is or is not dangerous (Griffin 1992, pp. 57–59).

Predator Classification

We have already seen how the selection of appropriate strategies depends on correct predator classification. The ability to classify predators is a significant cognitive capacity that is worthy of further investigation. A simple, conservative strategy is to accept a high rate of false negatives (Godfrey-Smith 1991). This is the strategy that seems to be favored by the abalone mentioned above. There are many events that cause sudden changes in light intensity, and relatively few of them are associated with predators. Nonetheless, so long as the cost of forgoing some feeding time while clamped firmly to the substrate is not too high, this simple strategy is an effective way to avoid being eaten. If, however, the environment were to change so that light levels were changing frequently and abalones were spending too much time clamped to the rock, there would be selective pressure in favor of better discrimination of predators from nonpredators.

Under specific conditions there will also be selective pressure in favor of better discrimination *among* predators. An adaptive response to one predator may not be an adaptive response to another, and so an organism that can discriminate among predators can select a response that suits the immediate threat. The extent to which such discriminations and responses may be innate can be investigated using the methods of cognitive ethology. Infant vervets begin by giving recognizable "eagle" alarm calls to a variety of birds and even to leaves falling from trees, but as they get older the calls become more specific to those species of eagles that prey on vervets (Seyfarth et al. 1980). In this case it seems reasonable to hypothesize that the vervets have an innate understanding of aerial threat but no innate concept of the specific raptors that are aerial predators. Adult reinforcement of the categories occurs when an infant's alarm call is echoed by an adult, and typically this happens only when there is a genuine threat.

Of interest here is the question of what concept the vervets acquire by this process, and the related question of what the call means. It is very easy to apply human-derived labels such as "eagle" or "leopard" to the various calls that the vervets emit, but this makes it easy for critics to wonder about the appropriateness of using such terms (see chapter 5). What is needed is an orientation that takes the animals' points of view into account. With respect to predators, it may be a mistake to think of a classification scheme that is heavily biased toward morphology. Instead, predators may be conceptualized according to what they typically do (Allen and Saidel 1997). In support of this, consider that vervet infants' "mistakes" in emitting "eagle" alarm calls are most commonly directed toward nonpredatory species diving rapidly from the sky or closely approaching the vervets, and that such errors not associated merely with morphological similarity (Cheney and Seyfarth 1986). Because diving and approaching closely are behaviors that may reasonably be associated with predation, and because moving objects are more easily discriminated from background than static objects, it would be unsurprising if vervets are innately disposed to react to such events. This suggests the hypothesis that, insofar as these calls refer to objects, the objects are initially classified in terms of their behaviors or actions. This is consistent with a discovery by Evans and Marler (1995) that a moving image of a raccoon shown to a chickens on a video monitor mounted overhead elicited "aerial predator" calls at a higher rate than "terrestrial predator" calls (although such calls were less reliably elicited than by video footage of a raptor on the overhead monitor).

These studies go some way toward providing the more sophisticated attributions of content that were discussed in chapter 5. Allen and Hauser (1991) criticized the common laboratory technique of using responses to photographs to investigate concept acquisition in nonhuman animals on the ground that, because such studies do not establish anything more than an ability to sort exemplars on the basis of morphological characteristics, they ignore the importance of relationships between concepts. Furthermore, as McLean and Rhodes (1991, p.180) point out, the results of laboratory studies are often confusing:

> . . . in a recent paper on concept learning in pigeons Roberts and Mazmanian (1988) showed that pigeons learned to distinguish pictures of kingfishers from pictures of other birds. The pigeons had great difficulty distinguishing pictures of animals from nonanimals (which they eventually learned to do), and pictures of birds from pictures of other kinds of animals (which they never learned to do). The authors found this result puzzling, because the birds could learn the most concrete specific category (kingfisher) and the least specific category (animal), but not one at an intermediate level of abstractness (bird).

McLean and Rhodes suggest that the ability to discriminate kingfishers may have been due to Roberts and Mazmanian's having picked a species that is a possible predator, and they go on to say that it is important to consider biological significance when designing laboratory studies of animal cognition. We agree, and we reiterate our point from chapter 5 that the fact that the conceptual schemes of nonhuman animals do not exactly correspond to classifications that are of anthropocentric interest does not mean that more precise specification of the intentional content of the cognitive states of nonhuman animals is impossible.

Much more needs to be discovered about the capacities and mechanisms for predator classification and recognition. McLean and Rhodes (1991, pp. 176–177) point out the following:

> A reflexive system [of predator recognition] would be appropriate when speed is critical, when the class of objects to be recognized is fixed, when simple cues signal the presence of a member of that class, when the cost of failure to respond rapidly is high, when an invariant response is usually successful and when the risk associated with making that response is low and fixed. A more flexible cognitive system would be appropriate when the organism must be able to respond to new stimuli, when the members of the class cannot be recognized using simple, physically specifiable cues, when a variety of responses (whose utility depends on context) are possible, and when the risks associated with each response are either high or variable.

The sheer importance of predation suggests that much could be learned about animal cognition in a variety of species by pursuing these ideas.

Vigilance, Information Gathering, and Representation

Classification of a predator depends on noticing the predator, and noticing depends on vigilance. Thus, the mechanisms and the range of vigilance behaviors are important determinants of subsequent capacities to classify predators and respond appropriately.

Vigilance is especially important in the context of feeding. This is because most animals must seek food away from safe areas, and in doing so they expose themselves to conditions that are not under their control. In addition, individuals of many species must trade off feeding and scanning if they cannot do both at the same time. For these reasons, studies of vigilance often look at its relationship to feeding. For organisms that rely heavily on sight, the ratio of time spent scanning to time spent feeding is often used as the basic measure of vigilance. This is potentially problematic for two reasons: because the activities for some species are not necessarily exclusive, and because factors not related to predation can affect the scanning behaviors of individual organisms. Feeding animals may not only need to minimize their exposure to predators; they may also, for example, be faced with competition for food from conspecifics and from rival species. There is a lot of flexibility in scanning patterns. When vigilance is considered in the broader context of multiple functions, a more interesting picture of the cognitive capacities underlying this flexibility emerges. When scanning, in addition to gaining information about the detection of possible predators, an individual can also gain information about events (such as what other members of its group are doing, and where they are) or about resources (including the type of food on which others are feeding or the quantity of food that is available (Templeton and Giraldeau 1995, 1996)). That is, they can acquire knowledge about the behavior of other group members or about (local) resources, and this is information that might influence what a scanning bird does next.

The acquisition of information about what group members are doing also applies to the behavior of nonhuman primates. For example, Caine and Marra (1988) and Rose and Fedigan (1995) observed that the vigilance of individuals was more focused on other group members than on predator detection.

Bekoff's (1995c) study of western evening grosbeaks concerned the sorts of information accessible to these birds as they feed in small and medium-sized groups and scan for potential predators and the expectations they might have about the behavior of other flock members. Here we compare his data to some preliminary results from a study of scanning behavior in Steller's jays suggesting a different set of expectations about other conspecifics (Allen et al. 1997 a,b). Both the jays and the grosbeaks are highly social, but they show quite different patterns of feeding and vigilance. Here we will be concerned primarily with their visual scanning; although it is possible that auditory cues are important (see, e.g., Sullivan, 1984), most studies have focused on vision.

The primary methodological problem facing studies of vigilance is how to determine whether an individual is really being vigilant. Here ethologists have traditionally relied on the intersubjective agreement that is involved in the construction of an ethogram. However, Lazarus (1990, p. 65) notes that in most cases "researchers have simply assumed that the behavior in question is vigilance, and have then sought its function." Lima

Figure 7.1
Grosbeaks arranged in a circle while feeding.

(1996) also noted that there seem to have been no direct examinations of whether foragers pay any attention to the behavior of other group members; he concluded that very little is known about the perceptions of the animals being studied, and that many models of vigilance reflect mainly the perceptions of the modelers themselves. (Lima is aware, of course, that much is known about the perceptual systems of animals; what he is referring to is the relative lack of knowledge about how these basic perceptions are integrated with knowledge and memory systems to produce behavior.) One assumption challenged by Lima (1995a) is that all members of a group are alerted to an attack when at least one member of the group detects it. He was able to show that in mixed flocks of emberizid sparrows, individuals who did not directly detect an (artificial) attack could not distinguish between birds that left the feeding area because of the threat and birds that left for some other reason. However, he also found that the sparrows were sensitive to multiple departures from the flock. They were particularly sensitive to departures of birds from the periphery of the feeding group, and to departures from areas with little cover. Lima also stressed the importance of individual vigilance.

A central question in comparative research on vigilance is how the behavior of individuals varies in groups of different sizes (Elgar 1989; Lima and Dill 1990; Lima 1996). Generally, it has been found that in small groups there is a negative relationship between group size and rates of scanning by individuals and a positive relationship between group size and the probability of predator detection. This is because there are more eyes and perhaps other sense organs that can be used to scan for or to detect predators. Perhaps a more important question, and one to which very little attention has been directed, is why this relationship between group size and scanning rates typically fails to hold for larger groups. It may seem easy to dismiss these data as statistical noise; however, in view of our suggestion in chapter 4 that many items of cognitive interest get overlooked in the search for statistical significance, it seems important to use these observations to inform and motivate new research and reanalysis of old data. Pooling data from individuals living in flocks of the same size but organized in different geometric arrays may mask interesting differences that might help answer the question of why the relationship between group size and scanning rates is not found, and also might inform cognitive analyses of scanning behavior.

A cognitive analysis of vigilance would involve asking various questions, some of which may not be directly related to cognitive inquiry but all of which could inform and motivate such an approach. Some are also very basic, but this return to basics seems necessary (Lima 1995b). One basic question is "What is a group?" Studies of vigilance during feeding typically count the number of animals in a predetermined area to determine group size. But it is not clear whether such measures accurately represent the perceptions of the animals themselves. The spatial boundaries of a group tend to be rather indistinct, and to vary among species. Although Elgar et al. (1984) found that a house sparrow who was in visual contact with other house sparrows but separated by 1.2 meters scanned as if it was alone, measures such as these are likely to be confounded by a number of variables, including the activities of the other animals and the geometry of their distribution. Treves (1997) noted from his work on monkeys that lower-level measures of aggregation (such as near-neighbor clusters) may have better predictive power than the distribution of the entire group. There are also species differences with respect to group composition. Some species feed primarily with other members of the same species, whereas others typically feed with members of other species. In mixed flocks of

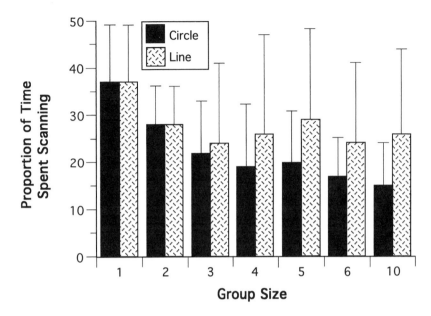

Figure 7.2
Proportion of time spent scanning as a function of group size and group geometry. Source: Bekoff 1995c.

birds there are sometimes "sentinel" species who provide predator warnings for the entire flock, perhaps in return for the protection afforded by larger groups and the increased access to food (Munn 1986).

In the face of these and other complexities, it is not clear what is meant by the statement that an individual is a member of a group. Nor is it clear whether our conception of a group is the same as the animals'. The questions that inform the conception of group membership include the following:

What types of behavioral criteria can be used to assess whether an individual animal thinks it is a member of a group?

Is there a critical distance between individuals below which we can say with some degree of certainty that they are members of the same group?

Need individuals spend a certain amount of time together within a certain distance to qualify as a group?

In our study of Steller's jays, we have found that the notion of a group may have to be spatially extended, for it seems that what we consider to be (for example) three groups of two birds might actually be (to the birds) a single group of six birds (Allen et al. 1997b). This question deserves special consideration on its own; even if we can come up with a working definition of group, we also need to be able to present measures of instantaneous and long-term effective group size. In studies of vigilance (and of other activities), variations in group size are often used to explain variation in other patterns of behavior, such as individual scanning rates, and precise measurements of group size are essential.

Another basic question is "Does the geometric distribution or the orientation of individuals influence individual vigilance?" Little attention has been paid to group geometry. Some authors write about visual obstructions but do not consider the actual geometry of the group (Elgar 1989; Quenette 1990). For example, Elgar does not directly refer to geometry as a variable influencing scanning for predators, but he does write about visual obstructions in terms of how they might influence vigilance and risk of predation. Likewise, in his review of vigilance in mammals, Quenette (1990) writes about visual obstructions and their effect on vigilance because they influence how information is received from the environment. Elgar et al. (1984, p. 221) report data that strongly suggest that "it is necessary for [house sparrows] to be able to continuously see their flockmates." Elgar et al. also review a literature which shows that, in general, scanning rates in small passerines do not decrease significantly with flocks larger than eight or nine birds. "It is possible," they write, "that sparrows simply cannot estimate the number of birds in larger flocks." An inability to estimate precisely the number of birds in larger flocks could be due to an inability to discriminate larger numbers, or it could just be that large flocks are typically organized in such a way that visual inspection is difficult or impossible.

How does the geometric distribution of individuals influence individual scanning? The location of an individual in a group, whether at the center or periphery, is known to influence that individual's pattern of vigilance (Elgar 1989; Lipetz and Bekoff 1982; Bednekoff and Ritter 1994). Generally, individuals on the edge of a group are more vigilant than those in the center. It remains to be studied how the geometry of the group influences the ease with which an individual is able to assess what others are doing by seeing (or hearing) them. For example, it seems that it would be

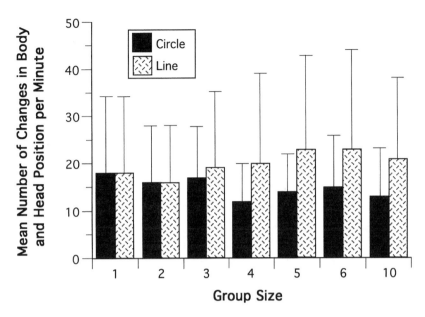

Figure 7.3
Mean number of changes in body and head position as a function of group size and group geometry. Source: Bekoff 1995c.

easier to see and to estimate how many animals are in a group and what others are doing if the individuals are organized in a circle rather than in a straight line, since in a straight line individuals can block the view of others.

To answer questions about possible relationships among flock size, flock geometry, and individual patterns of vigilance and other behaviors, Bekoff (1995c) studied western evening grosbeaks in the mountains near Boulder, Colorado. The scanning behavior of these birds was compared for two different geometrical organizations: a line and a rough circle (figure 7.1). Analysis revealed that the birds arranged in a line were more vigilant (figure 7.2), changed their head and body positions more often to orient toward other flock members (figure 7.3), reacted more slowly to changes in group size, showed less coordination in head movements, and showed more variability on all measures. The differences were most pronounced in groups larger than four birds. Statistical analyses reveal that a large percentage of the variation can be explained by group size. Birds organized in lines showed a longer and more significant delay in response to changes in group size. For birds arranged in a line, about three quarters of this delay can be accounted for by group size; for birds in a circle, only 1 percent of the variation is accounted for by group size.

The differences in behavior between birds organized in circular arrays and birds organized in linear arrays can be explained by individuals' attempts to learn, via visual monitoring, about what other flock members are doing. Although grosbeaks are able to do some scanning while feeding (Bekoff 1995c), knowledge about the behavior of other flock members is important to an individual grosbeak who must decide what proportion of time to spend exclusively feeding or scanning. If it believes other birds are scanning, then an individual may rely less on its own scanning for the detection of predators. Thus, it may be that individuals form beliefs about what others are most likely doing and predicate their own future behavior on these beliefs. Elgar et al. (1984) and Metcalfe (1984a,b) hypothesize that some birds do attempt to inspect visually other flock members (see also McBride et al. 1963). However, Lima (1994) points out that changes in behavior with changes in group size do not necessarily imply that group members monitor one another's behavior. In agreement with the data gathered on the grosbeaks, Metcalfe (1984a) and Redpath (1988) found that obscured vision can lead to increases in vigilance in other avian species (but see Lima 1987). With respect to possible influences of group geometry, Joel Berger told us that in his work on group size and foraging efficiency in bighorn sheep differences in group geometry might have accounted for the large range of variance in behaviors influenced by group size. (See Berger 1991, pp. 68–69.)

The data discussed here suggest that visual obstructions provided by other birds in a flock can interfere with an individual's monitoring of the behavior of other individuals (see also Templeton and Giraldeau 1996), and that individuals change their behavior on the basis of what they are able to see. Grosbeaks spend a good deal of time scanning for predators; they are also socially vigilant (see also Yäber and Herrera 1994), probably gathering information about the size of the flock, what others are doing, where others are, which individuals are present, phenotypic features of flock members, and food resources. Scheel (1993) noted that various herbivorous mammals also vary their scan rates in response to environmental changes. Further research into the cognitive capacities that are required for this kind of adaptive versatility would help to provide a sophisticated understanding of Griffin's (1992) suggestion that behavioral flexibility is a criterion for consciousness in animals.

Bird Brains Counting: How Is Group Size Assessed?

The capacities so far implicated in the flexible vigilance behavior of birds and mammals include the assessment of group size by individual animals. Ever since the Clever Hans debacle, scientists have been reluctant to attribute arithmetical abilities to nonhuman animals. This has been changing as various attempts have been made using laboratory animals to establish that they can count, add, or make other numerical judgments. Studies of chimpanzees (Boysen and Capaldi 1993; Premack 1986), an African grey parrot (Pepperberg 1990), pigeons (Emmerton and Delius 1993), cotton-top tamarins (Hauser and Carey 1997), and rhesus macaques (ibid.) have all provided some evidence of cognitive abilities with respect to numbers and (in some cases) numerals. There are many other studies that also suggest that many avian species are capable of discriminating precisely between quantities from one up to about eight (reviewed by Skutch 1996). It is controversial whether these abilities represent a capacity for counting (i.e., using an ordinal sequence to discriminate the absolute number of a set of items) or one for "subitizing" (rapidly assigning numerical tags to small quantities of items in a simultaneously presented array). (For discussions see Davis and Perusse 1988 and Boysen and Capaldi 1993.)

Continuing work with captive animals will be needed to sort out these proposals, but the successful transference of research techniques used on species commonly held in captivity to a broader range of species is not assured. For example, the study of chimpanzees by Boysen and Capaldi and the study of African grey parrots by Pepperberg both relied on extensive language training. Also, the techniques described by Hauser and Carey depend on measurements of time spent looking at artificial displays and on the animals' being sufficiently motivated to attend to such displays. Vigilance while feeding provides a naturalistic context in which animals are highly motivated, making it possible to collect data from a broader range of subjects. Although it may be more difficult to ascertain mechanisms under such conditions, much work can and must be done simply to delineate the competences. More data on other taxa are needed to assess if the inverse relationship between group size and individual scanning rate levels off or fails because of the inability of individuals to monitor the behavior of "too many other animals" (who might also be difficult to see). (It is also important to note that there may be trade-offs—for example, although it is easier for birds to see what other flock members are doing when they are arranged in a specific geometric array, it may also be easier for potential predators to see the group or specific individuals.) Vigilance by no means provides the only naturalistic domain in which to ascertain numeric competency, but it does provide a context which is common to many species and which might therefore provide examples of convergent solutions to common problems.

As group size and geometry change, there is also a change in how individuals interact. In order for an individual to gain information about these variables, it may be sufficient to use heuristics derived from encounter rates rather than directly counting individuals or subitizing groups (Gordon et al. 1993; Deneubourg and Goss 1989; Warburton and Lazarus 1991).

At least three different ways in which animals might represent numbers have been considered (Hauser and Carey 1997). One way uses mental symbols for numbers, a second uses an analog accumulator mechanism, and the third requires a mental model of the objects that tracks the distinct identity of each pair of objects represented in it. Careful field observation has the potential for helping to discriminate between these hypotheses for a very broad range of species. For example, it has been suggested that animals may change their behavior on the basis of encounter rate rather than actual group size (Gordon et al. 1993; Deneubourg and Goss 1989; Warburton and Lazarus 1991). For such an organism, a small population of rapidly shifting individuals might be indiscriminable from a larger population of more static individuals, because each would lead to the same rate of encounters. Careful field observation could help to determine whether in fact scanning rates are correlated more with movement patterns than with actual group size. The other two mechanisms might also differ in their predictions with respect to the speed of group-size assessment. The mental-symbol hypothesis sug-

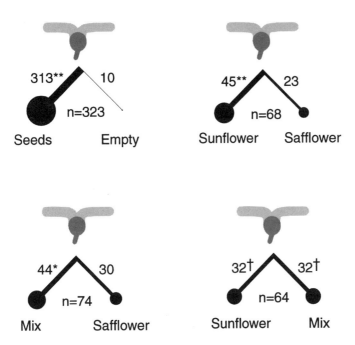

Figure 7.4
Feeder preferences according to food type available when no other jays were present. Relative thicknesses of lines and circles indicate proportions. Statistical significance of difference between two proportions is also indicated. Single asterisk represents $p < 0.05$; double asterisk represents $p < 0.01$; dagger represents $p > 0.05$.

gests that time required to assess group size should be a linear function of group size, whereas the mental-model hypothesis suggests that this relationship should be exponential because the number of pairwise relationships grows as an exponential function of the number of objects represented. Again, careful field observation could be used to discriminate these hypotheses. The mental-model hypothesis also suggests that the failure of birds to differentiate between larger groups of different sizes need not reflect an inability to make the differentiation but might reflect the fact that the amount of time to compute the larger size outweighs the potential benefit of reduced need for individual vigilance in larger groups. (This is not to say that animals *can* assess the larger numbers either!) Of course, the difficulty of studying these questions is enormous, but trying to get answers to them should be an exciting venture.

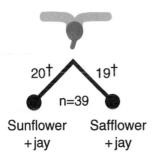

Sunflower   Safflower
+jay   +jay

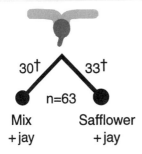

Mix   Safflower
+jay   +jay

Figure 7.5
Food-type preferences disappear when other jays are present at feeders. Dagger
represents $p > 0.05$.

In the simplest model of vigilance, it is assumed that animals alternate
between feeding and scanning for predators. We have discussed data that
show that animals may also be assessing the size of their group while scanning and feeding. Thus, for some animals, the choice is not simply between
feeding and looking for predators; it is among feeding, looking for predators, and assessing the size of the feeding group. We now wish to argue
that even this may be too narrow a conception. Our studies have revealed
that Steller's jays are also sensitive to a range of different activities in which
their conspecifics are engaged. When given a choice, the jays prefer to feed
at a feeder that is stocked with either sunflower seeds or a mixture rather
than one stocked with safflower seeds (Allen et al. 1997a; figure 7.4 here),
but they also prefer not to share a platform with another jay (figures 7.5,
7.6). When two nearby feeders are stocked with different seeds, socially
dominant jays are more likely to be found at the feeder with the preferred

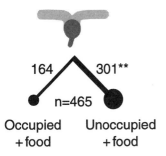

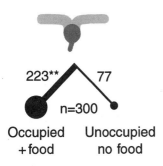

Figure 7.6
Feeder preferences are influenced by presence of other jays in presence or in absence of food. Relative thicknesses of lines and circles indicate proportions. Statistical significance of difference between two proportions is also indicated. Double asterisk represents $p < 0.001$.

food. Jays feeding on sunflower seeds appear to move around more and spend more time scanning between pecks than those feeding on a mixture or on safflower seeds. This may be because the probability of another jay's attempting to land at the same feeder is greater for this preferred food. Moving and spending more time scanning facilitate monitoring the social environment for this purpose (Allen et al. 1997b).

Evening grosbeaks are far more social feeders than Steller's jays. Grosbeaks have been observed to gather in flocks of twenty or more on each of the feeding platforms (Bekoff and Scott 1989; Bekoff 1995c), whereas Steller's jays were much more likely to occupy a platform alone or in conjunction with just one other jay. In 30 hours of film, there were only five brief occasions when three jays were seen on a single feeder. However, the number of jays on a given feeding platform was typically less than the number of jays alternating between the platforms and the surrounding trees. These data suggest that the notion of group size may require special attention when certain species are under study, especially when spatial parameters are used by researchers to make estimates of group size. The results indicating that jays sharing a feeder peck at a lower rate than a jay alone at a feeder are in contrast to the inverse relationship between group size and vigilance times that is commonly reported for other avian species (Elgar 1989; Lima 1995b, 1996; Lima and Dill 1990). Typically, the Steller's jays at this study site shuttled among feeders, the surrounding trees, and ground locations where they apparently cache seeds. It is therefore possible that the number of jays actually on the feeders at any moment is not an adequate measure of the size of the feeding group. Further investigation is necessary to see whether a spatially extended view of the feeding group would result in confirmation of the commonly reported decrease in time spent being vigilant with increased group size. It is also possible, however, that a direct relationship between group size and interpeck intervals would be found, which could be explained by the jays' need be more vigilant of one another than of potential predators.

Jays pecked at a significantly lower rate when sharing a feeder ("same-feeder" condition) than when no other jays were around ("clear" condition) or when another jay was located at the other feeder ("other-occupied" condition). These data differ from what is known for many other species of birds concerning the direct relationship between group size and feeding rates, perhaps because a group of Steller's jays should not be defined only in terms of close proximity. Jays flying by, or perched in trees or on the rail between the feeders, were associated with pecking rates intermediate between the lower rate associated with the same-feeder condition, and the higher rates associated with the clear and other-occupied conditions, but not significantly different from either. Jays flying by or in the trees were typically at least 3 meters from the feeding jay, and jays on the rail were less than 1.5 m from the feeding jay. This indicates that the increased pecking rate with a jay at the other feeder cannot be explained purely in terms of distance between jays. This contrasts with the previously mentioned discovery by Elgar et al. (1984) that a house sparrow in visual contact with other house sparrows but separated by 1.2 m scanned as if it was alone. If longer interpeck intervals are associated with greater social vigilance, these results suggest, interestingly, that the context in which the other jay appears is important. It is possible that a jay with its own food supply is not perceived to be as significant a competitor or threat as a jay at the same feeder or a jay that is nearby and not feeding. It seems that the jays are doing much more than merely monitoring the presence of conspecifics.

Concluding Remarks

Not only would the results of cognitive studies of vigilance further our knowledge of antipredatory scanning; they also would inform and motivate other studies (e.g., assessments of dominance) concerned with how individuals assess what they know and what others know either on the basis of direct interactions with them or by observing how others interact with individuals with whom they have not had direct encounters (observational learning). In large groups it probably would not be possible to know about every possible paired interaction, nor might it be possible or desirable for an individual to be able to interact with every other individual. Thus, in these instances, having the ability to read interaction patterns among others and then to use this information in one's own encounters would be extremely useful. It is also important to consider how individuals glean information (e.g., the location of a potential predator or a safe place) from their nonsocial environments, and how this information influences whether and how rapidly assessments of group size, group geometry, and changes in group size and geometry are made. We may also learn more about the accuracy of folk-psychological explanations for many of the behavior patterns that are of great interest to us.

What are some reasons for advocating cognitive-ethology analyses and intentional or representational explanations of animal behavior—especially the behavior of animals for whom such explanations seem far-fetched to some? Watanabe et al. (1993, p. 372) state: "The question is not whether pigeons have been proved beyond a reasonable doubt to possess and use concepts, but whether it has proved fruitful to ask whether they do." McLean and Rhodes (1991, p. 77) also recognize the utility of using cognitive models and intentional explanations in studies of enemy recognition in birds: "The main advantage of such a [cognitive] system is its flexibility. New knowledge can be acquired, either through direct experience or cultural transmission of information, so that the organism can learn and new ways of coping can be developed." Why might cognitive explanations be the best explanations to which we can appeal in some instances to help us come to terms with the comparative and evolutionary study of animal minds? That the explanatory power of our theorizing is increased is one reason. Furthermore, it is obvious that a cognitive approach will generate new ideas that can be tested empirically, will help in evaluations of extant explanations, will lead to the development of new predictive models, and may lead to the reconsideration of old data, some of which might have resisted explanation without a cognitive perspective (Bekoff 1996).

Cognitive explanations of vigilance in grosbeaks (and perhaps other animals) also account for the observed flexibility better than rule-of-thumb explanations (e.g., that grosbeaks scan one way if there are this number of individuals in this geometric array and scan another way if there are that number of individuals in that geometric array). For example, the ways in which flock size and flock geometry might interact to produce changes in the behavior of individuals that were previously explained (or unexplained) by appealing solely to flock size would not have been pursued without taking into account questions about representation. Furthermore, consideration of the possibility of the importance of visual representations for group-living birds motivated studies of other aspects of behavior, including rates of body and head movements and delays in response to changes in group size. When the results of these analyses were combined, a stronger case could be made for the utility of representational accounts to explain both the failure to find a significant negative relationship between group size and proportion of time spent scanning and other differences in the behavior of birds living in different geometric arrays.

The study of antipredatory behavior combines numerous elements that are critical to a cognitive approach. Vigilance, classification, conceptualization, estimation of number, social cooperation, and communication are all likely to have had their evolution affected by predation.

8

Consciousness: Essential, or Dispensable?

A Griffin bat is a miniature physics lab. So imagine the consternation among behavioristic ethologists when Mr. Griffin came out a decade ago, with "The Question of Animal Awareness," as a sentimental softy. . . . For Mr. Griffin, all this [cleverness] suggests consciousness. He's wrong. If such cleverness were enough to demonstrate consciousness, scientists could do the job over coffee and philosophers could have packed up their scholarly apparatus years ago.

—Helena Cronin (1992, p. 14)

. . . *if* dumb animals are aware of things, have conscious experience, we can never know what it is like, since they cannot tell us. In supposing that the awareness we posit on the basis of clever behavior is at all *like* human awareness of the sort we make introspective reports about, we only follow the actual, ordinary paths laid down by ordinary usage, but in following these paths we are led to error and confusion.

—Daniel Dennett (1969, p. 119)

We submit that it is this very goal of investigating animal consciousness that, although grand and romantic, falls far outside the scope of a scientific psychology that has struggled for the better part of the past century to eschew such tantalizing, but ultimately unsubstantiable, analyses of subjective mental experience.

—Mark Blumberg and Edward Wasserman (1995, p. 133)

In this chapter we approach questions of animal consciousness with the idea that empirical tractability is of paramount importance. We are interested in how ethology might contribute to the study of consciousness by focusing on why consciousness has evolved. This approach includes asking what functions consciousness might serve as animals negotiate their social and nonsocial terrains, and whether a conscious organism might be better equipped to deal with environmental instability and complexity than a nonconscious one. Dawkins (1993) points out that, although at present it is difficult to know what to look for in studies of consciousness, this does not mean that it is impossible and indefensible to make serious attempts to learn what characteristics are distinctive among animals who can be said to have conscious experiences. We do not rule out the possibility that humans are the only individuals who are conscious, but we believe that it is too soon to make such a judgment. As Bateson (1991, p. 830) stresses, "it would be as irresponsible as it would be illogical to suggest that because continuities might not be found, they do not exist."

Because of our emphasis on the functions of consciousness, our approach differs from much of the recent literature on the nature and origins of consciousness. We will not review that literature here, but it includes books by McGinn (1991), Tye (1995), Lycan (1987), Crick (1994), Edelman (1992), Searle (1992), Dennett (1991), Flanagan (1992), Dretske (1995), Penrose (1994), Metzinger (1995), Chalmers (1996), and Hameroff, Kaszniak, and Scott (1996). Many of these books are concerned specifically with human consciousness, and, particularly in the recent philosophical literature, there is a concentration on ontological questions about what consciousness is and the attention that has been given to epistemological questions often has been in the service of making ontological claims. Because of this, the literature provides relatively little direction for ethologists and comparative psychologists who wish to study animal consciousness.

We believe that this situation can be improved by deeper attention to questions about the biological functions of consciousness. Many philosophers' theories of what consciousness *is* make it hard to see what consciousness *does* for organisms that possess it. Such accounts often lead to epiphenomenalism—the view that consciousness is a causally inert side effect of neurological processes. If epiphenomenalism were true, then there could not be an evolutionary explanation of consciousness, because selection can only work on the effects of a trait. (There could, of course, be an evolutionary explanation for why organisms have the underlying neurological processes, but not one that explains it in terms of the conscious side effects of those processes.) An evolutionary approach to consciousness is dependent on the view that consciousness has functions that affect organismic fitness. Dawkins (1995) makes a similar point.

Although some authors have taken an evolutionary approach to consciousness, their suggestions are far from complete. Throughout his work, Donald Griffin suggests that consciousness evolved to allow adaptively flexible behavior. According to this suggestion, adaptively flexible behavior provides evidence of consciousness. It has also been suggested that consciousness evolved in social situations where it is important to be able to anticipate the flexible and adaptive behavior of others (Jolly 1968; Humphrey 1976; Byrne and Whiten 1988; Byrne 1995). If this is true, then complex social skills might be taken as evidence of consciousness. Other authors have assumed that consciousness provides an organism with a means of gaining knowledge or information about the environment (Dretske 1995). If this is so, then perceptual capacities provide evidence of consciousness. It seems to us, however, that none of these suggestions properly explains the connection between the proposed evidence and attributions of consciousness. If attributions of consciousness are to be justified as inferences to the best explanation, then it is necessary to explain more carefully the relationship between behavioral evidence and those attributions. Our approach represents an effort to do this more thoroughly than any others that have been put forward, although there are still crucial ways in which our account is incomplete.

What Is The Question?

A common starting point for recent discussions of animal consciousness is Thomas Nagel's (1974) question "What is it like to be a bat?" This question has captured the imaginations of many philosophers and scientists interested in other species of consciousness. Griffin was directly stimulated to write his 1976 book about animal awareness by interactions he had with Nagel while they were both at the Rockefeller University (Griffin, personal communication). Partly, perhaps, because Nagel's distinction between objective and subjective phenomena resonates so well with Jakob von Uexküll's distinction between *Umwelt* and *Innenwelt*, Nagel's work continues to motivate cognitive ethologists. For example, Cheney and Seyfarth (1990) start their book *How Monkeys See the World* with a chapter titled "What is it like to be a monkey?"

Nagel's influence on cognitive ethology is somewhat remarkable given his pessimistic conclusion that it is difficult to see how objective science could provide us with the essentially subjective knowledge of what it is like to be a bat. Seyfarth and Cheney (1990, p. 2) explicitly dispute his skepticism, writing that Nagel has "been too pessimistic and declared impossible what is merely difficult—and fascinating." Our view is that this difference of opinion arises from the fact that Nagel and the cognitive ethologists have, to a large degree, talked past one another. Ethologists have paid little more than lip service to the issue that is at the core of Nagel's question. They are, we shall argue, no worse off for this, because it is also the case that this core issue is of scant importance for ethologists at this stage of their investigations. Even if one cannot know what it is like to be another organism, an empirical investigation of the *distribution* of conscious experience among the members of different species is not ruled out. If we are correct, it will be possible to investigate which organisms have conscious states and what their biological functions may be.

The ethological objective of understanding the distribution and the biological functions of consciousness can be pursued while remaining neutral about Nagel's pessimistic conclusion. This is because justified belief *that* an experience is conscious is possible even if one does not know *what it is like* to have that experience. For example, if one lacked the neurochemical receptors necessary for the psychedelic effects of a particular drug, one might not be capable of knowing what it is like to have those psychedelic experiences; however, one could still believe with justification *that* the psychedelic experiences caused by that drug are conscious experiences. Even if it is correct that we can never know what it is like to be a bat because we lack the necessary neurological mechanisms, the project of understanding the distribution and the functions of consciousness would not be condemned, provided that it remains possible to approach attributions of consciousness to nonhuman organisms in a rigorous manner. The more fundamental question is "*Are* bats conscious?"

Despite his pessimism about knowing what it is like to be a bat, we do not believe that Nagel would be hostile to the points we have made here.

After all, he willingly assumes that bats are conscious—that there is indeed something that it is like to be a bat. Some psychologists (exemplified by the quote from Blumberg and Wasserman above) think that any such assumption is not scientifically defensible. Such views are more skeptical than Nagel's about the prospects for a scientific understanding of animal consciousness. Our objective in this chapter is to challenge this more extreme form of skepticism.

On (Not) Defining Consciousness

So far we have proceeded without an explicit discussion of what is meant by "consciousness." The term itself is a piece of folk psychology with a multitude of uses that may not be resolvable into a single, coherent concept (Dennett 1969, 1991; Wilkes 1984, 1995; Nelkin 1993). A traditional and plodding approach at this point would be to catalog those different uses carefully and then attempt to consider each of them as it applies to nonhuman animals. Historically, however, this approach has not been of much service to cognitive ethologists, so we propose to treat it in a perfunctory fashion. It is trivial that some animals are conscious in quite ordinary senses. Organisms are sometimes awake (conscious) and sometimes asleep (unconscious), and they sometimes perceive or attend to (are conscious of) features of their environments and sometimes fail to perceive or are oblivious to (unconscious of) those features. Ironically, the *lack* of consciousness in these senses is sometimes harder to account for in terms of biological function than its presence. Sleep, for example, would seem to expose the animal to greater risk of predation, so one would expect selection pressure against it or selection pressure for behaviors that mitigate the risks, such as seeking or constructing safe sleeping areas that enable the organism to get by with a lower level of sensitivity to environmental stimuli. Similar points apply to any lack of sensitivity or attention to various environmental features while the organism is awake. Consciousness in these senses is surely not at the heart of the dispute between cognitive ethologists and their critics. Although Beer (1992, p. 79) has suggested that if ethologists would restrict their claims for animal awareness to sensation and perception then "even tough-minded critics would be more receptive," perhaps progress on the more controversial questions will ultimately be more exciting than rapprochement with the critics.

Two remaining senses of consciousness that are at the heart of the dispute are self-consciousness and the qualitative nature of conscious experiences (known to philosophers as "qualia"). We are inclined to think of self-consciousness as a secondary notion, so we postpone its discussion until further below. The core remaining sense concerns the qualitative, phenomenological properties of experience: the fact that such experiences *feel* like something to subjects who possess them. There are plenty of philosophical theories of qualia on offer, including Dennett's (1988) eliminativism, but none of them provides clear methodological suggestions for ethologists. This is not necessarily a condemnation of those theories, for they have not typically had empirical tractability as an objective (especially with respect to nonhuman animals). Indeed, insofar as empirical tractability enters the equation at all, it is common to insist (correctly) that there is no *conceptual* connection between consciousness and observable behavior. But it does not follow that behavior provides no evidence of consciousness. Similarly, though Cronin is right that "clever behavior" does not infallibly *demonstrate* consciousness, we think her implicit equation of demonstration with suggestion in the criticism of Griffin (quoted above) is incorrect. A victim's blood on a sock does not demonstrate that the sock's owner was present at the murder scene, but it may suggest it. Likewise, clever behavior may suggest consciousness. Mere suggestion is, of course, an inadequate basis for a scientific theory of animal consciousness. And because Griffin (like many other proponents of animal consciousness) lacks a more theoretical account of the relationship between behavior and consciousness, his strategy of piling up examples of clever behavior by animals is unsatisfactory (Bekoff 1993; Jamieson and Bekoff 1993). The challenge is to articulate specific ways in which behavioral observations could be used to support attributions of consciousness.

Descartes famously thought that nothing short of conversational ability in a human language could support the attribution of consciousness to animals. Dennett (1969) turns the epistemological point into an axiom by defining two kinds of awareness: the awareness of language-speaking organisms and the awareness of "dumb animals." Though it is certainly convenient to pretend that there are two different phenomena here, one really should not prejudge the empirical question of continuity of consciousness by making such a definitional move. It is true that we cannot simply ask animals in English or Urdu to tell us about their experiences, but it is prematurely defeatist to think that we cannot gather evidence from other forms of behavior. What might such evidence look like? This is the question that will occupy us in the next few sections.

If our unwillingness to provide a specific definition of consciousness causes uneasiness, we refer our readers to a point made in our discussion of definitions of play in chapter 6. Satisfactory definition is, to reiterate, an endpoint of scientific investigation, not a starting point. It might be thought, however, that the category of play is in much better shape than consciousness, for play can be identified relatively uncontroversially by observational methods, whereas it is often thought to be much more controversial to claim that the same is true of consciousness. However, we think that this objection to the proposed approach rests on too narrow a view of scientific method. Because particular diseases may not always be directly observed or defined in terms of their symptoms, any diagnosis must be regarded as tentative in the early stages of investigation of the disease. Nonetheless, the tentative diagnoses made on this basis may form the basis of rigorous investigation. Likewise, although consciousness may not be *defined* in terms of its behavioral "symptoms," those behavioral capacities may be taken as a good first guide to the phenomena worth investigating further. Our objective in this chapter is to indicate a class of behavioral phenomena that fall into the category of being worth further investigation.

Sensation and Information

A great number, perhaps the majority, of phenomenologically salient experiences for humans are intimately connected with sensory events. Although not all sensory events involve consciousness, it is reasonable to surmise that a proper understanding of the functions of consciousness requires a proper understanding of the functions of sensory systems. Thus, we begin with a general discussion of sensory systems that includes even those that would not support attributions of consciousness.

Individual cells and organisms possess mechanisms that are specially adapted for transducing environmental energy. In multicellular animals these mechanisms may be concentrated into sensory organs or distributed as specialized nerve endings over the surface of the body. Unicellular organisms and the individual cells that make up multicellular organisms have highly specific protein channels embedded in the cell membranes that enable the cell to detect molecules in its immediate environment.

In a great many cases the capacities afforded by these mechanisms are biologically significant because they orient the organism (or the cell) to distal conditions. A bacterium possesses detectors for specific molecules that enable it to follow a chemical gradient, not because following the gradient is intrinsically useful, but because moving along the gradient increases the probability of finding something ingestible and digestible (Manson 1992). The same point applies to the sensory mechanisms of multicellular organisms. Vervet monkeys possess mechanisms that can detect and discriminate between different vocalizations not because detecting those vocalizations is intrinsically useful, but because running into a tree in response to a particular vocalization decreases the probability of being ingested by a leopard and looking at the ground in response to another vocalization decreases the probability of becoming a snack for a snake.

It is common to think of these capabilities in informational terms. A bacterium's chemical sensors provide information about the location of food. A vervet's auditory mechanisms provide information about the presence and type of predators. There are various ways of explicating the notion of information that is involved here (Allen and Hauser 1993), but the details need not concern us at present. Some of these conceptions of information also allow there to be a sense in which a bacterium or a vervet may be misinformed by stimuli that do not have their normal causes. In such cases a bacterium may follow a chemical gradient and find nothing that helps it to survive. When there is no actual threat from a leopard, a vervet may hear a "leopard" alarm call and run into a tree because someone was playing tricks with a tape recorder. It may be appropriate to characterize these as cases of misinformation, because it is a function of the sensory mechanisms of bacteria and vervets to provide information about food and predators respectively (cf. Millikan 1984). Dretske (1986) argues that multiple sensory pathways and associative learning are required before we should say that an organism can be misinformed by its sensory system. If he is correct, our characterization of the bacterium as misinformed about the presence of food may be overblown, but the case is still adequate to illustrate the points we wish to make.

Many organisms obtain information about distal events in their environments through sensory mechanisms. Are such sensory capabilities sufficient to support the claim that these organisms have conscious experiences? One of our reasons for choosing bacteria to illustrate the issues was, of course, to prime the reader to answer this question in the negative. It can also be pointed out that some plants appear to obtain information about distal events related to predation by detecting the byproducts of such predation drifting downwind from neighboring trees (Hughes 1990; Allen and Hauser 1993; Allen 1995b). Only the most committed panpsychists are likely to consider plant phenomenology a serious likelihood. Although it is a conceptual possibility that trees, bacteria, and even rocks are conscious, we believe that nothing is gained by adopting the panpsychist view.

At this point it is worth becoming a little more circumspect about the nature of our project. We do not expect to give an analysis or definition of consciousness. Rather, we wish to argue that a certain type of behavioral evidence warrants the attribution of conscious experience to an organism. It is quite consistent with this goal that the criteria for attributing consciousness differ from the conditions for possessing consciousness. Indeed, satisfying these criteria may be neither necessary nor sufficient for the possession of consciousness, just as meeting the criteria for a guilty verdict in a courtroom is neither necessary nor sufficient for the accused's actually having committed the crime. Nonetheless, the criteria applied to the attribution of the property may be considered reasonable guides to the possession of the property if it can be explained why they are relevant. Our aim, then, is to outline some behavioral and functional criteria for attributing consciousness and then argue for their relevance to consciousness. We reiterate, however, that these criteria should not be considered either necessary or sufficient conditions for the possession of consciousness.

The criteria we shall consider concern the capacity for detecting misinformation. First we shall explain what we mean by this. The ideas to be presented are based upon but also an extension of those presented by Allen (1997). Having explained what we mean by detecting misinformation, we shall then consider the relevance of these criteria to the notion of conscious experience.

Detecting Misinformation

Organisms respond to many different sensory stimuli. Some responses are intrinsically valuable (such as removing a limb from a fire). Others are only instrumentally valuable (such as moving toward a food source). For every such instrumental act there is the possibility that the act goes unrewarded. This may happen in various ways. One way is that the conditions giving rise to the sensory stimulation are not biologically normal. Perhaps a bacterium follows a chemical gradient emanating from a piece of food that is too big for it to ingest, or emanating from the pipette of a lab scientist. In either case there is misinformation because there was nothing ingestible and digestible causing the sensory events. The response of moving along the gradient goes unrewarded by the event that it is biologically designed to bring about. Another way in which the act may go unrewarded involves biologically normal conditions. The chemical gradient emanates from an ingestible, digestible morsel but perhaps our subject bacterium is just a bit slow off the mark, or perhaps it has further to travel than a close relative, and is beaten to it. In this case there was no misinformation, but the response failed to produce its biologically intended effect anyway.

Suppose an organism is capable of altering its subsequent response to the stimulus in response to the fact that the response is not rewarded. There are various ways in which this may occur. One simple way is that it may increase or decrease its sensitivity to the stimulus by increasing or decreasing the number or the sensitivity of its receptors. Another is that it may maintain the same level of receptiveness for the stimulus but strengthen or weaken the internal connection between the stimulus and the particular response. There are many more complicated schemes. Not all schemes, however, are equally appropriate for the two ways in which the behavior failed to result in a reward. For example, if an organism is frequently beaten to a food item, then it would be to its advantage to respond more vigorously the next time. Alternatively, if an organism is misinformed and hence attracted to non-ingestible items, then so long as it has other methods for finding food it may be to its advantage to respond less vigorously to future stimuli of this type. Thus, different ways of failing may recommend rather different adjustments.

An organism with severely limited sensory capacities may be unable to distinguish failures caused by misinformation from failures caused by competition for the same resources (this, almost certainly, is the lot of even the most talented bacterium). Such an organism could not, therefore, make internal adjustments geared to the specific causes of its failure to be rewarded, although it may make sophisticated adjustments in its threshold for signal detection to provide optimal responses across the range of conditions (Godfrey-Smith 1991). In conditions where the costs of responding inappropriately are sufficiently high, there may also be a selective advantage for organisms that can make more sophisticated discriminations. Thus, under those conditions there will be selection for mechanisms that allow for failure due to misinformation to be discriminated from failure for other reasons.

An ability to discriminate between tokens of a given stimulus type according to whether those tokens carry misinformation or information is present in humans for some stimuli. In some cases the discrimination is retrospective and must therefore involve memory. One may subsequently realize that one was fooled by an earlier stimulus. In other cases the discrimination may be simultaneous. For example, one may learn that one is the subject of an optical illusion while the illusion persists. There may be various ways of implementing the capacity to discriminate information from misinformation for different stimuli. Whether the members of a species have this capacity, and with respect to which stimuli they have it, can be empirically investigated by presenting animals with stimuli that carry conflicting information and seeing how capable they are of adjusting their responses to misinformation while not losing their ability to detect features of the original stimulus.

It is important to understand that the suggestion we are making does not amount to simple habituation. Cheney and Seyfarth (1988) found that vervet monkeys ceased responding to acoustically different social calls from a single individual after they had been exposed to repeated misinformative playbacks of a single social call made by that individual. This generalized habituation to the social calls of that individual appears to be a generalization about a semantic feature of the calls, not about their syntactic features. Thus, the experiments provide evidence of semantic processing or intentionality at some level. Without further elaboration, they tell us less about consciousness, for it is not clear whether the other vervets continue to hear the call and access its normal meaning while not responding overtly, or whether the call is, so to speak, tuned out. The data are not available, but modifications of these experiments would have the potential to reveal much more about vervets' abilities to deal with misinformation generally, and specifically about their ability to process the normal meaning of a signal while simultaneously rejecting that meaning.

If the ability to detect misinformation is found in more than one species, then there is also room for a wide range of variation with respect to the stimuli and the responses for which it is possible. These differences would be ecologically relevant variables governing the general evolution of cognitive abilities.

Why Is This Relevant?

Some skeptical readers may be wondering how all this discussion of behavioral capacities can be at all relevant to questions about conscious experiences. The most extreme form of this skepticism is evident in those who believe that it is possible to have a zombie who behaves just like a human but lacks any conscious experience at all. If such a thing were a relevant possibility, then no amount of behavioral evidence could ever be brought to bear on the epistemological question of who is conscious. Epiphenomenalism also lends support to the view that it is not possible to study consciousness scientifically, for if consciousness has no effects on observable behavior then there can be nothing behaviorally to distinguish a conscious organism from a nonconscious one, and consciousness would be undetectable as well as invisible to natural selection.

Philosophical zombies ("phi-zombies") are, of course, a philosophical myth. They are assumed to be behaviorally indistinguishable from normal human beings. But they are not like the zombies of the cult horror classics, whose glazed eyes, expressionless faces, and stiff movements are, pardon the pun, dead giveaways. Give a phi-zombie a glass of wine and ask him what he thinks and he may gush about a pleasant bouquet, and a flavor that has a slight taste of tannin, reminiscent of leather with a slight chocolatey aftertaste. But we are asked to imagine, despite all this behavior that there is "nobody home," no subject having conscious experiences at all—that there is nothing that it is like to be a phi-zombie. (One should, however, expect quite an argument to the contrary from the phi-zombie himself.) But on our view, the imaginability of phi-zombies no more shows that consciousness is irrelevant to the explanation of behavior than the fact that we can imagine cutting into a zombie's head and finding no brain would establish that brains are irrelevant to the explanation of behavior. It is simply question-begging to assume that the imaginability of phi-zombies should be taken as a serious objection to the explanatory relevance of consciousness. (See Chalmers 1996 for dissent.)

The philosophical confusion in this area stems from a far too unimaginative and simplistic view of the relationship among sensory input, consciousness, and behavior. If one imagines a direct causal chain from external event to sensory stimulation to behavior, then it is clear that merely inserting a bulb of consciousness between sensory stimulation and behavior is gratuitous. For many organisms, attributing consciousness to them would be gratuitous in just this way. This probably applies to most if not all bacteria and plants, a large proportion of invertebrates, and perhaps some vertebrates. This is not to state outright that qualitative experience is not a feature of their sensory lives; it is just that it is hard to see what attributing consciousness to them provides in the way of explanatory payoff. This point can be made vivid by an example involving decapitated alligators, whose forelimbs will swipe quite precisely at the point of a scalpel incision in the headless torso (J. Kleister, personal communication). On the reasonable assumption that a headless organism feels no pain, it can be seen that attributing pain to help explain responses precisely targeted to the removal of noxious stimuli is of no obvious explanatory benefit. If conscious pain does have functions, we suggest they include the ability of an organism to use the sensation as a fallible indicator of the urgency of responding in a way that will terminate the pain, rather than as an infallible indicator of the need for a response.

For the more sophisticated capabilities with respect to misinformation that we have described above, we argue that attributions of consciousness play a useful explanatory role. Consideration of a perceptual illusions can help show why this is so. Take the Müller-Lyer illusion as an example. In this illusion, two lines of equal length are perceived to be different in length when the arrowheads at their ends point in opposite directions. Lines ended thus: <—> are seen as shorter than lines ended thus: >—<. It seems that humans, given typical exposure to buildings and other rectangular objects, cannot help but see one line as longer than the other when presented with appropriately drawn Müller-Lyer figures. There is no choice in this matter. Once one has been informed about the illusion, one continues to see one line as longer than the other while judging simultaneously that they are of the same length and recognizing that one's visual experience contains misinformation about the world. It is significant in this case that one does not simply cease to see the two lines as having different lengths. In other words, the perceptual system does not change its sensitivity to the inputs. Given feedback about the actual lengths of the lines, an entirely different type of organism might in fact cease to be able to respond to these lines as if they had different lengths. But this kind of adjustment might also lead to errors with three-dimensional objects where the information encoded in the retinal pattern is properly caused by edges of different lengths. This is the dilemma, described in the previous section, that faces organisms incapable of detecting misinformation.

In the case of the Müller-Lyer illusion, there is a very natural sense in which the organism is capable of distinguishing between the way the world is (the judgment about the relative lengths of the lines) and the way the world appears to be (the deliverances of the perceptual system). Because humans are able to exploit the difference between appearances and judged reality, this distinction plays an explanatory role in understanding certain aspects of our behavior. The general capacity for treating perception and belief independently is an empirically testable phenomenon even in the absence of linguistic report. Behavioral evidence that an organism is subject to an illusion yet can make choices that depend on rejecting the illusory properties can replace direct verbal reporting.

If one takes seriously the idea that an organism can discriminate its appearance states from its judgments (beliefs) about the environment, then one is committed to the distinction between the way things appear to the organism and its beliefs about them. In our view, attributing conscious, subjective experiences may provide the best explanation for the ability of some organisms to make this distinction. Evidence for consciousness (but *not* its definition or analysis) lies in its ability to account for the separation of perception from judgment.

Where Next?

No doubt many questions remain, but at this point it would be premature to declare victory for either side in the attempt to definitively answer the question of whether conscious experience is a uniquely human property. We think that the approach we have outlined provides a tractable approach to at least some questions about the attribution of consciousness to nonhuman animals. It avoids Griffin's puzzling view that consciousness might help organisms such as honeybees by compensating for the limited processing power afforded by their relatively small nervous systems. This suggestion seems odd in light of evidence suggesting that consciousness is a phenomenon arising from large, interconnected networks of neurons (Shallice 1988)—networks vastly bigger than anything found in a honeybee. Nonetheless, it is possible to account for the importance of behavioral flexibility as evidence for consciousness, and for several other commonly cited features, within the framework we have described.

Along with behavioral flexibility, features commonly cited to support attributions of consciousness include the integration of information from multisensory sources and language abilities. Behavioral flexibility is relevant to attributions of consciousness because it is connected to an organism's monitoring of its own performance. An organism that cannot detect when its states misrepresent its environment will be much more limited with respect to the adjustments it can make when those states are caused by abnormal proximal stimuli. There is much room for variation here. All organisms, including humans, are less flexible with respect to some stimuli than with respect to others. Something akin to so-called degrees of consciousness may be found here, for the capacities of some animals for error detection will be approximate subsets of the capacities of others. Multimodal integration—the ability to access a common representation through different sensory pathways—is relevant because separate sensory pathways provide a mechanism by which the capacity to detect misinformation may be implemented. The ability to compare an integrated representation of the world against the representation provided by a single sensory modality would support the detection of perceptual error in an obvious way. Language is relevant because it provides a representational scheme that is relatively detached from particular sensory mechanisms and thus, like multimodal representations, provides a way to implement the detection of sensory misinformation.

The extent to which various organisms can detect and respond to their own errors is an empirical question, and there is plenty of room for matters of degree—for different species of mind. Various areas appear to be promising places to look. One such area is social play, which involves responding to behaviors that would elicit different responses in nonplay contexts. (There is also an interesting developmental connection in human children between the concepts of pretense and appearance; see Flavell et al. 1987.) Another area is social communication, particularly where signals are used deceptively or withheld in conditions where they would be appropriate. Surprise, embarrassment, and rapid learning (often involving just one or a few experiences with the conditions that caused the error) are all reactions that might be shown by organisms who have epistemic access to their own errors. From this perspective, it is possible to understand the passing comment at the end of Chisholm's (1957) classic discussion of Brentano and intentionality, where he suggested that the most promising place to look for intentionality in nonhuman animals is expectation. For example, some animals appear surprised when their play signals are responded to with aggression—they seem to expect that play will follow (Bekoff 1995a). There is, of course, a sense of expectation that is compatible with behavioral conditioning, but differing responses to violations of expectation will support different hypotheses about the mechanisms underlying those responses (see also Hauser and Carey 1997).

Back to Bats and Monkeys

Would knowing more details about *whether* an organism is conscious of various features of its sensory world provide any insight into *what* that consciousness is like? Clearly, the mere fact that bats use echolocation is insufficient to answer the question "What it is like to be a bat?" It would be no more sensible to try to answer the question "What is it like to be a primate?" if given only the information that humans and ringtailed lemurs both have forward-facing eyes (and presumably, therefore, stereoscopic vision). There are approximately 800 species of bats, and among mammals only rodents form a more diverse group. Among the species of bats that use echolocation (about 30 species from the genus *Rousettus* in the suborder *Megachiroptera*, and all of the approximately 660 species in the suborder *Microchiroptera*) there are at least three kinds of echolocation (constant frequency, frequency sweep, and short burst), and they differ with respect to whether outgoing ultrasound is produced orally or nasally. Each of these differences has consequences for the sensory ecology of the animals, affecting the kinds of discriminations that can be made, the kinds of obstacles that can be avoided, and the kinds of prey that can be hunted. Presumably there is no one thing it is "like to be a bat," any more than there is one thing it is "like to be a primate."

Of course, the burden of proof is on those who think that more of the scientific details would help, and Nagel has an argument for the conclusion that they won't help. We have not rebutted that argument here (for criticism, see Lycan 1987 and Akins 1993), because we have argued that knowing what it is like to be a bat is less important to cognitive ethology than knowing whether it is like anything at all. With respect to the second topic, the details of bat echolocation must be investigated case by case. If, for example, a bat can discriminate different obstacles it does not follow that different (or any) qualitative experiences are involved (although there will, of course, be some difference in neural processing to account for the discrimination). But if a bat can detect when it is being misinformed about an obstacle and can adjust its behavior appropriately, and if it is possible to obtain evidence that the bat still perceives the obstacle in the distorted way, then it may be possible to gain evidence that its perceptions of the obstacle have a qualitative component.

For the most part, despite their overt references to Nagel's question, ethologists have stayed away from Nagel's focus on knowledge of what it is like to have the qualia in question. Cheney and Seyfarth (1990) do not address it at all in their chapter named after Nagel's paper. Their explicitly stated intention to "use consciousness and self-awareness interchangeably" (1990, p. 240) belies the apparent overlap of their interests with Nagel, and there is nothing in their book that would lead Nagel to recant his argument about objective scientific knowledge of the subjective experiences of monkeys. Indeed, the notions of subjectivity and qualia do not figure anywhere in Cheney and Seyfarth's book. Nagel would, we think, agree that there is much to be learned about the objective properties of the discriminatory abilities of vervet monkeys (and of the various species of bat), while denying that it could tell us what it is like to be those organisms. If we are right, however, this is of relatively little importance for understanding the functional properties of conscious experience.

By driving a wedge between the two questions of the existence and the character of conscious experience, it is possible to put in greater focus the question of what role conscious experiences might play in evolutionary theory. Consider two organisms that are capable of making exactly the same discriminations as each other but whose qualitative experiences are different from other. Readers familiar with current philosophy of mind will be familiar with "inverted-spectrum" thought experiments in which color experiences are imagined to be complementary between two subjects. If inverted spectra are neurologically possible (Hardin (1996) argues that they may not be), what consequences would this have for the fitness of the organisms? The answer here depends on whether different qualia produce different emotional or physiological effects. For example, if experiencing red qualia raises heart rates and experiencing blue lowers them, an organism confronted with a predator that it experiences as red might be better prepared for flight than the organism that experiences the same predator as blue. But if one assumes that the functional correlates are also mirrored, then the difference in subjective experiences can cause no relative fitness advantage for one organism over the other for by hypothesis the two are functionally equivalent. But then the question of exactly what it is like to have certain experiences is not relevant to the fitness of the organisms concerned, and hence not relevant to an evolutionary account. The most that can matter is that there are conscious experiences.

Consciousness and Self-Consciousness

We mentioned above that Cheney and Seyfarth are concerned with self-consciousness rather than qualia. A fascination with self-consciousness is common among ethologists and comparative scientists and has largely been engendered by work on mirror self-recognition in primates (Gallup 1970; Parker et al. 1994; Povinelli 1994b, 1996; Hauser et al. 1995). We quote Cheney and Seyfarth (1990, p. 240) at some length on the difference between self-awareness and self-recognition, for they introduce some important distinctions:

> Operational definitions of consciousness are slippery at best, primarily because self-recognition and self-awareness are multifaceted and can be manifested in different ways in different contexts. Although we use consciousness and self-awareness interchangeably here, we distinguish consciousness from self-recognition. Self-recognition is a more conservative term than consciousness and refers only to the ability to distinguish oneself from others without implying any awareness of so doing. There is ample evidence from studies of children, for example, that many aspects of self-recognition do not require active self-reflection. . . . Consciousness however, is a kind of meta-self-awareness; it implies that the individual is aware of his own state of mind and can use this awareness to predict and explain the behavior of both himself and others.

With the confusions that this passage might engender (for instance, is consciousness to be understood as self-awareness or as meta-self-awareness, and what is the difference?) set aside, there are two important points that we agree with. First, the point about the relative inadequacy of operational definitions because of the heterogeneity of the phenomena under discussion is well taken and is fully in accord with our own attitudes toward such definitions (expressed above; see also Allen and Bekoff 1994). Far from being an acid test for self-awareness, mirror tests are but one domain within which self-awareness or self-recognition might be studied. Second, the distinction between conscious awareness of self and other versus nonconscious representation of the self is a good one that we shall attempt to place in a slightly different context further below. We disagree, however, with the claim made at the end of this passage that consciousness entails the ability to predict and explain the behavior of self and others. As Barresi and Moore (1996) have recently argued, there is room for several levels of sophistication between complete lack of self-knowledge and full social understanding.

According to Barresi and Moore, at the simplest level of self-representation an agent represents his or her intentional relations to the objects of his or her own activity. For example, agents distinguish real movement of external objects in the sensory field from the apparent movements of such objects that are due to their own motion. Thus, according to Barresi and Moore (ibid., p. 109), the experiences of any motile organism "must always involve objects and events in the world in relation to its own activities directed at those objects or events but need not include itself as an agent." At the second level of complexity, an organism is capable of integrating its first-person information with perceptual information about other agents in order to achieve a certain degree of coordinated activity. At the third level, the agent can combine perceived information about himself with imagined representations of other, or vice versa, allowing an even greater degree of coordination and social manipulation. And at the fourth and highest level in their scheme, the agent is capable of imagining both first-agent and other-agent points of view. We do not agree with the sweeping phylogenetic claims that Barresi and Moore base on their four level framework (Allen 1996), but it does provide a more sophisticated framework than is available elsewhere for comparative studies of self-awareness and its relation to social understanding.

Despite the possibility afforded by such schemes for the fine-grained analysis of the functional aspects of self-recognition and self-awareness, there remains the question of what the relationship is between such capabilities and attributions of qualitative consciousness. The prejudice that seems to operate with many authors is that qualitative states of awareness are associated only with the most sophisticated kinds of self-awareness, such as at level 4 of the Barresi-Moore hierarchy. We think, however, that this is not correct. Although it is true that an organism at level 4 will have the kind of capacities that support attributions of consciousness, we believe that the capacity for detecting misinformation can be implemented by means of resources that are available at the second level of their hierarchy.

Concluding Remarks

Without a doubt, the difficulty of understanding consciousness is the biggest bludgeon used to bash cognitive ethology. This is undoubtedly due in part to Griffin's insistence on pushing animal consciousness to the top of his agenda. But we think that to focus on the difficulty of understanding consciousness is essentially unfair to cognitive ethologists, for many interesting questions about the evolution of mentality can be pursued in the absence of closure on problems about consciousness. Our project of expli-cating the use of mentalistic terms in ethology would not collapse if this chapter on consciousness were to be omitted from our book. Nonetheless, it might have been seen as a failure of nerve on our part if we had omitted the topic of animal consciousness. At least this chapter does not leave us open to a charge of shirking. But, of course, we hope that it has done more by helping to distinguish some issues that when not carefully distinguished make discussions of animal consciousness such a mess. And we hope to have convinced the reader that some questions about animal conscious-ness may be empirically tractable.

Many philosophers have focused on what it is like to be in a particular conscious state. This has motivated a preponderance of opinion favoring the view that consciousness cannot be investigated in a scientific fashion, particularly when the subjects are nonhuman animals. We have argued that this particular epistemological worry is misplaced, and that the more fundamental questions concern which organisms have conscious states rather than what it is like to be those organisms.

For many philosophers, however, the epistemological problems of con-sciousness pale in comparison to the ontological problem of saying just what consciousness is. There is no opinion on this issue so bizarre that it has not been held at some time by a philosopher—not to mention physi-cists! The ontological problem of consciousness has produced a range of theories, including the view that it is a property of immaterial souls (Descartes), the view that it is a quantum gravitational effect in the micro-tubules of neurons (Penrose 1994), and the view that it is a basic proper-ty of matter akin to charge and mass (Chalmers 1996). It has also produced the defeatist position that humans are too stupid ever to be able to figure it out (McGinn 1991), or that we can't figure it out because isn't real (Dennett 1991). We have had nothing explicit to say about the onto-logical problem of consciousness (what it is) except that we are skeptical of Cartesian dualistic views. Nonetheless, we think that we have done what is necessary for the project facing cognitive ethologists and com-parative psychologists. For these purposes it is enough to point to empir-ical phenomena that exhibit some of the characteristics associated with consciousness and target those for further investigation. Only further research will tell whether those characteristics are the right ones to be pointing to.

9

Toward an Interdisciplinary Science of Cognitive Ethology: Synthesizing Field, Laboratory, and Armchair Approaches

> . . . [cognitive] ethologists, having cast off the straitjacket of behaviorism and kicked off its weighted overshoes, are looking around somewhat insecurely for something presentable to wear.
> —Daniel Dennett (1983, p. 343)

> It is perhaps at this moment that the cognitive ethologist decides to hang up his field glasses, become a cognitive psychologist, and have nothing further to do with talk about consciousness or intention.
> —Cecilia Heyes (1987a, p. 124)

Surplus straitjackets, often cleverly reconditioned as laboratory coats, are still being promoted by more or less reformed behaviorists using the sales pitch that they can see right through the cognitive ethologists' mentalistic garb. This campaign may be of limited effectiveness. Field biologists, after all, are not exactly famous for being concerned about their clothing. Indeed, we know some who might be quite happy to wear nothing but a pair of field glasses, so long as they are left alone to conduct their research. Yet even the most committed naturalists need occasionally to attend conferences with colleagues who take delight in unraveling costumes by pulling on any loose threads. Dennett's (1983, 1987) cut of the intentional cloth provides one of the few lines designed explicitly for cognitive ethologists who do not wish to appear uncovered. Some critics, including Rachlin (1991), find this line unsuitable for any occasion. Others, including Heyes and Dickinson (1990), believe that, although Dennett's products may be suitable as undergarments for a lab coat, they are not suited for use in the field.

We think that cognitive ethologists would do best to keep their research methods and their clothing options as open as possible. At present there is no one garment in which a cognitive ethologist can be dressed with a guarantee of no loose threads. The line that Dennett offers is distinctive and of considerable utility for ethologists in the field and in the laboratory, but ultimately (as we shall explain below) it may not be durable enough for everyone's purposes. Millikan's (1984, 1993) biofunctional line of intentional products also provides some useful items for ethologists' wardrobes. Lab coats, too, belong in the wardrobe. Since Niko Tinbergen (1951, 1963), both laboratory experimentation and fieldwork have always been essential to ethology. Cognitive ethologists especially have much to gain by finding ways to transfer experimental methods from lab to field and back—see, e.g., Hauser and Carey 1997.

The comparative psychologists Heyes and Dickinson (1990, 1995) reject ethological fieldwork as unsuited to the investigation of intentional states in nonhuman animals, but they accept that Dennett's methods supply the necessary framework for laboratory investigation of intentionality. In this chapter we will argue that the experiments they describe are not as easily interpreted as they believe and that cognitive investigations should not be conducted exclusively in the laboratory.

Stimulus Control and Dirty Coats

A spotless white laboratory coat symbolizes the laboratory scientist's quest for complete experimental control. If every detail of the environment in which observations are made can be controlled, stray causal factors can be eliminated and hypotheses can be tested rigorously. Natural habitats are inherently messy and uncontrollable. Though white lab coats may look good under artificial light, they have never worn well in the field; they tend to show the dirt (besides disturbing the animals). But even if it is aesthetically preferable to watch animals in nature, the principles of laboratory science favor the observation of animals in cages. We doubt, however, that laboratory scientists can achieve the level of control that they seek. Because animals in certain situations can be manipulated in ways that are unnatural for them, one must also be concerned that the results of lab observation may be research artifacts that do not provide a clear window on animal mentality.

It is important, however, not to downplay the difficulties involved in field research, including lack of control over the behavior of animals being studied, lack of control over variables that influence the behavior of the animals being studied, and the potential for individuals who are conducting the research to interfere unwittingly with natural behavior patterns. Furthermore, because animals living in field conditions are generally more difficult to observe than animals living in more confined conditions, various manipulations are often used to make them more accessible to study. These manipulations include handling, trapping, tagging, banding, and fitting with radio collars that transmit physiological and behavioral information. Any of these manipulations may affect behavior, both of organisms that are directly handled and of organisms that interact with them. Filming animals so that permanent records can be obtained also can have a negative influence on the animals being filmed; reflections from camera bodies or lenses, the noise of motor-driven cameras and other sorts of video devices, and the heat and brightness of spotlights can all be disruptive. Finally, "just being there," or visiting individuals, groups, nests, dens, and ranging areas, can also have a significant influence on the behavior of the animals (for details see Bekoff 1995d and Bekoff and Jamieson 1996b). Although none of these problems is unique to field studies, all can have important and diverse effects on wild animals, who may not be accustomed to handling by humans, to the presence of humans, or to carrying instruments as they go about their daily routines.

The effects of human interference, both deliberate and accidental, can be quite surprising. What seem to be minor or insignificant intrusions from our point of view can actually be major intrusions in the lives of animals. The following examples, all involving birds, suggest that much more work is needed concerning how various manipulations influence the behavior of individuals in species from all taxa:

(1) Major (1990) reported that, in white-fronted chats, nests that were visited daily suffered higher nest predation than nests that were visited only once (at the end of a typical period of incubation).

(2) Wilson et al. (1991) found that Adélie penguins exposed to aircraft and directly to humans showed profound changes in behavior, including deviation from a direct course back to a nest and increased nest abandonment. They also found substantial increases in penguins' heart rates. Trumpeter swans do not show such adverse effects to aircraft (Henson and

Grant 1991); however, the noise and visible presence of stopped vehicles did produce changes in incubation behavior by female swans that could result in decreased productivity due to increases in the mortality of eggs and hatchlings.

(3) Kinkel (1989) reported that fewer wing-tagged ring-billed gulls returned to their colony site than leg-banded individuals, that pair bonds of tagged birds were broken more frequently than pair bonds of banded birds, and that most tagged females who returned to their colony were unable to acquire mates. However, Pineau et al. (1992) did not find that little egrets suffered from the effects of capture and wing tagging.

(4) Burley et al. (1982) found mate choice in zebra finches to be influenced by the colors of the leg bands used to mark individuals. There may be other influences of this sort that have not been documented. Females with black rings and males with red rings had higher reproductive success than birds with other colors. Blue and green rings were especially unattractive on both females and males.

(5) Osztreiher (1995) found not only that observers influenced the frequency of the "morning dance" in Arabian babblers but also that different observers observed different dance frequencies. For example, if a group of babblers remained unobserved for a single day, the frequency of dancing increased. Also, dance frequency witnessed by an observer decreased with observer's experience.

All in all, it is very difficult in field studies to gather "before" and "after" data. However, the above examples show clearly that observer presence and bias can influence the sorts of data that are collected and also influence the behavior of the animals being studied. Though these effects do not doom field studies, observer-animal interactions must be given serious consideration. (See also Davis and Balfour 1992; Bekoff 1994a.)

Although carefully conducted field experiments are often able to control for the influence of variables that might affect the expression of behavioral responses, there usually remains some possibility that the influence of some variables cannot be accounted for. Cheney and Seyfarth (1990) conducted fieldwork on the capacity of vervet monkeys to attribute knowledge to each other by playing back taped vocalizations of familiar individuals to other group members. In trying to assess the role of auditory cues alone, these researchers were concerned about their inability to eliminate "all visual or auditory evidence of the [familiar] animal's physical presence" (ibid., p. 230). We would suggest, however, that this inability to gain total control may not be problematic if the goal is to understand how monkeys see the world. Typically, in most social situations the physical presence of individuals and access to stimuli from different modalities may be important to consider. Vervets, other nonhumans, and humans may attribute mental states using a combination of variables that are difficult to separate experimentally. Negative or inconclusive experimental results concerning vervets' or other animals' attribution of mind to other individuals may stem from the impoverishment of their normal environment caused by the removal of information that they normally use in attribution (Bekoff et al. 1994).

It is not at all clear that the apparently greater experimental control afforded by captive studies constitutes a step in the right direction. It is known that the presence of visitors to zoos can result in the disruption of the behavior of zoo animals, and this has been particularly well documented for the social behavior of primates (Kreger and Mench 1995). These data are especially important because a good deal of research on animal cognition is focused on social interactions, and it is important to realize that those social interactions may be different in the presence of human observers. The problem of observer interference with normal patterns of behavior is every bit as acute for laboratory animals as it is for field research. Getting animals accustomed to test situations that may be unnatural, or getting them used to unfamiliar equipment such as mirrors, may also greatly influence results.

Testing Hypotheses: Making Cognitive Ethology Tractable

A major factor motivating the concern with experimental control is the scientific objective of rigorous hypothesis testing. Alert to this objective but wanting to support research in the field, Dennett (1983) suggested what he called the "Sherlock Holmes method" for field testing intentional hypotheses, which involves placing animals in situations likely to cause them to reveal what they know if they are motivated to achieve a specific goal. Dennett's "intentional stance" requires one to adopt the idealization that an organism is fully rational and to use this idealization to deduce an organism's behavior on the basis of specific hypotheses about its beliefs and desires. If an animal fails to behave as predicted, then the hypothesized intentional attributions are false. According to this approach, one cannot abandon the assumption of ideal rationality without abandoning the intentional stance. Dennett has implied (1983, p. 343) that intentional idioms provide a vocabulary for ethologists to use in the interim until neuroscientific explanations can be provided for animal behavior. Not everyone is as confident as Dennett that a Golden Age of neuroscience will provide all that he promises, but even without a belief in the Promised Coming it is possible to assess the utility of the intentional stance for the systematic attribution of intentional states to nonhuman animals. Dennett had the opportunity to test his line under the hot African sun when he visited Cheney and Seyfarth's research site. Having returned with a deepened appreciation of the difficulties of fieldwork, he admitted that it was no simple matter to apply the Sherlock Holmes method in the field (Dennett 1987). Colin Allen had the opportunity to conduct the fieldwork on Steller's jays described in chapter 8, and he can vouch for how difficult and time-consuming such work can be—especially the tedium of tabulating bird behaviors by watching video footage one frame at a time.

Heyes and Dickinson (1990, 1995) are convinced that the limitations of fieldwork make it incapable of supporting intentional attributions to nonhuman animals; however, they believe that the intentional stance can be effectively employed in the laboratory, and they regard Dennett's rationality assumption as indispensable for rigorous investigation of intentional hypotheses. As we have already indicated, we accept that laboratory research is an important part of the quest for an understanding of other species of mind, but we reject the idea that field studies have nothing to contribute. We have a number of quarrels with the details of Heyes and Dickinson's argument, and we turn to those issues next. Our discussion borrows heavily from Allen and Bekoff 1995b.

The Challenge from the Lab

It is worth delving into Heyes and Dickinson's arguments in considerable detail because rarely does one find such explicit criteria for justifying mentalistic explanations. It is tempting to think that what cognitive ethologists need and lack are formal criteria that could be applied to any behavior to determine the appropriateness of a mentalistic explanation. We think it is unlikely that anyone can fulfill that need. This is not to say that formal specifications have no place in the study of animal cognition. What we object to is the idea that any single criterion or simple set of criteria can be considered suitable for every application. Formal criteria derived from different philosophical theories of mind can suggest different and not necessarily incompatible bases for comparison. Cognitive ethology is, in part, a phylogenetic project, and phylogenetic studies typically involve comparison along multiple dimensions. There is no reason to think that things should be any different with respect to a phylogeny-motivated investigation of mental characteristics.

Heyes and Dickinson's analysis of intentional action gives rise to two behavioral criteria that they claim must both be met in order to justify an intentional interpretation for the behavior. The first is the "belief criterion," for which it is necessary to establish that the behavior in question was caused by an "instrumental" belief having the form that a piece of behavior or action A whose intentionality is under investigation caused the organism to gain access to some desired object O. Heyes and Dickinson call this kind of belief about the causal relationship between action and goal satisfaction a "simple instrumental belief." Their second criterion is the "desire criterion": it must be shown that a desire for access to O is causally implicated in the behavior A.

Heyes and Dickinson focus specifically on the widespread behavior of approaching food, and they consider when it would be reasonable to explain such behavior intentionally. The core of their argument can be reconstructed as follows:

(1) An action A warrants an intentional account only if it is caused by an (instrumental) belief of the form "Action A causes access to some desired object O."

(2) If an action A would be acquired or persist under contingencies that do not support the instrumental belief that A causes access to O, then A is not caused by that belief.

(3) The action of approaching food (A) is acquired (by rats) and persists (in chicks) under contingencies that do not support the belief that approaching food (O) causes access to the food.

Hence,

(4) The action of approaching food performed by chicks, by rats, and by other species (e.g. cats) does not warrant an intentional account.

We shall determine the merits of this argument by considering each premise in turn and then assessing the degree to which the premises support the conclusion.

Premise 1
This premise states the belief criterion for intentional characterization that is derived from Heyes and Dickinson's analysis of intentional action. Heyes and Dickinson explicitly align their discussion with Dennett (1983, 1987), who is concerned with intentionality of mental states in the technical sense that they possess representational content. Understood this way, we think, the belief criterion is not true: intentional accounts may be warranted even when an action is not caused by a belief, if it is caused by some other kind of representation. Consider, for example, a predator whose attack is mediated by a particular representation (e.g. a search image or prototypical representation of its prey). In this case, specific characteristics of the search image may be causally implicated in the behavior. A predator may, for instance, chase a small antelope but ignore a large one because of a closer match between its search image and the perceived prey. There may have been learning or natural selection for a representation that matches smaller prey, because, historically, small antelope have been easier to catch. Or, to select an actual example from cognitive ethology, consider the attribution of cognitive maps to help explain why bees will not fly to the middle of a lake but will fly across the lake when presented with dances that indicate a food source in those locations (Gould 1986; Gould and Gould 1994). In both of these cases, the causal relevance of states with intentional content does not depend on desires or instrumental beliefs—we don't, for example, have to imagine that bees or antelopes believe that their actions cause access to a desired object. Nonetheless their behaviors are directed by internal representations of the environment. And if it is correct to say that an animal's behavior is controlled by a representation of its local environment, then the behavior warrants an intentional account in Brentano's technical sense (although perhaps not in the ordinary sense of being deliberate).

Heyes and Dickinson focus on "simple instrumental acts" on the ground that "any intentional account of higher 'cognitive' processes must in the end assume that they are expressed in behavior through an instrumental act; such acts must be the final common pathway in any intentional account of behavior" (1990, p. 102). The "higher 'cognitive' processes" that they have in mind include Premack's (1986) work with Sarah (a chimpanzee) and Pepperberg's (1987) work with Alex (a parrot), both of whom have demonstrated the capacity for making same/different judgments. Although the examples we have cited above may not fall under the restricted class of simple instrumental acts, neither do they fall into the category of higher cognitive processes. Nor are we convinced that simple instrumental acts must be the final common pathway in any intentional account of behavior. Some theories of intentionality (e.g. Millikan 1984) make intentional-state attributions legitimate even for organisms that do not have instrumental beliefs. Since Heyes and Dickinson have the broader aim of criticizing intentional-state attributions by cognitive ethologists, it is not legitimate to restrict attention to the simple instrumental cases. However, even if one heeds Heyes and Dickinson's restriction to simple instrumental acts, we believe their argument fails for other reasons.

The notions of intentional state and representation to which we have appealed are deliberately broad. We regard questions about the types of representation implicated in the causation of animal behavior, and their roles, as requiring serious empirical investigation. For instance, Stich (1978) distinguishes between the role of representations in beliefs and subdoxastic (merely cognitive) states, such that the former but not the latter are accessible to consciousness. In chapter 8 we discussed ways in which a similar distinction might be investigated in nonhuman animals by investigating the capacity to detect misrepresentation (see also Allen 1997). In general, however, we assume the availability of a naturalistic account of intentionality and representation. The naturalistic accounts provided by Millikan (1984) and Dretske (1986) neither presuppose that representations occur only as conscious intentional states nor presuppose that they interact with other intentional states in any particularly sophisticated ways.

In their response to Allen and Bekoff 1995b, Heyes and Dickinson (1995) object to our use of the notions of search image and cognitive map:

> How would we ever know whether the "search image" of a predator or the "cognitive map" of a bee has intentional properties (for the predator or bee, rather than the human observer) unless it can control behavior that is rational with respect to the content of these states? It is not

sufficient to appeal to the adaptiveness of the behavior because the rationality that matters with respect to intentionality is that of the psychological processes of the individual agent, not of the evolutionary process.

Their commitment to what they take as Dennett's conception of intentionality, which makes rationality essential, is what drives this particular line of questioning. Ironically, Dennett (1987) himself does not embrace the distinction between intentionality derived from evolutionary processes and that of "the individual agent" (which he regards to be wholly derivative of biological function). This point of Dennett's is admittedly controversial and not widely accepted among philosophers, but it owes much to Millikan's (1984, 1993) theory of intentionality, which we introduced in chapter 6.

Millikan's theory provides two things for our argument here. First, it suggests a way to dispute Dennett's rationality assumption, for the failure of an individual organism to appear perfectly rational does not condemn an intentional attribution any more than the failure of a sperm to penetrate an egg condemns the claim that its function is to do so. Intentional attributions are a species of functional attribution, and as such they may frequently fail to produce their "intended" results. Second, Millikan's theory emphasizes the importance of historical criteria for the attribution of intentional states. These criteria look to the ancestral history of selection that led to current organism's production of a particular internal state. This account of intentionality explains how the connection between a bee's internal representation of its environment and its behavior may be both (proximally) mechanistic and (ultimately) intentional. According to Millikan's account, a bee's internal state is intentional if it is produced as the result of a process whose function is to control behavior in virtue of an established correspondence between features of the internal state and the bee's environment. Although their reasons are not correct, Heyes and Dickinson are right to assert that it is not sufficient to appeal to the adaptiveness of the individual bee's behavior to justify an intentional attribution. We endorse this assertion because an individual action may turn out to be accidentally adaptive, whereas Millikan's account requires that there be a systematic relationship between the mechanism and reproductive fitness that is mediated by the correspondence between the mechanism and the environment.

By allowing that mechanistic and intentional approaches are not rivals, have we started down the slope toward intentional explanations of the "phototaxis of sunflowers and tactile sensitivity of mimosa" (Heyes and Dickinson 1995, p. 330)? We submit that this is not a very slippery slope. The phototaxis of sunflowers and the ability of mimosa to close their leaves in response to touch are highly stimulus-bound behaviors that are not sensitive to alternative sources of information (chapter 4). Nor do they involve cooperation between communicating "devices" (chapter 6). Thus, they are not the kinds of candidates of behavior for which we have argued that cognitive explanations are warranted.

Premise 2

Heyes and Dickinson justify their second premise by the pointing out that the belief criterion is a causal requirement and hence is satisfied only if a certain counterfactual is true: namely that, all other things being equal, the action would not have occurred if the belief were absent. According to Heyes and Dickinson, when environmental conditions do not support the belief that a given behavior will produce a desired result, to persist in the behavior would not be rational. Furthermore (by appeal to Dennett's intentional stance), they claim that the rationality assumption is required in order to generate predictions from the intentional stance; so, if the belief criterion makes an empirically testable claim, behavior that is not sensitive to the available evidence must be taken as evidence against the attribution of the belief. It is possible to deny this premise if it can be made plausible that the persistence of "irrational" behavior is compatible with the behavior's being caused by the instrumental belief that the behavior will cause access to the desired object.

What may seem irrational from one perspective may not seem irrational at all from another perspective. In ethology, this point was recognized by Jakob von Uexküll (1909; see also Burghardt 1973), who insisted that it is important to understand both an organism's *Umwelt* and its *Innenwelt* in order to understand its behavior. We will consider the specific case of approaching food in our discussion of the third premise; in the general case, the phenomenon of belief persistence in the face of undermining evidence has received much attention and it is by no means clear that from an evolutionary perspective this phenomenon provides evidence of irrationality. (See selections in Kornblith 1985, especially Harman 1984.) Thus, the persistence of a behavior that is not appropriate to the evidentiary conditions does not automatically provide evidence of irrationality.

We are also concerned about the "single-factor" approach to belief attribution that Heyes and Dickinson adopt. In our view, single-belief attributions, rather like scientific hypotheses, are not testable in isolation. The Quine-Duhem thesis (chapter 4) entails that any apparent falsification of a scientific hypothesis can be discounted by a revision in the background assumptions. In general there is no algorithm for determining when an hypothesis should be rejected, although, of course, various defenses can seem more or less plausible. Similarly, when an organism behaves in a way that is surprising in relation to a belief that one has attributed to it, one has the option of either withdrawing the attribution of belief or revising other assumptions that one has made about the situation. This means that it is impossible to prove that a particular belief attribution is correct. But one should be only as concerned about this as about the impossibility of scientific certainty in general.

Heyes and Dickinson (1995) acknowledge the Quine-Duhem point, but they continue to insist that our approach fails to offer "a clear, behavioral basis" (p. 332) for drawing a distinction between intentionally but irrationally caused behavior and behavior that is caused by states without intentional content. This demand for a strictly behavioral test for intentionality is at odds with various analyses of intentionality, including Millikan's, as we have explained.

Premise 3

In this premise Heyes and Dickinson apply the criterion for belief attribution to specific empirical results involving animals in artificially constructed versions of the looking-glass world. Heyes and Dickinson (1990, p. 90) cite two studies, the first being that of Hershberger (1986), who, they note, "arranged a looking glass environment for some chicks: their food bowl receded from them at twice the rate the walked toward it, and approached them at twice the rate they retreated from it." They continue: "In spite of the fact that they could easily have gained access to food by walking away from the bowl, the chicks persisted in chasing the bowl away. After 100 trials the chicks succeeded in gaining access to the food bowl only 30 percent of the time." The plausibility of Heyes and Dickinson's claim about this experimental situation depends on the plausibility of their claim that the experimentally provided contingencies really do not support the belief that approaching the food causes access to the food. We are inclined to dispute this interpretation for two reasons:

(i) As Heyes and Dickinson themselves note, the general experience of the chicks with objects outside the experimental situation supports the more general belief that approaching arbitrary objects causes access to those objects, so these results could be seen as cases of persistence of an adaptive, more general belief that entails the more specific belief that approaching food causes access to food. Thus, it is not obvious that the contingencies facing the chicks do not support this belief.

(ii) Most predators face a situation where potential food runs away from them. Capture success rates for most predators are far below 30 percent (Curio 1976; Estes 1991), so any hunting strategy that results in a 30 percent capture rate is actually relatively successful; the same may be true of other forms of foraging. Thus, it may be quite reasonable for chicks to believe that whatever they are doing is an appropriate way to obtain food, and it may be quite adaptive for them to persist in this belief even if food that is approached is observed to recede.

In response to an objection similar to (i), Heyes and Dickinson cite studies in which Dickinson and Dawson (1988, 1989) attempted to rule out the possibility that a subject's behavior might be caused by a belief that is acquired outside the experimental situation and is highly resistant to change. Dickinson and Dawson (ibid.) showed that rats will acquire the "maladaptive" (Heyes and Dickinson 1990, p. 90) habit of approaching a food bowl during the sounding of a tone even if food is withheld unless they wait until after the tone to start approaching the bowl. Heyes and Dickinson claim that reinforcement outside the experimental situation cannot account for the acquisition of this novel behavior. Heyes and Dickinson represent this behavior as *approach-tone* and claim that neither experimental nor external contingencies support the belief that performing the *approach-tone* action causes access to food. Perhaps. But why should one believe that approaching the bowl *during* the tone is the proper interpretation of what rats have learned to do? From a different perspective, one might regard the rats as acquiring the behavior of approaching the food bowl *after the initiation* of the tone. In the experimental situation, food was delivered if the rat did not begin its approach before the tone ends and was not delivered otherwise. If the rats fail to distinguish approaches occurring during the tone from those occurring after the termination of the tone, then the experimental situation amounts to a variable reward schedule for approaching after initiation of the tone. Variable reward schedules are well known to be very effective reinforcers (often more effective than consistent rewards). Thus, it is not surprising that the rats learned to approach the bowl more often when the tone had just sounded than at other times.

In response to (ii): We surmised (Allen and Bekoff 1995b) that Heyes and Dickinson might object to our interpretation of the looking-glass results on the ground that, for the chicks, whatever they are doing that is responsible for obtaining food in 30 percent of the cases is not approaching the food, so we have not controverted Heyes and Dickinson's claim that the belief that approaching the food causes access to food is untenable in the circumstances. Although we agree that the chicks could do better by performing the action of leaving the food, the behavior they engage in, which includes approaching the food, coincides with an acceptable return rate and thus provides no incentive for noticing that another behavior might be better.

An organism attending to the different return rates of approaching and leaving the food might notice that the latter is less effective than the former. But one cannot require that a belief-maintenance system attend to every piece of information that is relevant to its beliefs (or consider its behavior with respect to every environmental variable). Omniscience is not a reasonable requirement for belief attribution. In view of the 30 percent success of chicks in gaining access to food, there may be no incentive for noticing the different return rates of approaching and leaving; the belief that approaching the food causes access to the food is quite tenable in the circumstances.

If one were to continue to insist on the untenability of the belief, then the response could be put in the form of another objection to premise 2: Folk remedies persist because of the human tendency to act on beliefs of the form that ingesting some elixir causes access to improved health. That most people fail to notice the evidence that would make these beliefs untenable does not call into question the intentionality of the action of ingesting the elixir; likewise for chicks and rats. Omniscience has no place in a theory of rational belief maintenance. Yet another way to make this point is to note that rats and chicks are probably not insensitive to every manipulation that would change the reward contingencies. Although we have not done the empirical work, we would predict that if there had never been any food in the bowl the approach behavior would be extinguished or never acquired in chicks and rats.

As it turned out, Heyes and Dickinson (1995) objected to our suggestion that the chicks might simply be failing to notice that approach and withdrawal have different return rates by describing the behavior of a pigeon that is first trained with a stimulus that signals a food reward and is then placed on an "omission schedule" where pecking causes no food to be delivered. Once the pigeon ceases to peck, the relationship between stimulus and food is reinstated and the bird begins to peck again; however, this causes reintroduction of the omission schedule. Heyes and Dickinson claim that this cycle of acquisition and extinction will continue indefinitely, and that because the pecking results in the decrease in food it is a maladaptive behavior. Thus, they make the following claim (1995, p. 331): "It is not, as Allen and Bekoff suggest, that animals on omission schedules merely fail to contact the omission contingency and hence to notice that withdrawal or inhibition of approach (and pecking) is more successful. Instead, and irrationally, it is exposure to the very success of response inhibition that re-establishes the maladaptive behavior." Clearly the pigeon does "contact the omission contingency" in the sense that the omission contingency has an effect on its behavior. But imagine that you are the subject of this experiment. First, you notice that a stimulus indicates food, so you engage in a normal feeding behavior. Then, as you do so, the stimulus becomes very unreliable as an indicator of food, so you lose interest in it and you cease to engage in that behavior. Then, the stimulus becomes reliable again, so you resume your normal feeding behavior. This cycle repeats, and you never notice that it is your own tendency to engage in the feeding behavior that causes the connection between the stimulus and food to be severed. Does this mean that your feeding behavior is irrational and hence not intentional, or does it mean that you are perhaps a bit slow on the uptake? We think that the latter is at least as plausible an interpretation as the former.

The Conclusion and the Validity of the Argument

In the course of their argument, Heyes and Dickinson (1990) offered a pair of descriptions of the behavior of their experimental subjects: *approach(food)* and *approach-tone* (i.e., approaching during the tone). We have also considered a third description: approaching the bowl after the initiation of a tone (either during the tone or after it has finished sounding). The argument, as we formulated it in steps 1–4 above, was phrased entirely in terms of *approach(food)*. Even if under one description a piece of behavior fails to be intentional, it does not follow that it is not intentional under any description at all. The conclusion of the argument (step 4) is correspondingly ambiguous. On one reading it says only that the behavior is not intentional under the specific description *approach(food)*. Under the other reading it says that the behavior is not intentional under any description. Even if all the premises were granted as true, the conclusion would be supported only under the first interpretation. Thus, one should not conclude that the approaching behavior is not intentional under any description unless one has specific arguments against the plausible descriptions other than *approach(food)*.

In addition to the problems just mentioned, Heyes and Dickinson never clearly dissociate their discussion from the ordinary purposive sense of intentionality. Cognitive ethology is clearly concerned also with Brentano style intentionality; however, if the premises of Heyes and Dickinson's argument are plausible only when "intentional" is read in the ordinary sense of "purposeful," the conclusion could be interpreted only as saying that the action of approaching food is not purposeful in chicks and rats. This limited application of the result to purposefulness, however, misses its target of the wider role of intentional terms in cognitive ethology to provide a vocabulary for any explanation that makes use of the notion of representation. Furthermore, we think that it is unfortunate that Heyes and Dickinson attempt to generalize an all-embracing conclusion about the food-approach behavior in a variety of nonhuman species on the basis of a composite of different results from studies of chicks, rats, and pigeons , none of which are completely interpretable in the absence of information about the ethology of these species.

Stimulus Control and Impoverished Environments

Despite the often-stated motivation of gaining more control by bringing the study of animal cognition into the laboratory, we wonder whether the experiments Heyes and Dickinson describe are, in fact, properly controlled. They refer to the fictional character of Alice, who adapted rapidly to the fictional looking-glass world, and it is natural to assume (as they did) that this represents a general human ability. We do not doubt that some adult humans could adapt to the experimental situation faced by Hershberger's chicks, but we are not sure that any experiment on humans would be as controlled as one might initially think. For instance, many of us when growing up played some variant or other of the game "red light, green light," the object of which is to creep up and touch one player by moving only when that player is not looking. Experiences such as these may make adults in Hershberger's situation more likely to notice the correlation between inattention to the food and their access to it. Dogs and cats, too, often play in a manner such that mock attacks occur only when the play partner looks away. It would be interesting to see whether early experiences of this type were correlated with the ability to respond in an Alice-like way to Hershberger's experimental situation. It is also worth noting that the animals used in laboratory experiments are often deprived of opportunities for social play that may be important for the development of certain cognitive abilities. Here is a case where experimental control is potentially a form of overcontrol.

Heyes and Dickinson (1990, p. 87) criticize cognitive ethologists for attributing "intentional states to animals on the basis of passive observation of their behavior under free-living conditions." We believe, however, that this represents an unfairly narrow view of what those researchers were attempting to do. Cognitive ethologists, as we are sure Heyes and Dickinson acknowledge, do conduct experiments in the field (Cheney and Seyfarth 1990; Ristau 1991). Even under nonexperimental conditions, one may observe changes in reward contingencies that occur naturally. Although the statistical analysis of behavior observed under natural or field-experimental conditions may be less robust than in the case of laboratory experiments, the information that such studies provide is essential for the proper interpretation of laboratory work. Different organisms respond differently with changes in reward contingencies, and there may be a variety of explanations available in each case. As the example of a 30 percent reward rate shows, it is difficult to interpret an organism's response (or failure to respond) in a given situation without information about the histories of the individuals and species involved. Furthermore, the illusion of control that exists in the laboratory makes interpreting the results difficult. For instance, without ethological information about the history and evolution of play for members of a given species, one might not think of the consequences of play deprivation in caged animals.

Toward a Synthesis of Ethology, Comparative Psychology, and Philosophy

We believe that both laboratory experiments and fieldwork are essential for a complete understanding of animal cognition. In chapter 3 we described the four questions that Hinde (1982) claims are crucial to ethology: What are the immediate causes of behavior? How does behavior develop? What is the function of behavior? How did it evolve? These four questions have their roots in Tinbergen's (1951, 1963) identification of four overlapping areas with which ethological investigations should be concerned: evolution (phylogeny), adaptation (function), causation, and development (ontogeny). The methods for answering questions in each of these areas vary, but all begin with careful observation and description of the behavior patterns that are performed by the animals under study. The information afforded by these initial observations allow a researcher to exploit an animal's normal behavioral repertoire to answer questions about the evolution, function, causation, and development of the behaviors in that repertoire.

This reference to the normal behavioral repertoire should not be understood in terms of statistical frequency. Rather we have in mind something akin to Millikan's (1984) capitalized "Normal" which refers to situations that have played a role in the selection history of the specific trait being considered. Even rarely performed behaviors may be normal in this sense, for they may have proved critical to the survival and reproduction of the organisms that performed them in the past. Rare behaviors may, however, be linked to highly specific conditions that are difficult to reproduce, and it would be a mistake to try to elicit such a behavior experimentally under different conditions. Although obvious in one sense, in designing studies it is important to try only to ask animals to do what is within their capabilities. Without prior knowledge of those capabilities, putting this piece of advice into practice can be hard to do. According to Mitani (1995) the most prudent route is to put questions of interest to the animals themselves.

For similar reasons, it is important to know as much as possible about the sensory world of the animals being studied. Experiments should not be designed that ask animals to do things that they are unable to do because they are insensitive to the experimental stimuli or unmotivated by the stimuli. The relationship between normal ecological conditions and differences between the capabilities of animals to acquire, process, and respond to information is the domain of a growing field called "sensory ecology" (Dusenbery 1992).

To reiterate: Cognitive ethologists, never having been limited to "passive observation . . . under free-living conditions" (Heyes and Dickinson 1990, p. 87) are in need of a good theoretical framework for attributing intentional states. Both laboratory and field studies are important for assessing continuity across different taxa. Criteria like those suggested by Heyes and Dickinson have, we believe, a role to play in comparative studies of animal cognition. However, we reject the view that mental states can be assigned or withheld on the basis of simple behavioristic tests that are confined to the laboratory.

Concluding Remarks

The approach that we urge is interdisciplinary, naturalistic, strongly evolutionary, ecological, and comparative. There are, quite simply, no grounds for hope that anyone will be able to provide a simple set of behavioral criteria for the attribution of mental states. Nervous systems are enormously complex and support a wide range of functions. Some of these functions are shared between species; others are not. There need not be a tidy hierarchy of functionality; it is quite possible, for instance, that function *F1* is shared by traits found in members of species *S1* and *S2* and not in *S3*, whereas traits with function *F2* are found in *S2* and *S3*, but absent in *S1*.

As Dennett (1983) has pointed out, it is quite likely that animals will present a confusing array of abilities to meet certain criteria for intelligence while failing others. These differences will seem especially confusing in the absence of a proper understanding of evolutionary and ecological contexts.

Situations where there are many dimensions for comparison are well known to those who study phylogeny. Organisms are melanges of homologous traits (traits similar in form to those of other species, owing to differentiation from a common ancestor), homomorphous traits (traits similar in form to those of other species but with different underlying structure, attributable to convergent evolution), analogous traits (traits similar in function to those of other species, despite different structure and origin), unique adaptations to specific circumstances, and traits that may lack any evolutionary significance at all. In view of the complexity of this situation, the best one can hope to do is formulate many empirically tractable bases for comparison and then let empirical results drive the development of theories and the formulation of alternative and not always mutually exclusive explanations.

We are a long way from having an adequate database from which to make stipulative claims about the taxonomic distribution of various cognitive skills or to claim to have a theory of mind. As we mentioned in chapter 2, some monkeys cannot perform imitation tasks that some mice can (Whiten and Ham 1992). Does this count as an example of what Dennett (1983) calls "demoting" data—e.g., data showing that monkeys are not as clever as one might have thought? If the point was to answer the question "Are monkeys smarter than mice?" this is a confusion, for there is no reason to expect a single linear scale of intelligence. In the world of mice it may be more important to be able to do some things than it is in the world of monkeys, but in other respects a monkey may have capacities that a mouse lacks. There also is much variation within species, and this also must be documented more fully.

Science is not likely to make complete contact with the nature of animal minds at any single point—many methods will be useful, and competing hypotheses should be evaluated. Both "soft" anecdotal information and "hard" empirical data (data amenable to detailed statistical analysis) are needed to inform and to motivate further empirical experimental research. The various naturalistic theories of mind currently being fashioned by philosophers will continue to provide valuable ideas to cognitive ethologists who are seeking to fashion something that will fit them well and that will in turn help philosophers to improve their products. We believe that everyone interested in the nature of animal minds has much to gain by trying on their adversaries' clothes instead of trying simply to disrobe them.

A major goal of this book has been to indicate how a viable empirical research program could be developed and sustained. We believe that we have achieved this in our extensive discussions of play and antipredatory behavior. Of course there are many other examples that we have not addressed in such great detail. Though only time will tell whether an empirical research program in cognitive ethology will be successful, we believe that we have done at least enough to show that the future of cognitive ethology is an open question that cannot be summarily dismissed.

References

Akins, K. A. 1993. A bat without qualities. In *Consciousness*, ed. M. Davies and G. Humphreys. Blackwell.

Allen, C. 1992a. Mental content. *British Journal for the Philosophy of Science* 43: 537–553.

Allen, C. 1992b. Mental content and evolutionary explanation. *Biology and Philosophy* 7: 1–12.

Allen, C. 1995a. It isn't what you think: A new idea about intentional causation. *Noûs* 29: 115–126.

Allen, C. 1995b. Intentionality: Natural and artificial. In *Comparative Approaches to Cognitive Science*, ed. H. Roitblat and J.-A.Meyer. MIT Press.

Allen, C. 1996. Comparative psychology not folk phylogeny. *Behavioral and Brain Sciences* 19: 122–123.

Allen, C. 1997. Animal cognition and animal minds. In *Philosophy and the Sciences of the Mind*, ed. P. Machamer and M. Carrier. Pittsburgh University Press.

Allen, C., and Bekoff, M. 1994. Intentionality, social play, and definition. *Biology and Philosophy* 9: 63–74.

Allen, C., and Bekoff, M. 1995a. Function, natural design, and animal behavior: Philosophical and ethological considerations. *Perspectives on Ethology* 11: 1–46.

Allen, C., and Bekoff, M. 1995b. Cognitive ethology and the intentionality of animal behavior. *Mind and Language* 10: 313–328.

Allen, C., and Hauser, M. D. 1991. Concept attribution in nonhuman animals: Theoretical and methodological problems in ascribing complex mental processes. *Philosophy of Science* 58: 221–240.

Allen, C., and Hauser, M. D. 1993. Communication and cognition: Is information the connection? *Philosophy of Science Association* 2: 81–91.

Allen, C., and Saidel, E. 1997. The evolution of reference. In *The Evolution of Mind*, ed. D. Cummins and C. Allen. Oxford University Press.

Allen, C., Bekoff, M., and Grant, M. C. 1997a. Where, what, and with whom to eat? Choices made by Steller's jays (*Cyanocitta stelleri*). In preparation.

Allen, C., Bekoff, M., and Wolfe, A. 1997b. Feeding rates in Steller's jays (*Cyanocitta stelleri*): Effects of food type and social conditions. In preparation.

Altmann, S. A. 1962. Social behavior of anthropoid primates: Analysis of recent concepts. In *Roots of Behavior*, ed. E. Bliss. Harper.

Baron-Cohen, S. 1995. *Mindblindness: An Essay on Autism and Theory of Mind*. MIT Press.

Barresi, J., and Moore, C. 1996. Intentional relations and social understanding. *Behavioral and Brain Sciences* 19: 107–154.

Bateson, P. P. G. 1991. Assessment of pain in animals. *Animal Behaviour* 42: 827–839.

Beck, B. B. 1982. Chimpocentrism: Bias in cognitive ethology. *Journal of Human Evolution* 11: 3–17.

Bednekoff, P. A., and Ritter, R. 1994. Vigilance in Nxai Pan springbok, *Antidorcas marsupialis*. *Behaviour* 129: 1–11.

Beer, C. G. 1982. Review of Lorenz, *The Foundations of Ethology*. *American Scientist* 70: 326.

Beer, C. G. 1991. From folk psychology to cognitive ethology. In *Cognitive Ethology*, ed. C. Ristau. Erlbaum.

Beer, C. 1992. Conceptual issues in cognitive ethology. *Advances in the Study of Behavior* 21: 69–109.

Bekoff, M. 1972. The development of social interaction, play, and metacommunication in mammals: An ethological perspective. *Quarterly Review of Biology* 47: 412–434.

Bekoff, M. 1974. Social play and play-soliciting by infant canids. *American Zoologist* 14: 323–340.

Bekoff, M. 1975. The communication of play intention: Are play signals functional? *Semiotica* 15: 231–239.

Bekoff, M. 1976. Animal play: Problems and perspectives. *Perspectives in Ethology* 2: 165–188.

Bekoff, M. 1977a. Social communication in canids: Evidence for the evolution of a stereotyped mammalian display. *Science* 197: 1097–1099.

Bekoff, M. 1977b. Mammalian dispersal and the ontogeny of individual behavioral phenotypes. *American Naturalist* 111: 715–732.

Bekoff, M. 1978a. Behavioral development in coyotes and Eastern coyotes: Biology, behavior and management. In *Coyotes*, ed. M. Bekoff. Academic Press.

Bekoff, M. 1978b. Social play: Structure, function, and the evolution of a cooperative social behavior. In *The Development of Behavior*, ed. G. Burghardt and M. Bekoff. Garland.

Bekoff, M. 1992. Description and explanation: A plea for plurality. *Behavioral and Brain Sciences* 15: 269–270.

Bekoff, M. 1993. Review of Griffin, *Animal Minds*. *Ethology* 95: 166–170.

Bekoff, M. 1994a. Cognitive ethology and the treatment of nonhuman animals: How matters of mind inform matters of welfare. *Animal Welfare* 3: 75–96.

Bekoff, M. 1994b But is it research? What price interdisciplinary interests. *Biology and Philosophy* 9: 249–251.

Bekoff, M. 1995a. Play signals as punctuation: The structure of social play in canids. *Behaviour* 132: 419–429.

Bekoff, M. 1995b Cognitive ethology and the explanation of nonhuman animal behavior. In *Comparative Approaches to Cognitive Science*, ed. H. Roitblat and J.-A. Meyer. MIT Press.

Bekoff, M. 1995c. Vigilance, flock size, and flock geometry: Information gathering by western evening grosbeaks (Aves, fringillidae). *Ethology* 99: 150–161.

Bekoff, M. 1995d. Marking , trapping, and manipulating animals: Some methodological and ethical considerations. In *Wildlife Mammals as Research Models*, ed. K. Bayne and M. Kreger. Scientists' Center for Animal Welfare.

Bekoff, M. 1996. Cognitive ethology, vigilance, information gathering, and representation: Who might know what and why? *Behavioural Processes* 35: 225–237.

Bekoff, M., and Allen, C. 1992. Intentional icons: Towards an evolutionary cognitive ethology. *Ethology* 91: 1–16.

Bekoff, M., and Allen, C. 1997. Cognitive ethology: Slayers, skeptics, and proponents. In *Anthropomorphism, Anecdote, and Animals*, ed. R. Mitchell et al. SUNY Press.

Bekoff, M., and Byers, J. A. 1981. A critical reanalysis of the ontogeny of mammalian social and locomotor play: An ethological hornet's nest. In *Behavioral Development*, ed. K. Immelmann et al. Cambridge University Press.

Bekoff, M., and Byers, J. A., eds. 1998. *Animal Play: Evolutionary, Comparative, and Ecological Approaches*. Cambridge University Press.

Bekoff, M., and Jamieson, D., eds. 1990a. *Interpretation and Explanation in the Study of Animal Behavior*, volume 1: *Interpretation, Intentionality, and Communication*. Westview.

Bekoff, M., and Jamieson, D., eds. 1990b. *Interpretation and Explanation in the Study of Animal Behavior*, volume 2: *Explanation, Evolution, and Adaptation*. Westview.

Bekoff, M., and Jamieson, D., eds. 1996a. *Readings in Animal Cognition*. MIT Press.

Bekoff, M., and Jamieson, D. 1996b. Ethics and the study of carnivores: Doing science while respecting animals. In *Carnivore Behavior, Ecology, and Evolution*, volume 2. Cornell University Press.

Bekoff, M., and Scott, A. C. 1989. Aggression, dominance, and social organization in evening grosbeaks. *Ethology* 83: 177–194.

Bekoff, M., Townsend, S. E., and Jamieson, D. 1994. Beyond monkey minds: Towards a richer cognitive ethology. *Behavioral and Brain Sciences* 17: 571–572.

Berger, J. 1979. "Predator harassment" as a defensive strategy in ungulates. *American Midland Naturalist* 102: 197–199.

Berger, J. 1991. Pregnancy incentives, predation constraints and habitat shifts: Experimental and field evidence for wild bighorn sheep. *Animal Behaviour* 41: 61–77.

Blumberg, M., and Wasserman, E. A. 1995. Animal mind and the argument from design. *American Psychologist* 50: 133–144.

Boakes, R. A. 1984. *From Darwin to Behaviorism: Psychology and the Minds of Animals*. Cambridge University Press.

Bogdan, R. J., ed. 1991. *Belief: Form, Content and Function*. Oxford University Press.

Bower, G. H., and Hilgard, E. R. 1981. *Theories of Learning*. Fifth edition. Prentice-Hall.

Boysen, S. T., and Capaldi, E. J., eds. 1993. *The Development of Numerical Competence: Animal and Human Models*. Erlbaum.

Brentano, F. 1874. *Psychologie vom empirischen Standpunkt*. Leipzig.

Burghardt, G. 1973. Instinct and innate behavior: Toward an ethological psychology. In *The Study of Behavior*, ed. J. Nevin and G. Reynolds. Scott, Foresman.

Burghardt, G. 1985. Animal awareness. *American Psychologist* 40: 905–919.

Burghardt, G. 1996. Play. In *Encyclopedia of Comparative Psychology*, ed. G. Greenberg and M. Haraway. Garland.

Burkhardt, R. W., Jr. 1981. On the emergence of ethology as a scientific discipline. *Conspectus of History* 1: 62–81.

Burkhardt, R. W., Jr. 1983. The development of an evolutionary ethology. In *Evolution from Molecules to Men*, ed. D. Bendall. Cambridge University Press.

Burkhardt, R. W., Jr. 1997. The founders of ethology and the problem of animal subjective experience. In *Animal Consciousness and Animal Ethics*, ed. M. Dol et al. Van Gorcum.

Burley, N., Krantzberg, G., and Radman, P. 1982. Influence of color-banding on the conspecific preferences of zebra finches. *Animal Behaviour* 30: 444–455.

Byrne, R. 1995. *The Thinking Ape: Evolutionary Origins of Intelligence*. Oxford University Press.

Byrne, R., and Whiten, A. 1988. *Machiavellian Intelligence: Social Expertise and the Evolution of Intellect in Monkeys, Apes, and Humans*. Oxford University Press.

Caine, N. G., and Marra, S. L. 1988. Vigilance and social organization in two species of primates. *Animal Behaviour* 36: 897–904.

Caro, T, M. 1986. The functions of stotting in Thomson's gazelles: Some tests of the predictions. *Animal Behaviour* 34: 663–684.

Caudill, M. 1992. *In Our Own Image: Building An Artificial Person*. Oxford University Press.

Chalmers, D. J. 1996. *The Conscious Mind: In Search of a Fundamental Theory*. Oxford University Press.

Cheney, D. L., and Seyfarth, R. M. 1986. Vocal development in vervet monkeys. *Animal Behaviour* 34: 1640–1658.

Cheney, D. L., and Seyfarth, R. M. 1988. Assessment of meaning and detection of unreliable signals by vervet monkeys. *Animal Behaviour* 36: 477–486.

Cheney, D. L., and Seyfarth, R. M. 1990. *How Monkeys See the World: Inside the Mind of Another Species.* University of Chicago Press.

Cheney, D. L., and Seyfarth, R. M. 1992. Précis of *How Monkeys See the World. Behavioral and Brain Sciences* 15: 135–182.

Chisholm, R. M. 1957. *Perceiving: A Philosophical Study.* Cornell University Press.

Christensen, S. M., and Turner, D. R., eds. 1993. *Folk Psychology and the Philosophy of Mind.* Erlbaum.

Churchland, P. M. 1981. Eliminative materialism and the propositional attitudes. *Journal of Philosophy* 78: 67–90.

Churchland, P. M. 1995. *The Engine of Reason, the Seat of the Soul: A Philosophical Journey into the Brain.* MIT Press.

Clark, A. 1993. Mice, shrews, and misrepresentation. *Journal of Philosophy* 90: 290–310.

Colgan, P. 1989. *Animal Motivation.* Chapman and Hall.

Cosmides, L., and Tooby, J. 1997. In *The Evolution of Mind*, ed. D. Cummins and C. Allen. Oxford University Press.

Crick, F. 1994. *The Astonishing Hypothesis: The Scientific Search for the Soul.* Scribner.

Crist, E.1996. Darwin's anthropomorphism: an argument for animal-human continuity. *Advances in Human Ecology* 5: 33-83.

Cronin, H. 1992. Review of Griffin, *Animal Minds. New York Times Book Review*, November 1: 14.

Cummins, D. 1996. Evidence for the innateness of deontic reasoning. *Mind and Language* 11: 160-190.

Cummins, D., and Allen, C., eds. 1997. *The Evolution of Mind.* Oxford University Press.

Cummins, R. 1975. Functional analysis. *Journal of Philosophy* 72: 741–765.

Curio, E. M. 1976. *The Ethology of Predation.* Springer-Verlag.

Dahlbohm, B. 1993. Introduction. In *Dennett and His Critics* ed. B. Dahlbohm. Blackwell.

Darwin, C. 1871. *The Descent of Man and Selection in Relation to Sex.* Reprinted by Random House (Modern Library) in 1936. (Page numbers cited are from 1936 edition.)

Darwin, C. 1872. *The Expression of the Emotions in Man and Animals.* Appleton.

Darwin, C. 1896. *Insectivorous Plants.* Appleton.

Davis, H., and Balfour, D. eds. 1992. *The Inevitable Bond: Examining Scientist-Animal Interactions*. Cambridge University Press.

Davis, H., and Pérusse, R. 1988. Numerical competence in animals: Definitional issues, current evidence, and a new research agenda. *Behavioral and Brain Sciences* 11: 561–615.

Dawkins, M. S. 1993. *Through Our Eyes Only?* Freeman.

Dawkins, M. S. 1995. *Unravelling Animal Behavior*. Second edition. Wiley.

Dawkins, R., and Krebs, J. 1978. Animal signals: Information or manipulation? In *Behavioral Ecology*, ed. J. Krebs and N. Davies. Sinauer.

Deneubourg, J. L., and Goss, C. 1989. Collective patterns and decision making. *Ethology Ecology, and Evolution* 1: 295–311.

Dennett, D. C. 1969. *Content and Consciousness*. Routledge and Kegan Paul.

Dennett, D. C. 1983. Intentional systems in cognitive ethology: The "Panglossian paradigm" defended. *Behavioral and Brain Sciences* 6: 343–390.

Dennett, D. C. 1987. *The Intentional Stance*. MIT Press.

Dennett, D. C. 1988. Quining qualia. In *Consciousness in Contemporary Science*, ed. A. Marcel and E. Bisiach. Oxford University Press.

Dennett, D. C. 1991. *Consciousness Explained*. Little, Brown.

Dennett, D. C. 1995. *Darwin's Dangerous Idea: Evolution and the Meanings of Life*. Simon and Schuster.

Dennett, D. C. 1996. *Kinds of Minds*. Basic Books.

Dewsbury, D. A. 1989. A brief history of the study of animal behavior in North America. *Perspectives in Ethology* 8: 85–122.

Dewsbury, D. A. 1990. Nikolaas Tinbergen (1907–1988). *American Psychologist* 45: 67–68.

Dickinson, A., and Dawson, G. R. 1988. Motivational control of instrumental performance: The role of prior experience of the reinforcer. *Quarterly Journal of Experimental Psychology* 40B: 113–134.

Dickinson, A., and Dawson, G. R. 1989. Incentive learning and the motivational control of instrumental performance. *Quarterly Journal of Experimental Psychology* 41B: 99–112.

Donald, M. 1991. *Origins of the Modern Mind: Three Stages in the Evolution of Culture and Cognition*. Harvard University Press.

Dretske, F. 1986. Misrepresentation. In *Belief*, ed. R. Bogdan. Oxford University Press.

Dretske, F. 1988. *Explaining Behavior: Reasons in a World of Causes*. MIT Press.

Dretske, F. 1995. *Naturalizing the Mind*. MIT Press.

Dusenberry, D. B. 1992. *Sensory Ecology: How Organisms Acquire and Respond to Information*. Freeman.

Edelman, G. M. 1992. *Bright Air, Brilliant Fire: On the Matter of the Mind*. Basic Books.

Eibl-Eibesfeldt, I. 1975. *Ethology: The Biology of Behavior*, second edition. Holt, Rinehart, and Winston.

Elgar, M. A. 1989. Predator vigilance and group size in mammals and birds: A critical review of the empirical evidence. *Biological Reviews* 64: 13–33.

Elgar, M. A., Burren, P. J., and Posen, M. 1984. Vigilance and perception of flock size in foraging house sparrows *Passer domesticus* L. *Behaviour* 90: 215–223.

Emmerton, J., and Delius, J. D. 1993. Beyond sensation: Visual cognition in pigeons. In *Vision, Brain, and Behavior in Birds*, ed. H. Zeigler and H.-J. Bischof. MIT Press.

Enç, B. 1995. Units of behavior. *Philosophy of Science* 62: 523–542.

Estes, R. D. 1991. *The Behaviour Guide to African Mammals Including Hoofed Mammals, Carnivores, and Primates*. University of California Press.

Evans, C., and Marler, P. 1995. Language and animal communication: Parallels and contrasts. In *Comparative Approaches to Cognitive Science*, ed. H. Roitblat and J.-A. Meyer. MIT Press.

Fagen, R. 1981. *Animal Play Behavior*. Oxford University Press.

Fagen, R. 1993. Primate juveniles and primate play. In *Juvenile Primates*, ed. M. Pereira and L. Fairbanks. Oxford University Press.

Feddersen-Petersen, D. 1991. The ontogeny of social play and agonistic behaviour in selected canid species. *Bonn Zoologische Beitrage* 42: 97–114.

Fernald, L. D. 1984. *The Hans Legacy: A Story of Science*. Erlbaum.

Fisher, J. A. 1996. The myth of anthropomorphism. In *Readings in Animal Cognition*, ed. M. Bekoff and D. Jamieson. MIT Press.

Flanagan, O. J. 1992. *Consciousness Reconsidered*. MIT Press.

Flavell, J., Flavell, E., and Green, F. 1987. Young children's knowledge about the apparent-real and pretend-real distinctions. *Developmental Psychology* 23, no. 6: 816–822.

Fodor, J. A. 1987. *Psychosemantics: The Problem of Meaning in the Philosophy of Mind*. MIT Press.

Fodor, J. A. 1994. *The Elm and the Expert*. MIT Press.

Frey, R. G. 1980. *Interests and Rights: The Case against Animals*. Oxford University Press.

Galef, B. G., Jr. 1996a. Tradition in animals: Field observations and laboratory analyses. In *Readings in Animal Cognition*, ed. M. Bekoff and D. Jamieson. MIT Press.

Galef, B. G., Jr. 1996b. Tradition and imitation in animals. In *Encyclopedia of Comparative Psychology*, ed. G. Greenberg and M. Haraway. Garland.

Gallup, G. G., Jr. 1970. Chimpanzees: Self-recognition. *Science* 167: 86–87.

Gerstner, G. E., and Fazio, V. A. 1995. Evidence of a universal perceptual unit in mammals. *Ethology* 101: 89–100.

Godfrey-Smith, P. 1988. Review of Millikan, *Language, Thought, and Other Biological Categories. Australasian Journal of Philosophy* 66: 25–28.

Godfrey-Smith, P. 1991. Signal, decision, action. *Journal of Philosophy* 91: 709–722.

Golani, I. 1992. A mobility gradient in the organization of movement: The perception of movement through symbolic language. *Behavioral and Brain Sciences* 15: 249–308.

Gopnik, A. 1993. Psychopsychology. *Consciousness and Cognition* 2: 264–280.

Gordon, D. M. 1992. Wittgenstein and ant-watching. *Biology and Philosophy* 7: 13–25.

Gordon, D. M., Paul, R. E., and Thorpe, K. 1993. What is the function of encounter patterns in ant colonies? *Animal Behaviour* 45: 1083–1100.

Gould, J. L. 1986. The locale map of honey bees: Do insects have cognitive maps? *Science* 232: 860–863.

Gould, J. L., and Gould, C. G. 1994. *The Animal Mind*. Scientific American Library, W. H. Freeman.

Greenwood, J. D., ed. 1991. *The Future of Folk Psychology: Intentionality and Cognitive Science*. Cambridge University Press.

Gregory, R. L. 1986. *Odd Perceptions*. Methuen.

Grice, H. P. 1957. Meaning. *Philosophical Review* 66: 377-388.

Griffin, D. R. 1976. *The Question of Animal Awareness: Evolutionary Continuity of Mental Experience*. Rockefeller University Press (second edition: 1981).

Griffin, D. R. 1978. Prospects for a cognitive ethology. *Behavioral and Brain Sciences* 4: 527–538.

Griffin, D. R. 1984. *Animal Thinking*. Harvard University Press.

Griffin, D. R. 1992. *Animal Minds*. University of Chicago Press.

Guilford, T., and Dawkins, M. S. 1991. Receiver psychology and the evolution of animal signals. *Animal Behaviour* 42: 1–14.

Guthrie, E. R. 1952. *The Psychology of Learning*. Harper.

Hailman, J. P. 1967. *An Introduction to Animal Behavior: Ethology's First Century*. Prentice-Hall.

Hailman, J. P. 1977. *Optical Signals: Animal Communication and Light*. Indiana University Press.

Hameroff, S. R., Kaszniak, A. W., and Scott, A. C., eds. 1996. *Toward a Science of Consciousness: The First Tucson Discussions and Debates*. MIT Press.

Hardin, C. L. 1996. *Color for Philosophers: Unweaving the Rainbow*. Hackett.

Harman, G. 1984. Positive versus negative undermining in belief revision. *Noûs* 18: 39–50.

Hauser, M. D. 1988. Invention and social transmission: New data from wild vervet monkeys. In *Machiavellian Intelligence*, ed. R. Byrne and A. Whiten. Oxford University Press.

Hauser, M. D., and Carey, S. 1997. Building a cognitive creature from a set of primitives: Evolutionary and developmental insights. In *The Evolution of Mind*, ed. D. Cummins and C. Allen. Oxford University Press.

Hauser, M. D., and Marler, P. 1993a. Food associated calls in rhesus macaques (*Macaca mulatta*). I. Socioecological factors. *Behavioral Ecology* 4: 194–205.

Hauser, M. D., and Marler, P. 1993b. Food associated calls in rhesus macaques (*Macaca mulatta*). II. Costs and benefits of call production and suppression. *Behavioral Ecology* 4: 206–212.

Hauser, M. D., and Nelson, D. A. 1991. "Intentional" signaling in animal communication. *Trends in Ecology and Evolution* 6: 186–189.

Hauser, M. D., Kralik, J., Botto-Mahan, C., Garrett, M., and Oser, J. 1995. Self-recognition in primates: Phylogeny and the salience of species-typical features. *Proceedings of the National Academy of Sciences* 92: 10811–10814.

Hearst, E. 1975. The classical-instrumental distinction: Reflexes, voluntary behavior, and categories of associative learning. In *Handbook of Learning and Cognitive Processes*, volume 2, ed. W. Estes. Erlbaum.

Heinsohn, R., and Packer, C. 1995. Complex cooperative strategies in group-territorial African lions. *Science* 269: 1260–1262.

Henson, P., and Grant, T. A. 1991. The effects of human disturbance on trumpeter swan breeding behavior. *Wildlife Society Bulletin* 19: 248–257.

Hershberger, W. A. 1986. An approach through the looking-glass. *Animal Learning and Behavior* 14: 443–451.

Heyes, C. 1987a. Cognisance of consciousness in the study of animal knowledge. In *Evolutionary Epistemology*, ed. W. Callebaut and R. Pinxten. Reidel.

Heyes, C. 1987b. Contrasting approaches to the legitimation of intentional language within comparative psychology. *Behaviorism* 15: 41–50.

Heyes, C. 1993. Imitation, culture and cognition. *Animal Behaviour* 46: 999–1010.

Heyes, C. 1994a. Reflections on self-recognition in primates. *Animal Behaviour* 47: 909–919.

Heyes, C. 1994b. Social learning in animals: Categories and mechanisms. *Biological Review* 69: 207–231.

Heyes, C. 1994c. Social cognition in primates. In *Animal Learning and Cognition*, ed. N. MacIntosh. Academic.

Heyes, C. 1994d. Cues, convergence, and curmudgeon: A reply to Povinelli. *Animal Behaviour* 48: 242-244.

Heyes, C., and Dickinson, A. 1990. The intentionality of animal action. *Mind and Language* 5: 87–104.

Heyes, C., and Dickinson, A. 1995. Folk psychology won't go away: Response to Allen and Bekoff. *Mind and Language* 10: 329–332.

Hill, H. L., and Bekoff, M. 1977. The variability of some motor components of social play and agonistic behavior in infant Eastern coyotes *Canis latrans* var. *Animal Behaviour* 25: 907–909.

Hinde, R. A. 1970. *Animal Behavior: A Synthesis of Ethology and Comparative Psychology*. McGraw-Hill.

Hölldobler, B., and Wilson, E. O. 1990. *The Ants*. Harvard University Press.

Holley, A. J. F. 1993. Do brown hares signal to foxes? *Ethology* 94: 21–30.

Huber, P. 1810. *Recherches sur les moeurs des fourmis indigenes*. J. J. Paschoud.

Hughes, S. 1990. Antelope activate the acacia's alarm system. *New Scientist* 127, September 29: 19.

Hull, C. L. 1943. *Principles of Behavior: An Introduction to Behavior Theory*. Appleton-Century.

Humphrey, N. 1976. The social function of intellect. In *Growing Points in Ethology*, ed. P. Bateson and R. Hinde. Cambridge University Press. Reprinted in Byrne and Whiten 1988.

Humphrey, N. 1977. Review of Griffin, *The Question of Animal Awareness*. *Animal Behaviour* 25: 521–522.

Jackson, F. 1986. What Mary didn't know. *Journal of Philosophy* 83: 291-295.

Jamieson, D., and Bekoff, M. 1993. On aims and methods of cognitive ethology. *Philosophy of Science Association* 2: 110–124.

Jolly, A. 1966. Lemur social behavior and primate intelligence. *Science* 153: 501–506. Reprinted in Byrne and Whiten 1988.

Kamil, A. C. 1987. A synthetic approach to the study of animal intelligence. Reprinted in *Behavioral Mechanisms in Evolutionary Ecology*, ed. L. Real (University of Chicago Press, 1994).

Kandel, E. R., Schwartz, J. H., and Jessell, T. M. 1991. *Principles of Neural Science*, third edition. Elsevier.

Kennedy, J. S. 1992. *The New Anthropomorphism*. Cambridge University Press.

Kimble, G. A. 1994. A new formula for behaviorism. *Psychological Review* 101: 254–258.

Kinkel, L. K. 1989. Lasting effects of wing tags on ring-billed gulls. *Auk* 106: 619–624.

Klemm, W. R. 1992. Are there EEG correlates of mental states in animals? *Pharmacoelectroencephalography* 26: 151–165.

Konorski, J., and Miller, S. 1937a. On two types of conditioned reflex. *Journal of General Psychology* 16: 264–272.

Konorski, J., and Miller, S. 1937b. Further remarks on two types of conditioned reflex. *Journal of General Psychology* 17: 405–407.

Kornblith, H. 1985. *Naturalizing Epistemology*. MIT Press.

Krebs, J. R., and Dawkins, R. 1984. Animal signals: Mind-reading and manipulation. In *Behavioral Ecology*, ed. J. Krebs and N. Davies. Sinauer.

Kreger, M. D., and Mench, J. A. 1995. Visitor-animal interactions at the zoo. *Anthrozoös* 8: 143–158.

Kripke, S. 1972. *Naming and Necessity.* Harvard University Press.

Krushinsky, L. V. 1990. *Experimental Studies of Elementary Reasoning: Evolutionary, Physiological and Genetic Aspects of Behavior.* National Library of Medicine.

Lazarus, J. 1990. Looking for trouble. *New Scientist* 125: 62–65.

Lehner, P. N. 1996. *Handbook of Ethological Methods.* Cambridge University Press.

Lehrman, D. S. 1953. A critique of Konrad Lorenz's theory of instinctive behavior. *Quarterly Review of Biology* 28: 337-363.

Lehrman, D. S. 1970. Semantic and conceptual issues in the nature-nurture problem. In *Development and Evolution of Behavior*, ed. L. Aronson et al. Freeman.

Leslie, A. M. 1987. Pretense and representation: The origins of "theory of mind." *Psychological Review* 94: 412–426.

Lima, S. L. 1987. Distance to cover, visual obstructions, and vigilance in house sparrows. *Behaviour* 102: 231–238.

Lima, S. L. 1994. On the personal benefits of anti-predatory vigilance. *Animal Behaviour* 48: 734–736.

Lima, S. L. 1995a. Collective detection of predatory attack by social foragers: Fraught with ambiguity? *Animal Behaviour* 50: 1097–1108.

Lima, S. L. 1995b. Back to the basics of anti-predatory vigilance: The group size effect. *Animal Behaviour* 49: 11–20.

Lima, S. L. 1996. The influence of models on the interpretation of vigilance. In *Readings in Animal Cognition*, ed. M. Bekoff and D. Jamieson. MIT Press.

Lima, S. L., and Dill, L. M. 1990. Behavioral decisions made under the risk of predation: A review and prospectus. *Canadian Journal of Zoology* 68: 619–640.

Lipetz, V. E., and Bekoff, M. 1980. Possible functions of predator harassment in pronghorn antelope. *Journal of Mammalogy* 61: 741–743.

Lipetz, V. E., and Bekoff, M. 1982. Group size and vigilance in pronghorns. *Zeitschrift für Tierpsychologie* 58: 203–216.

Lloyd Morgan, C. 1894. *An Introduction to Comparative Psychology.* Walter Scott.

Lorenz, K. Z. 1981. *The Foundations of Ethology.* Springer-Verlag.

Lorenz, K. Z. 1991. *Here Am I—Where Are You? The Behavior of the Greylag Goose.* Harcourt Brace Jovanovich.

Lorenz, K. Z. 1996. *The Natural Science of the Human Species: An Introduction to Comparative Behavioral Research.* MIT Press.

Lycan, W. G. 1987. *Consciousness.* MIT Press.

Lycan, W. G. 1996. Folk psychology and its discontents. In *Philosophy and the Sciences of the Mind*, ed. P. Machamer and M. Carrier. Pittsburgh University Press.

Macedonia, J. M., and Evans, C. S. 1993. Variation among mammalian alarm call systems and the problem of meaning in animal signals. *Ethology* 93: 177–197.

Major, R. E. 1990. The effect of human observers on the intensity of nest predation. *Ibis* 132: 608–612.

Malcolm, N. 1973. Thoughtless brutes. *Proceedings and Addresses of American Philosophical Association* 46 (November): 5–20.

Manson, M. D. 1992. Bacteria motility and chemotaxis. *Advances in Microbial Physiology* 33: 277–346.

Marler, P. 1968. Visual systems. In *Animal Communications*, ed. T. Sebeok. Indiana University Press.

Marler, C., and Evans, P. 1995. Bird calls: Just emotional displays or something more? *Ibis* 138: 26–33.

Marler, P., Karakashian, S., and Gyger, M. 1991. Do animals have the option of withholding signals when communication is inappropriate? The audience effect. In *Cognitive Ethology*, ed. C. Ristau. Erlbaum.

Martin, P. R., and Bateson, P. P. G. 1993. *Measuring Behavior: An Introductory Guide*. Second edition. Cambridge University Press.

Martin, P., and Caro, T. M. 1985. On the functions of play and its role in behavioral development. *Advances in the Study of Behavior* 15: 59–103.

Mather, J. A. 1995. Cognition in cephalopods. *Advances in the Study of Behavior* 24: 317–353.

McBride, G., James, J. W., and Shoffner, R. N. 1963. Social forces determining spacing and head orientation in a flock of domestic hens. *Nature* 197: 1272–1273.

McFarland, D., and Bösser, T. 1993. *Intelligent Behavior in Animals and Robots*. MIT Press.

McGinn, C. 1991. *The Problem of Consciousness: Essays toward a Resolution*. Blackwell.

McLean, I. G., and Rhodes, G. 1991. Enemy recognition and response in birds. *Current Ornithology* 8: 173–211.

Meltzoff, A., and Gopnik, A. 1993. The role of imitation in understanding persons and developing a theory of mind. In *Understanding Other Minds*, ed. S. Baron-Cohen et al. Oxford University Press.

Metcalfe, N. B. 1984a. The effects of habitat on the vigilance of shorebirds: Is visibility important? *Animal Behaviour* 32: 981–985.

Metcalfe, N. B. 1984b. The effects of mixed-species flocking on the vigilance of shorebirds: Who do they trust? *Animal Behaviour* 32: 986–993.

Metzinger, T., ed. 1995. *Conscious Experience*. Ferdinand Schoningh.

Millikan, R. G. 1984. *Language, Thought, and Other Biological Categories*. MIT Press.

Millikan, R. G. 1986. Thoughts without laws: Cognitive science without content. *Philosophical Review* 95: 47–80.

Millikan, R. G. 1989. In defense of proper functions. *Philosophy of Science* 56: 288-302.

Millikan, R. G. 1993. *White Queen Psychology and Other Essays for Alice*. MIT Press.

Mitani, J. 1995. Next of Kin. *Scientific American* 272, June: 116–117.

Mitchell, R. W. 1990: A theory of play. In *Interpretation and Explanation in the Study of Animal Behavior*, volume I, ed. M. Bekoff and D. Jamieson. Westview.

Mitchell, R. W. 1996. The history and method of anthropomorphic analysis of anecdotes about animals and God in Western Science. In *Anthropomorphism, Anecdote, and Animals*, ed. R. Mitchell et al. SUNY Press.

Morton, A. 1996. Folk psychology is not a predictive device. *Mind* 105: 119–137.

Munn, C. A. 1986. The deceptive use of alarm calls by sentinel species in mixed-species flocks of neotropical birds. In *Deception*, ed. R. Mitchell and N. Thompson. SUNY Press.

Nagel, T. 1974. What is it like to be a bat? *Philosophical Review* 83: 435–405.

Natsoulas, T. 1978. Consciousness. *American Psychologist* 33: 906–914.

Nelkin, N. 1993. What is consciousness? *Philosophy of Science* 60: 419–434.

Nicol, C. J. 1996. Farm animal cognition. *Animal Sciences* 62: 375-391.

Osztreiher, R. 1995. Influence of the observer on the frequency of the "morning dance" in Australian babblers. *Ethology* 100: 320–330.

Parker, S. T., Boccia, M. L., and Mitchell, R. W., eds. 1994. *Self-Awareness in Animals and Humans*. Cambridge University Press.

Parker, S. T., and Milbrath, C. 1994. Contributions of imitation and role-playing games to the construction of self in primates. In *Self-Awareness in Animals and Humans: Developmental Perspectives*, ed. S. Parker et al. Cambridge University Press.

Pearce. J. M. 1987. *Introduction to Animal Cognition*. Erlbaum.

Penrose, R. 1994. *Shadows of the Mind: A Search for the Missing Science of Consciousness*. Oxford University Press.

Pepperberg, I. M. 1987: Acquisition of the same/different concept by an African grey parrot (*Psittacus erithacus*): Learning with respect to categories of color, shape, and material. *Animal Learning and Behavior* 15: 423–432.

Pepperberg, I. M. 1990. Some cognitive capacities of an African grey parrot (*Psittacus erithacus*). *Advances in the Study of Behavior* 19: 357–409.

Pineau, O., Hafner, H., and Kayser, Y. 1992. Influence of capture and wing tagging on the little egret (*Egretta garzetta*) during the breeding season. *La Terre et la Vie* 47: 199–204.

Popper, K. R. 1959. *The Logic of Scientific Discovery*. Basic Books.

Povinelli, D. J. 1994a. Comparative studies of animal mental state attribution: a reply to Heyes. *Animal Behaviour* 48: 239-241.

Povinelli, D. J. 1994b. How to create self-recognizing gorillas (but don't try it on macaques). In *Self-Awareness in Animals and Humans*, ed. S. Parker et al. Cambridge University Press.

Povinelli, D. J. 1996. Chimpanzee theory of mind? The long road to strong inference. In *Theories of theories of mind*, ed. P. Carruthers and P. Smith. Cambridge University Press.

Povinelli, D. J., and Cant, J. G. H. 1995. Arboreal clambering and the evolution of self-conception. *Quarterly Review of Biology* 70: 393–421.

Povinelli, D. J., Nelson, K. E., and Boysen, S. T. 1990. Inferences about guessing and knowing by chimpanzees (*Pan troglodytes*). *Journal of Comparative Psychology* 105: 318-325.

Premack, D. 1986. *Gavagai! or the Future History of the Animal Language Controversy*. MIT Press.

Premack, D. 1988. "Does the chimpanzee have a theory of mind?" revisited. In *Machiavellian Intelligence*, ed. R. Byrne and A. Whiten. Oxford University Press.

Premack, D., and Woodruff, G. 1978. Does the chimpanzee have a theory of mind? *Behavioral and Brain Sciences* 4: 515–526.

Purton, A. C. 1978. Ethological categories of behavior and some consequences of their conflation. *Animal Behaviour* 26: 653–670.

Quenette, P.-Y. 1990. Functions of vigilance behavior in mammals: A review. *Acta Oecologica* 11: 801–818.

Quine, W. V. O. 1953. *From a Logical Point of View*. Harvard University Press.

Rachels, J. 1990. *Created from Animals: The Moral Implications of Darwinism*. Oxford University Press.

Rachlin, H. 1991. *Introduction to Modern Behaviorism*, Third edition. Freeman.

Redpath, S. 1988. Vigilance levels in preening Dunlin Calidris alpina. *Ibis* 130: 555–557.

Richards, R. J. 1987. *Darwin and the Emergence of Evolutionary Theories of Mind and Behavior*. University of Chicago Press.

Ristau, C. 1991. Aspects of the cognitive ethology of an injury-feigning bird, the piping plover. In *Cognitive Ethology*, ed. C. Ristau. Erlbaum.

Roberts, W. A., and Mazmanian, D. S. 1988. Concept learning at different levels of abstraction by pigeons, monkeys and people. *Journal of Experimental Psychology: Animal Behavior Proceedings* 14: 247–260.

Robinson, D. N. 1989. *Aristotle's Psychology*. Columbia University Press.

Roitblat, H. L., and J.-A. Meyer, eds. 1995. *Comparative Approaches to Cognitive Science*. MIT Press.

Rollin, B. E. 1989. *The Unheeded Cry: Animal Consciousness, Animal Pain and Science*. Oxford University Press.

Rollin, B. E. 1990. How the animals lost their minds: Animal mentation and scientific ideology. In *Interpretation and Explanation in the Study of Animal Behavior*, volume I, ed. M. Bekoff and D. Jamieson. Westview.

Romanes, G. J. 1883. *Animal Intelligence*. Appleton.

Rose, L. M., and Fedigan, L. M. 1994. Vigilance in white-faced capuchins, *Cebus capucinus*, in Costa Rica. *Animal Behaviour* 49: 63–70.

Rosenberg, A. 1988. *Philosophy of Social Science*. Westview.

Rosenberg, A. 1990. Is there an evolutionary biology of play? In *Interpretation and Explanation in the Study of Animal Behavior*, volume 1, ed. M. Bekoff and D. Jamieson. Westview.

Ryle, G. 1949. *The Concept of Mind*. Hutchinson.

Saidel, E. J. 1992. What price neurophilosophy? *Philosophy of Science Association* 1: 461–468.

Savage-Rumbaugh, E. S. 1990. Language as a cause-effect communication system. *Philosophical Psychology* 3: 55–76.

Savage-Rumbaugh, E. S., Williams, S. L., Furuichi, T., and Kano, T. 1996. Language perceived: *Paniscus* branches out. In *Great Ape Societies*, ed. W. McGrew et al. Cambridge University Press.

Schaller, G. B., and Lowther, G. R. 1969. The relevance of social carnivore behavior to the study of early hominids. *Southwest Journal of Anthropology* 25: 307–341.

Scheel, D. 1993. Watching for lions in the grass: The usefulness of scanning and its effects during hunts. *Animal Behaviour* 46: 695–704.

Searle, J. R. 1980. Minds, brains and programs. *Behavioral and Brain Sciences* 3: 417–424.

Searle, J. R. 1992. *The Rediscovery of the Mind*. MIT Press.

Seyfarth. R. M., Cheney, D. L., and Marler, P. 1980. Vervet monkey alarm calls: Semantic communication in a free-ranging primate. *Animal Behaviour* 28: 1070–1094.

Shallice, T. 1988. *From Neurophysiology to Mental Structure*. Cambridge University Press.

Shannon, C. E., and Weaver, W. 1949. *The Mathematical Theory of Communication*. University of Illinois Press.

Shapiro, L. 1992. Darwin and disjunction: Foraging theory and univocal assignments of content. *Philosophy of Science Association* 1: 469–480.

Shapiro, L. 1994. Behavior, ISO functionalism, and psychology. *Studies in History and Philosophy of Science* 25: 191–209.

Shapiro, L. 1997. The nature of nature: Rethinking naturalistic theories of thought. *Philosophical Psychology*, in press.

Shettleworth, S. J. 1993. Where is the comparison in comparative cognition? Alternative research programs. *Psychological Science* 3: 179–184.

Skinner, B. F. 1974. *About Behaviorism*. Knopf.

Skutch, A. F. 1996. *The Minds of Birds*. Texas A&M University Press.

Smith, L. D. 1986. *Behaviorism and Logical Positivism: A Reassessment of the Alliance*. Stanford University Press.

Smith, P. K., and Carruthers, P. 1996. *Theories of Theories of Mind*. Cambridge University Press.

Smith, W. J. 1977. *The Behavior of Communicating: An Ethological Approach*. Harvard University Press.

Sober, E. 1993. *Philosophy of Biology*. Westview Press.

Sober, E. 1997. Morgan's canon. In *The Evolution of Mind*, ed. D Cummins and C. Allen. Oxford University Press.

Sterelny, K. 1997. Navigating the social world: Simulation versus theory. *Philosophical Books*, in press.

Stich, S. P. 1978: Beliefs and subdoxastic states. *Philosophy of Science* 45: 499–518.

Stich, S. 1983. *From Folk Psychology to Cognitive Science*. MIT Press.

Stich, S. 1992. What is a theory of mental representation? *Mind* 101: 243–61.

Stich, S., and Ravenscroft, I. 1994. What *is* folk psychology? *Cognition* 50: 447–468.

Strawson, G. 1994. *Mental Reality*. MIT Press.

Sullivan, K. A. 1984. Information exploitation by downy woodpeckers in mixed-species flocks. *Behaviour* 91: 294–311.

Templeton, J. J., and Giraldeau, L.-A. 1995. Public information cues affect the scrounging decisions of starlings. *Animal Behaviour* 49: 1617-1626.

Templeton, J. J., and Giraldeau, L.-A. 1996. Vicarious sampling: the use of personal and public information by starlings foraging in a simple patchy environment. *Ecology and Sociobiology* 38: 105-114.

Thompson, K. V. 1996. Behavioral development and play. In *Wild Mammals in Captivity*, ed. D. Kleiman et al. University of Chicago Press.

Thorpe, W. H. 1979. *The Origins and Rise of Ethology*. Praeger.

Tinbergen, N. 1951. *The Study of Instinct*. Oxford University Press (1989 edition).

Tinbergen, N. 1963. On aims and methods of ethology. *Zeitschrift für Tierpsychologie* 20: 410–433.

Tinbergen, N. 1969. *Curious Naturalists*. Anchor Books.

Tinbergen, N. 1972. Foreword to Hans Kruuk, *The Spotted Hyena*. University of Chicago Press.

Tinbergen, E. A., and Tinbergen, N. 1972. Early childhood autism—an ethological approach. *Advances in Ethology* (supplement to *Zeitschrift für Tierpsychologie*) 10: 1–53.

Tinklepaugh, O. L. 1928. An experimental study of representative factors in monkeys. *Journal of Comparative Psychology* 8: 197–236.

Toates, F. 1995. Animal motivation and cognition. In *Comparative Approaches to Cognitive Science*, ed. H. Roitblat and J.-A. Meyer. MIT Press.

Tolman, E. C. 1951. *Purposive Behavior in Animals and Men.* Irvington.

Tomasello, M., B. L. George, A. C. Kruger, M. Jeffry, and F. A. Evans. 1985. The development of gestural communication in young chimpanzees. *Journal of Human Evolution* 14: 175–186.

Tomasello, M., D. Gust, and G. T. Frost. 1989. A longitudinal investigation of gestural communication in young chimpanzees. *Primates* 30: 35–50.

Treves, A. 1997. The influence of group size and near neighbors on vigilance in two species of arboreal monkeys. *Behaviour*, in press.

Triesman, M. 1975a. Predation and the evolution of gregariousness. I. Models for concealment and evasion. *Animal Behaviour* 23: 779–800.

Triesman, M. 1975b. Predation and the evolution of gregariousness. II. An economic model for predator-prey interactions. *Animal Behaviour* 23: 801–825.

Tye, M. 1992. Naturalism and the mental. *Mind* 101: 421–441.

Tye, M. 1995. *Ten Problems of Consciousness: A Representational Theory of the Phenomenal Mind.* MIT Press.

van den Bos, R. 1997. Reflections on the organisation of mind, brain and behavior. In *Animal Consciousness and Animal Ethics*, ed. M. Dol et al. Van Gorcum.

van Valen, L. M. 1996. On interdisciplinary and such. *Biology and Philosophy* 11: 255–257.

Vauclair, J. 1996. *Animal Cognition: An Introduction to Modern Comparative Psychology.* Harvard University Press.

Von Eckardt, B. 1993. *What Is Cognitive Science?* MIT Press.

von Uexküll, J. 1909. *Umwelt und Innenwelt der Tiere.* Springer-Verlag. Excerpted in *Foundations of Comparative Ethology*, ed. G. Burghardt (Van Nostrand Reinhold, 1985).

Warburton, K., and Lazarus, J. 1991. Tendency-distance models of social cohesion in animal groups. *Journal of Theoretical Biology* 150: 473–488.

Watanabe, S., Lea, S. E. G., and Dittrich, W. H. 1993. What can we learn from experiments on pigeon concept discrimination? In *Vision, Brain, and Behavior in Birds*, ed. H. Zeigler and H.-J. Bischof. MIT Press.

Watson, D. M., and Croft, D. B. 1996. Age-related differences in playfighting strategies of captive male red-necked wallabies (*Macropus rufogriseus banksianus*). *Ethology* 102: 336–346.

Watson, J. B. 1930. *Behaviorism.* Norton.

Whiten, A., and R. Ham 1992. On the nature and evolution of imitation in the animal kingdom: Reappraisal of a century of research. *Advances in the Study of Behavior* 21: 239–283.

Wicksten, M. 1980. Decorator crabs. *Scientific American* 242: 146-154.

Wilder, H. 1996. Interpretive cognitive ethology. In *Readings in Animal Cognition*, ed. M. Bekoff and D. Jamieson. MIT Press.

Wilkes, K. 1984. Is consciousness important? *British Journal for the Philosophy of Science* 35: 223–243.

Wilkes, K. 1995. Losing consciousness. In *Conscious Experience*, ed. T. Metzinger. Ferdinand Schoningh.

Williams, G. C. 1992. *Natural Selection: Domains, Levels, and Challenges*. Oxford University Press.

Wilson, R. P., Culik, B., Danfeld, R., and Adelung, D. 1991. People in Antarctica— how much do Adélie penguins *Pygoscelis adeliae* care? *Polar Biology* 11: 363–370.

Wittgenstein, L. 1953. *Philosophical Investigations*. Macmillan.

Yäber, M. C., and Herrera, E. A. 1994. Vigilance, group size and social status in capybaras. *Animal Behaviour* 48: 1301–1307.

Yoerg, S. I. 1991. Ecological frames of mind: The role of cognition in behavioral ecology. *Quarterly Review of Biology* 66: 287–301.

Yoerg, S. I., and Kamil, A. C. 1991. Integrating cognitive ethology with cognitive psychology. In *Cognitive Ethology*, ed. C. Ristau. Erlbaum.

Index

of behavior, 16, 26, 28, 35–36, 46,
48, 51, 56–58, 62, 68–69, 72,
75–85, 92, 106, 119, 128–130,
136–138, 151, 167
behavioristic, 28–31, 35, 57, 62
biological, 92
causal, 61–62, 66
cognitive, 35–36, 43, 58, 138, 171
evolutionary, 28, 61–62, 69–73, 92,
140–141
folk-psychological, 36, 58, 64,
73–84, 137
functional, 78
intentional, 92, 137–138, 167,
170–171, 176
of intentionality, 43, 51, 94–95, 107
mentalistic, 28, 35, 54–55, 58, 64,
78, 85, 166–167 (*see also* Folk
psychology)
metacausal, 78
normal, 107
and prediction, 75–78, 84, 94, 157
psychological, 28, 63, 166
reductionistic, 8, 35

Feeding, 89, 116, 121–126, 130–131,
134–137, 152, 175
silent, 61, 67–69
singular and social, 134–137
Field study. *See* Experimentation
Fighting, 98–99, 102, 104, 116–120
for dominance, 104
Fleeing, 116–120,
Fodor, J., 1, 58–59, 63, 82, 96
Folk psychology, 2–3, 15, 36, 58,
63–85, 143. *See also* Explanation
arguments against, 65–66, 75–76
and content, 66–69
developmental sequence of, 64
and intentionality, 14–15
Food, 56–57, 127, 130, 134–137,
146–149, 167–168, 171–176
approaching, 167
catching, 35, 123–124
concept of, 79–82

detection of, 60, 67
finding, 34–35, 60
sharing, 67–68, 70, 72
signaling, 60, 67–70
Freezing, 41–42, 76, 117
Frey, R., 39–41, 51
Function(s), 34, 44–47, 88–90, 96,
105, 108, 116, 119–120, 124, 147,
156, 158, 170, 178–180
adaptive, 13, 37, 46–47, 72, 95
biological, 15, 18, 71–72, 89, 93–95,
140–143, 162, 170
classification of, 44–47, 96
proper, 105–107
and structure, 94
Functional capacities, 13
Functional description, 44, 46, 72
Functional explanation. *See*
Explanation
Functional property, 13, 94, 156
Functional similarity, 36

Geese, 30–31
Geometric arrays, 126, 130–132, 138
circular, 130
linear, 130, 133
Gestures, 98–99, 111
Golani, I., 45–47
Gopnik, A., 65, 110
Griffin, D., 4, 12, 21–22, 32–37,
49–54, 120, 139
on behavioral flexibility, 24, 131,
141, 144
on cognition, 32, 36
on consciousness, 18, 32–36, 141,
144, 153, 158
Grosbeak, 124, 129–130, 135, 138
Group, size of, 126–137,

Habitat
natural, 12, 39, 59, 162
selection of, 35
Habituation, 149–150
Hare, 76–77, 120
Heinroth, O., 30